Rebels with a Cause

Rebels with a Cause

The Secret History of the Original Rolling Stones

Graham Gordon

List of Contents

Preface. ix

Part 1: The Breakthrough of the Rolling Stones · · · · · · · · · · · · · · · ·1
Chapter 1   The Ace of Hearts and the Russian Geezer. 3
Chapter 2   A Skinny Survivor and a Wannabe Politician 17
Chapter 3   "Hitting Civilisation on the Head". 30
Chapter 4   Entry of a Whizzkid 38
Chapter 5   Dancing in the Streets of Richmond 48

Part 2: Revolution in Tin Pan Alley ·59
Chapter 6   Marijuana, Stu and Nanker-Phelge 61
Chapter 7   Gasoline, Rubber and Route 66 65
Chapter 8   Dissolving the Fifties to an Exotic Dancer's Beat 71
Chapter 9   You Must Be Joking- and Why Not! 75
Chapter 10 Tall Tales of a Sexual Predator. 78
Chapter 11 "All Right, Keith, Come On!". 82
Chapter 12 Brian Jones Unleashed 87
Chapter 13 The Erotic Manifesto 91

Part 3: Welcome to Chicago-The Chess Sessions· · · · · · · · · · · · · · ·97
Chapter 14 'It's All Over Now'- Time to Man Up 99
Chapter 15 'I Can't Be Satisfied' 103
Chapter 16 2120 South Michigan Avenue 106
Chapter 17 Chicken Fried in Bacon Grease 110
Chapter 18 High Heel Sneakers and Old Crow Licquor. 113
Chapter 19 Sex Marathon. 116

Part 4: Farewell to Rhythm and Blues ·119
Chapter 20   Diversion into Soul. 121
Chapter 21   The Little Red Rooster and the Strange Kin People 123
Chapter 22   What a Shame - About Keith Richards 128
Chapter 23   'The Last Time' : First Progressive Pop Hit 131
Chapter 24   Satisfaction- for Some! 134

Part 5: The Rolling Stones' Peak of Progressive Pop· · · · · · · · · · · · ·141
Chapter 25   A Rolling Stone from Howard City, Michigan 143
Chapter 26   Gypsy Tunes, Frozen Steak and Valium. 148
Chapter 27   Trying to Re-arrange Her Mind 152
Chapter 28   'Ride On, Baby' – a Girl from an FBI File. 155
Chapter 29   Living in Sin and Loving It 159
Chapter 30   Waiting- But For Who Knows What ? 162
Chapter 31   'Lady Jane': Sounds from a Bygone Century 165
Chapter 32   Sexual Politics 169
Chapter 33   Out of Time in Swinging London 172
Chapter 34   'Paint It Black': Masterpiece of Grief. 175
Chapter 35   'Aftermath' and 'Revolver'. 181
Chapter 36   Standing in the Shadow. 187
Chapter 37   'Back Street Girl' : the Fate of
              a Working Class Mistress. 191
Chapter 38   Keith, Linda and Brian- the Story of 'Ruby Tuesday'. . . .196

Part 6: The Breakup of the Original Rolling Stones · · · · · · · · · · · · · ·205
Chapter 39   Drug Bust at Redlands, Treachery in Morocco 207
Chapter 40   Mick Jagger's Establishment Pardon 213
Chapter 41   'Child of the Moon' v 'Jumpin' Jack Flash' 222
Chapter 42   The Persecution of Brian Jones. 229
Chapter 43   Mick Jagger- Anarchist and Gentleman 236
Chapter 44   Keith Richards- " I Like to Whip 'Em So Hard" 239
Chapter 45   Exit Brian Jones. 243

Chapter 46   The Unmysterious Death of Brian Jones 251
Chapter 47   Jones, the Stones and the Sixties 254

                Postscript: The Rocking Stones .271
                Sources 277
                About the Author 281

Preface

SLOWLY BUT SURELY what happened on YouTube reconnected viewers – the older ones nostalgic, the younger ones curious – with the sounds of the original Rolling Stones. Junking the tongue and lips logo, sign of what the Stones became, uploaders sought out archive shots, mostly in black and white, of the Rolling Stones as they were in the Sixties.

What the uploaders created was the exact opposite of MTV videos where vacuous images try to disguise the musical banality of the so-called 'featured artist.' They revived the honourable function of the promo film which used pictures as secondary to music, a means of illustrating sounds with images. Beginning in October 2009 and ending in April 2014, a score of uploaders – whose usernames were sometimes as simple as sid 1396 and at other times as zany as Leonard Nosferatu – revitalised the Rolling Stones' progressive pop tracks from 1965-8.

Some of the songs which gained a new lease of life on YouTube were half forgotten, vaguely remembered hits such as 'The Last Time', 'It's All Over Now' and 'Ruby Tuesday.' But others were little-known gems such as 'Sittin' on a Fence', 'Ride On, Baby', 'Back Street Girl' and 'Child of the Moon.' It wasn't surprising that a number such as 'Out of Time', with its strong dance beat, should clock two million views. Yet it was left in the shade by the classic ballad, 'Lady Jane', which has reached three million.

It would no longer be possible for brain-dead DJs to use their glib putdown phrase, 'oldies', to write off music as beautiful as this. What's more, archive footage revealed the Rolling Stones not as garishly garbed stadium rockers, still less the 'steel wheelchair wrinklies', beloved of the tabloids. They reappeared as human young guys, wearing smart casuals, relaxed and laughing together as mates and musical comrades or side-by-side with their as yet unglamourised girlfriends. Younger YouTube viewers were moved to comment on the timelessness of the Rolling Stones' Sixties music -standing in contrast to their totally dated 'massive hits' and contradicting any notion of 'rock dinosaurs.'

The most obvious difference between the original Rolling Stones and the Stones of subsequent decades was of course the presence of the band's founder, Brian Jones. Dismissed by some as a drug- addled dandy, his death the subject of morbid fascination, Jones was in fact a multi-instrumental virtuoso. Physically weak, racked with asthma and undermined by epilepsy, he was also a highly intelligent musicologist, the first to suss links between R&B and world music. Basing his technique on great rhythm and blues musicians such as Elmore James and Little Walter, he emerged as the finest white exponent of both slide guitar and harmonica.

Yet the story of the original Rolling Stones goes well beyond Brian Jones alone. Keith Richards was very different then from the person he later became, the hard-boiled 'Keef' of rock legend. Not yet addicted to heroin, he was a superbly innovative guitarist and a truly creative composer, never content to churn out the same old stuff time after time. Dedicated student of blues guitar, he was also an ace with rock 'n' roll licks à la Chuck Berry. Richards was the one who ensured that the Rolling Stones' sound was dynamic rhythm and blues.

It couldn't be said that Mick Jagger was a different person from his later self. Jagger was always a man of multiple personalities – gymnast manque, wannabe politician, protean vocalist, sometime anarchist longing to become a gentleman. Yet he was rejected by polite society because of his facial appearance. Determined to get his own back on the Establishment, he reinvented himself as a libidinous dancer eager for acclaim as a sex symbol. When his mother, Eva Jagger, said "there's a side to Michael I'll never understand" she was in fact uttering an understatement. And while in interview Mick Jagger would habitually play down the meaning of songs which he'd written, he was actually a supremely gifted lyricist, an absolute master of internal rhyme and telling phrase.

Jagger's greatness as a lyricist can only be fully recognised by listening to his words on Rolling Stones records. The prohibitive cost of obtaining permission from those who hold publishing rights makes it virtually impossible to quote lyrics in a book.

The success of the Rolling Stones could not have been achieved without their superb rhythm section. But whereas with Charlie Watts what you saw was what you got, Bill Wyman was far more than a fine bassist. He was an intuitively creative musician and a perceptive diarist. Far beyond the tabloid caricature of a man obsessed with much younger women, Bill Wyman was a man of high emotional intelligence.

Although the Stones' second manager, Andrew Oldham, was of considerable importance in showbiz terms, his status as listed producer was a facade which cloaked his minimal musical significance. The Rolling Stones' effective producer at the peak of their powers in the mid-Sixties was an American listed only as an arranger, Jack Nitzsche. It was Nitzsche who guided the superb 'Aftermath' sessions recorded at RCA Studios in Los Angeles.

His importance revealed itself in the contrast between 'Aftermath' and the two failed albums which succeeded it, 'Between the Buttons' and 'Their Satanic Majesties Request.' These were recorded in London with Nitzsche not there and Oldham at the helm. Discipline slumped as a succession of hangers-on and 'Swinging London' celebrities loafed around in the Olympic Studios. As Bill Wyman succinctly remarked "these sessions were more notable for dopey camaraderie than for the music they produced."

Whilst Ian Stewart, co-founder of the band and splendid session keyboardist, is sometimes referred to as 'the sixth Stone', that accolade would be even more appropriate in the case of Jack Nitzsche. Brought up in Howard City, Michigan, Nitzsche perceived the Rolling Stones as the musical equivalents of his teenage hero, the renegade actor, James Dean, star of the movie 'Rebel Without a Cause.' But to Nitzsche, the Rolling Stones were rebels with a cause – that of rhythm and blues and later progressive pop.

The term 'pop' had been seen as synonymous with 'teen pop' and thus the object of snobbery originally from aficionados of classical music and later from rock critics. Yet Brian Jones thought different. He admired rhythm and blues as African-American pop, a music which combined the lyrical intensity of classic blues with the danceability of R&B and the melodic subtlety of songwriters such as Willie Dixon.

The Rolling Stones' rhythm and blues records would be brushed aside by rock critics as 'blues covers.' They were nothing of the kind. They were in fact brilliantly original reinterpretations of classic R&B tracks. It was no coincidence that the British Rhythm and Blues movement– perceived by Americans as 'British Invasion'- would give birth to the iconic pop of the mid-Sixties. Even the Beatles themselves, never part of BRB, were strongly influenced by rhythm and blues.

British Rhythm and Blues is a genre never recognised by rock critics, people who insist on strictly ethnic categories. It was named by the Rolling Stones' original manager, Russian-born Giorgio Gomelsky, the man who later managed the Yardbirds and promoted both the Animals and the Spencer Davis Group. Having failed to sign the Rolling Stones to a binding contract, Gomelsky was outflanked by Andrew Oldham. Yet without Gomelsky's promotion of the band, first at the Crawdaddy Club in Richmond and later at the Richmond Athletic Grounds, the Rolling Stones would never have broken through in the first place.

Once Andrew Oldham had seized control of the Stones, he operated from a strictly business point of view, dissipating the impact of the band's finest tracks by dispersing them on various different albums and, in the case of their finest album, 'Aftermath', topping up its great tracks with country crap. And, after Mick Jagger had ousted Oldham and become, together with Allen Klein, co-manager, he would have scant regard for the Rolling Stones' back catalogue.

Running parallel with the revival of the Rolling Stones' iconic pop on YouTube, uploaders effectively built videos by excavating further archive footage to revive the band's great rhythm and blues reinterpretations from 1963-4. These included the likes of 'I Just Want to Make Love to You', 'Little Red Rooster', 'Mona', 'Little by Little' and 'I'm a King Bee'– not to mention their original R&B instrumentals such as '2120 South Michigan Avenue' and 'Now I've Got a Witness.' These uploaded videos, together with the records they illustrate, are important primary sources for uncovering the true cultural history of the Sixties.

The lyrics of the Rolling Stones' tracks reveal much about their personal lives and consistently comment on the changing times in which they lived. That's why they're referred to here in detail. This is what makes 'Rebels with a Cause' a unique book, one which stands in total contrast to the many tomes which concentrate on the Stones as a rock band, something they only became when they released the album, 'Beggars Banquet' in 1968. Till then, through five fascinating years, they'd built on their inspiration in rhythm and blues to produce the peerless pop of the 'Swinging Sixties.'

Part 1: The Breakthrough of the Rolling Stones

CHAPTER 1

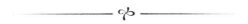

The Ace of Hearts and the Russian Geezer

HE WAS STARING out of the window in the middle of a daydream when the phone on his desk shrilled. He awoke to what he thought would be just another boring call about the routine business of Imperial Chemical Industries. It was nothing of the kind. His caller was one of the most extraordinary men ever to set foot on the London scene, as different from himself as chalk from cheese. The voice on the other end of the line was full of warmth even though the message was brief and to the point.

"Hi, Stu!" the caller said "Giorgio here. Listen, Hunt's let me down. Tell the guys the gig's theirs, they're on next Sunday. Leave the ads to me. Cheers!"

Ian Stewart had been gazing from the window of Imperial Chemical House, right in the heart of London overlooking the Thames, watching the snow falling relentlessly as it had done day after day during the god-forsaken winter of 1962-3. That was the coldest the capital had seen for two hundred and twenty three years.

Ian Stewart was a humble ICI clerk by day, no more than a wage slave, truth to tell, yet he was a free man on a Saturday night, playing boogie piano in a West End club. Now his spirits soared as he savoured the prospect of a residency. The venue might be in the back room of a pub fifteen miles out of town at remote Richmond but it would be an escape from the tyranny of the Dixieland Jazz fanatics, the so-called 'trad mafia', with their blind hatred of new music.

What seemed to Stewart no more than a stroke of luck was in fact the breakthrough of the Rolling Stones. More than that, although even his caller, Giorgio Gomelsky, could not have known it yet, it was the cultural birth of the Sixties, something which hadn't happened right on time on New Year's Day three years before but which would spring to life on the day of the upcoming Rolling Stones' gig at the Station Hotel in Richmond. That took place on February 24 1963.

Ian Stewart, known as Stu, wasn't the leader of the Rolling Stones but he was its co-founder. He was the only one who had a phone to receive messages from bookers and he alone had transport. Stu's vehicle might have been an old beat up Rover van but you could load Charlie Watts' drum kit into it and stash amps like Bill Wyman's AC30s. Stu had a clean driving licence and he took the band from gig to gig.

Had it been suggested to Ian Stewart's work colleagues or family members that he'd play a part in a musical revolution, they'd have laughed. Simply, he didn't look the part. Although Stu was just twenty-four, he seemed at least ten years older. He was thick set with a large head and a protruding jaw. The calcium deficiency which deformed his jaw was the unhappy legacy of a childhood bout of measles and, in his teens, he had corrective surgery which meant the jaw being clamped for six months. Self-conscious about this, he'd gone into his shell and would never express himself with any degree of confidence.

What applied for his looks was the same with his background. Ian Andrew Robert Stewart had been brought up in Sutton, Surrey, the son of an architect. He'd been to prep school in Cheam and grammar school in Kingston but he yearned for the holidays when he could head at once to his uncle's farm in Scotland. He'd been born in Fifeshire, in the village of Pittenweem and his hobbies were fishing and golf. In some ways he was still a Fifeshire farmer at heart. He'd never be interested in drugs, he relaxed with just a couple of beers and he kept well clear of the nascent groupie scene. He had a steady girlfriend and got married at twenty-nine. His only vice was hamburgers.

Beneath his homely exterior, however, Stu was devoted to jazz and rhythm and blues. He was a first-rate boogie woogie pianist, basing himself on Thirties kingpin Albert Ammons, banging out sixths with a propulsive left hand. But in the summer of 62 Stewart was transfixed when he heard a record which was in the Top Three on the Billboard Hot 100. This was 'Green Onions', an instrumental by Booker T and the MGs, already a number one hit on the R&B chart. It featured Booker T Jones on the Hammond M3 organ and it inspired Stewart to add organ to his keyboard armoury

IAN STEWART
The pianist who started the band with Brian Jones

Earlier in 62, Stu had been the first to respond to an ad in Jazz News, dated May 2, seeking rhythm and blues musicians for an audition at the Bricklayers Arms in Soho. It had been placed by the other co-founder of the Rolling Stones, Lewis Brian Hopkins Jones. Forget rockspeak about bands forming rather than being founded and forget the mythical blue plaque erected at Dartford railway station in 2015 attributing the formation of the Rolling Stones to a couple of others whose paths once crossed there. The nucleus of the band was present when Ian Stewart met Brian Jones at the Bricklayers Arms.

Brian Jones had already made a sensational debut on the London music scene. Alexis Korner, leader of Blues Incorporated, had begun playing Saturday night rhythm and blues gigs at the Ealing Jazz Club. It was there that Jones, introduced by Korner as 'Elmo Lewis' brought the house down with his fantastic slide guitar on Elmore James' 'Dust My Broom.'

Ian Stewart sailed through the audition at the Bricklayers Arms but was baffled by the personality of the guy who'd recruited him. Indeed he described Brian Jones to his friends as "an odd character." A devotee of African-American music, Jones himself was blond, blue-eyed and fair skinned. He was manifestly intelligent yet he'd been in an out of half a dozen dead end jobs by the time he was twenty. Jones spoke in a cultured accent with a hint of a lisp and his manner was somewhat fey. It had briefly crossed Stu's mind that Brian might be gay- until he saw his almost insatiable appetite for women. Indeed the twin lodestars of Brian Jones' life were the emerging rhythm and blues scene and the teenage girls which it attracted.

Unlike the other members of what soon became his band, Brian Jones was not a Londoner. He came from Cheltenham where he was born on February 28 1942. A Regency spa town lying on the edge of the beautiful Cotswold Hills, Cheltenham was widely considered the epitome of provincial respectability. In the Fifties, it had been stuffy, snobbish and furtive, the kind of place where people peeked out from behind lace curtains on a Sunday morning to see who was prematurely mowing their lawn. Yet there was a Cheltenham underbelly too. The town was surrounded by military bases, American as well as British, and that made it a haven of prostitution.

Living in the sedate suburb of Up Hatherley, Brian Jones' parents, Lewis and Louisa, were intelligent yet straitlaced, the products of the strict chapel -going culture of South Wales and pillars of their local denominational church. Lewis was a high -salaried aeronautical engineer. Louisa was a dedicated piano teacher who introduced Brian to the keyboard as a boy of six. But the Jones household was a repressive one in which Brian's friends never felt comfortable. There were few signs of overt affection from his father whilst his mother was ice-cold, warning him that, if he was naughty, he might have to 'go away' like his younger sister Pamela. In fact Pamela had died of leukaemia at the age of three.

At Cheltenham Grammar School aged twelve, Brian had been noted as an absolutely brilliant boy. His deputy headmaster later revealed that Brian had an IQ of 135 and remembered him "studying in an intellectual and rigorous way. He was the top of the A stream in which there were some very bright people who later gained starred entry to Oxbridge."

Brian Jones also had great musical gifts. Trained for classical music, he'd played Weber's First Clarinet Concerto with a youth orchestra in his early teens. Well-behaved and keen on cricket and model railways, he was viewed as an admirable student, someone certain of a career in the professions who, if he so chose, could alternatively become a notable orchestral musician.

Then his life totally changed. He became fascinated with jazz and enthralled by sex. Spending less and less time at home, he sneered at the sedate composers his mother cherished, the likes of Edward Elgar and Ralph Vaughan Williams. At school, Brian maintained a good exam record despite doing little work. A rebel before rebellion became fashionable, he objected to wearing school uniform and being obliged to take part in team sports. Fast -tracked into the Sixth Form, he obtained nine O Levels plus A Levels in Physics and Chemistry. But he failed A Level Biology and his two pass grades were moderate. He didn't get the grades needed for university.

Rock 'n' roll hit the UK when Brian was fourteen but he was quick to see through the raucous showmanship of Bill Haley and the Comets. He soon found modern jazz and, impressed by alto saxophonists Charlie Parker and Cannonball Adderley, he switched from clarinet to sax.

But above all Brian loved the sound of electric slide guitar When he heard Chicago bluesman Elmore James' record, 'Dust My Broom', he said it was "as if the earth shuddered on its axis." He improvised a dummy bottleneck from glass tubing he'd found in a junkyard and practiced till his fingers bled.

Brian Jones' sex life began when he was a fifteen-year-old school-boy. Almost at once he drew girls towards him with the greatest of ease. Some of it came from his looks – girls would talk to each other about "his lovely ivory skin", "his gorgeous blond hair" and "that mischievous smile." Others spoke about his personality – "he had something really naughty about him and that made him so interesting." Much of it came from his charisma – the way he could fascinate them with stories, the way he could make them laugh with his impersonations, the speed and dexterity with which he could shuffle a deck of cards and, above all, the way he played guitar. To those who believed in fortune-telling, Brian Jones' trump card would be the ace of hearts.

His first steady girlfriend was nicknamed Hope and she was at the local girls' Grammar School, Pate's. One day Hope's friends were startled to see a girl they thought was shy French kissing and fondling Brian Jones in the street with shocked old ladies averting their eyes. What Brian was openly getting from Hope was something most lads of his age in those repressive times could only dream of receiving on the back seats of a cinema – if they got it at all!

Suddenly Hope disappeared from school. She was pregnant with Brian Jones' child. Only her parents and his plus her headteacher knew the truth. Otherwise it was hushed up. She was left with only one option. In an age when abortion was illegal and single motherhood considered shameful, she had to give her baby up for adoption.

At seventeen Brian Jones was in a relationship with a slightly younger girl, Val Corbett. Corbett was also at Pate's Grammar School. She was an intelligent girl and an attractive one, full breasted with long brown hair. Her friends said she was deeply in love with Brian, she had eyes for no one else and all her thoughts were of him. The birth control pill was still several years down the line and Val got pregnant. This time Jones was expected to show responsibility. In 1959 there was no teenage marriage without parental consent but Val's dad quickly gave it.

Val was excited about what she thought would be her upcoming marriage but sensible about preparing to look after her child. Jones had clearly said he would marry her. Then he called it off-not face to face but in a letter. He said he'd only agreed under pressure from his father. This was false. Lewis Jones had been strongly opposed to the marriage.

Val Corbett's son, Barry David, was born on May 29 1960. She kept her little boy and before long was married to another young guy, one who was fully prepared to become a stepfather.

Pat Andrews was the next girl to fall under Brian Jones' spell. She met him on a blind date at the Aztec coffee bar on Cheltenham High Street. In future years the trainee beautician recalled her first impressions-"I couldn't speak, I literally couldn't speak – there was this light coming from I don't know where – I don't remember what he said – I was just so focused on this angelic blond hair." Going to gigs where he performed she added "when I listened to him playing, I was transported into another world, another realm."

It wasn't only girls of his own age for whom Brian Jones held a seductive fascination. In a jazz club at the Wooden Bridge Hotel in Guildford, late in 59, he met a twenty-three-year-old married woman by the name of Angeline. Although Jones was six years younger than her, it made no difference. They had a one night stand as a result of which Angeline became pregnant. Jones never knew about that but, when she told her husband, he forgave her and brought up the child, a girl they called Carol, as if she was his own.

Brian Jones had been on the point of starting a course at Cheltenham College of Art. But the offer of a place had been abruptly withdrawn after an anonymous letter blackened his character. No one knew exactly what was in that letter but many had speculated about its contents. It was bound to have been about sex. And in an era when sexual repression was still the norm –except only in London- any hint of deviance from the straight and narrow could have serious consequences.

In Cheltenham Brian Jones' affairs were the subject of many rumours, some with substance, others wildly exaggerated. He was said to have 'seduced' a fourteen year old schoolgirl –in fact he was barely older than that himself at the time – and he was believed to have had it off with several French girls, visiting the city on a student exchange scheme. Doubtless the gossip about him would have found its way into the letter received at Cheltenham College of Art.

Barred from art school at the age of seventeen, under pressure from his father, Jones enrolled on a course for trainee opticians at Northampton Institute in Clerkenwell. A big consolation was that he got to spend time in London but he did little work, failed the course and had to return to Cheltenham.

After that he scraped a meagre living doing a succession of jobs none of which lasted long. He worked in a chemist's shop, he drove a coal lorry and he was a clerk in an architect's office. But by night he was in his element on the music scene playing gig after gig.

When Alexis Korner, pioneer white bluesman, played at Cheltenham in October 61, the nineteen-year-old Jones boldly went backstage and astonished Korner, with his confidence and musical knowledge. In fact, he'd played on more than a hundred gigs while still living in Cheltenham, playing acoustic guitar with a De Armon pickup. He starred across the genres, sometimes with jazz bands, other times with rock'n' roll groups. While guitar and harmonica were his favourite instruments, he also shone on tenor and alto sax.

Jazz band leader John Keene later recalled-"Brian was streets ahead of us musically. He was very impressive on the guitar. We couldn't understand the chordal things he knew." Keene also said "he really knew what he wanted to do. He was ambitious and focused. He felt like a fish out of water in Cheltenham."

Infuriated by his way of life, Brian's mother changed the house locks and, to make sure he got the message, she packed his spare clothes into an old suitcase and dumped it on the front drive.

Aged eighteen when that happened, he took a cheap flat in rundown Bath Road which he shared with a jazz -loving friend. The pair of them had a whale of a time turning their pad into a hangout for visiting jazz musicians, keeping crates of ale on hand, charging music buffs for admission and picking up extra cash when they returned loads of empty bottles. But it all ended when they were kicked out for not paying the rent on time.

Travelling with jazz buffs who were also CND activists, Jones visited Oxford where he met Paul Pond, who was studying English Literature at Jesus College. They had a lot in common. Pond had been born the same week as Jones. He was also from a southern middle-class background, hailing from Portsmouth. What's more, Pond had started a rhythm and blues band. They talked not just music but art and foreign language films. On religion too they were in accord. Brian Jones had rejected his parents' fundamentalist beliefs and was an atheist. So was Pond, at that stage, though he become a Christian many years later, long after he'd changed his name to Paul Jones.

Paul Pond could scarcely believe his ears when he took a phone call from Brian Jones, one evening early in 62. "Listen, Paul," said Brian "from now on I'm taking it seriously. I'm coming to London, I'm getting a flat, I'm forming a band and I want you to be my lead singer."

Nothing Jones had said till this point had startled Pond. It was when Jones added the words- "and I'm going to be rich and famous" that his friend's incredulity kicked in. "Come off it, Brian, for God's sake!" replied Pond before turning the invitation down flat. "You won't do that playing the blues."

Two years after Jones was barred from art school, Pat Andrews gave birth to his son, Julian Mark Antony, on October 23 1961. He was quickly at the hospital with flowers, clothes and assurances of marriage. Yet, only a few months later, he moved to London without giving her his new address. When she traced him to Finchley, arriving with baby Julian in her arms, he seemed dismayed but reluctantly faced up to his responsibilities.

Undaunted, Jones got a part-time job in the Civil Service stores in The Strand. He moved from the cheap Finchley digs to a flat in Notting Hill, at rundown Powis Square. He lived there with Pat Andrews and Julian. Andrews worked off and on in a chemist's shop if she could find someone to mind the baby. But when Jones became a full-time musician, Pat and Julian returned to Cheltenham. After that, Pat continued to see Brian but only on sporadic visits to London.

BRIAN JONES
Master of more than a score of different instruments

Eager for potentially useful contacts on the London music scene, Jones had kept in constant touch with Alexis Korner after meeting him in Cheltenham. This had borne fruit when Korner summoned him on stage at the Ealing Jazz Club. But a more important figure was someone he got to know shortly after moving to London full-time. This was Giorgio Gomelsky, the man who would make that fateful phone call to Ian Stewart within a year.

Giorgio Gomelsky was a young journalist on Jazz News but his main interest was rhythm and blues. He'd visited Chicago several times and had seen Muddy Waters playing live. Talking to Brian Jones on and off during 62, Giorgio Gomelsky found the young English musician brilliantly gifted, knowledgeable and ambitious.

Gomelsky had started to promote R&B when he took over at the Cy Laurie Club in Soho's Ham Yard. But he'd soon been frozen out of the West End by the trad jazz mafia who relentlessly badmouthed new music. He took heart from the spread of Chicago rhythm and blues interest in the UK. Yet, as Gomelsky saw things, however admirable it was that a bluesman like Alexis Korner had founded Blues Incorporated, that would mean nothing till a young English band emerged which played all out rhythm and blues not old school blues.

For more open-minded than other jazz journalists, who looked down on rock 'n' roll, Gomelsky had already met the pre-fame Beatles in Hamburg and had clocked the vitality of their rock 'n' roll-based set. If a young English rhythm and blues band showed signs of rock 'n' roll influence, he would have no problem whatever with that. Yet the 62 Rolling Stones were being held back by their lack of a good rhythm section. This was a drawback of which Brian Jones was only too keenly aware and he was doing his best to recruit a top-class drummer and bassist. Meanwhile he sensed that Giorgio Gomelsky would be just the guy to promote his band as soon as he could get an out-of-town venue up and running.

On the London music scene, Giorgio Gomelsky -the so-called "Russian geezer with the Italian name" was nicknamed 'Rasputin.' No doubt about it, Gomelsky was chock full of intimidating charisma. He was tall, burly, dark and bearded, with a tumbling forelock of jet black hair, and his eyes had a fierce gleam under beetle brows.

But first impressions were deceptive. Gomelsky would soon celebrate his twenty-ninth birthday. He was toasted by a wide circle of friends, to whom he replied in a heavy accent which mingled the half a dozen languages he spoke. His speech was typically humorous, frequently witty and reflected a genuinely friendly personality. He was adored by his English girlfriend who rejoiced in the ultimately conventional name of Enid Tidy but whom Giorgio described as "a really cool girl."

Enid was one of the few who knew the full, astonishing life story of Giorgio Gomelsky. He'd been born on a ship travelling the Black Sea between Odessa and Tbilisi. His mother was French, a fashion designer from Monte Carlo and his father was a Ukrainian surgeon. By the time Giorgio was born, in 1934, Soviet Russia had become a very different place from the land of revolution only seventeen years before. Joseph Stalin was now its dictator and he detested what he called "rootless cosmopolitans." Without question the Gomelsky family were the epitome of that.

When Giorgio was a boy of four, his parents escaped from Russia and settled for a while in Italy. When Giorgio was nine years old, the Nazis invaded Italy in the last years of the Second World War. Defying the curfew, Giorgio and his pals discovered some old jazz records in an attic and defiantly blasted them out of an open window from an ancient gramophone. Amazingly, the boys weren't arrested and Giorgio survived to see black American GIs in the Allied army of Liberation. He asked them about blues and he absorbed everything he was told. As he would later say "I had no homeland of my own so blues became my homeland."

After the war the Gomelskys moved to Switzerland. But, as he grew up, Giorgio found himself right out of step with the strict Swiss way of life. In his teens he proposed a jazz festival in Zürich. It was banned by the city fathers but Giorgio and his buddies staged a protest, mooning in the streets. The authorities were disgusted but they grudgingly relented.

By this time his parents had divorced and his mother had relocated to London. His imagination fired by copies of the Melody Maker she sent him, he resolved to do the same. He arrived, aged twenty-one, in 1955.

Much as he flourished on the London jazz scene, Giorgio Gomelsky was bitterly disappointed by the London to which he relocated. It was still stuck in the Fusty Fifties, burdened with coal fires and notorious for pea soup smog. By 1962, however, Gomelsky believed the metropolis was on the cusp of societal change. Two things facilitated this. One was the growth of coffee bar culture – he himself had opened the first coffee bar (the Olympic, off the King's Road) – which enabled young people to gather together after the pubs had to close. The other factor was the advent of cheaply available Italian scooters which freed young men and their girlfriends from dependence on the Tube.

By the beginning of 1963, big changes had taken place. The Rolling Stones had acquired a brilliant bassist and the best young drummer in London. And Giorgio Gomelsky had started promoting R&B on the weekend in suburban Richmond, at the Station Hotel. But Gomelsky was stuck with a modestly talented outfit, the Dave Hunt Rhythm and Blues Band. As a man of honour, he didn't want to just sack Hunt without a good reason.

In fact Hunt didn't last long. He and his band failed to turn up for a gig one night. And that was what led Giorgio Gomelsky to phone Ian Stewart the very next day with a message to be passed on to Brian Jones.

GIORGIO GOMELSKY
He said "when music changes, the walls of the city start to crumble"

CHAPTER 2

A Skinny Survivor and a Wannabe Politician

TWO HOURS AFTER taking Giorgio Gomelsky's momentous message, Ian Stewart was on his lunch break heading for the Wimpy bar at Earls Court. That's where he'd meet up with Brian Jones and two other members of the original Rolling Stones. They were always glad to see him because he had luncheon vouchers which he fiddled from ICI. Although not quite at starvation level, they were desperately hungry most of the time. Two of them were unemployed (Jones had been sacked from his job for pilfering) the other was a student whose grant was thrown into the kitty because without it they'd survive only by cadging and shoplifting. But by the look on big Stu's face they rapidly surmised he had more than grub on his mind.

The smaller of the two was an almost waiflike nineteen-year-old, shy and spotty with sticky out ears and a slack jaw. Only the burning brown eyes betrayed the ambition which consumed him. He was a brilliantly gifted guitarist who'd already effected a musical synthesis which was key to the early sound of the Rolling Stones. Much as he loved Chicago electric blues, Muddy Waters and the Chess masters, Keith Richards dug Chuck Berry with an equal fervour.

They might look down their noses in scorn at Chuck Berry in the West End jazz clubs, they might dismiss him as "that loathsome rock 'n' roll merchant" but this lad knew better than that. Brought up on jazz himself, the grandson of a Thirties bandleader by the name of Gus Dupree, only son of an acutely intelligent mother whose tastes spanned Ellington to Mozart, he'd seen Berry in the movie 'Jazz on a Summer's Day.' And he'd sussed the duck-walking singer–songwriter/stellar guitarist for what he really 1was. In short, the most gifted man the world of rhythm and blues had ever produced, albeit in self-imposed rock'n'roll exile, eager to make a fast buck from American teens with a short attention span.

What Keith Richards knew – and what the left-leaning, sandal -wearing blues buffs would never realise – was that Chuck Berry was the missing link between Chicago blues and a vital and viable new pop which would depend on musicianship as well as chart appeal. Much as Keith loved Berry's rock 'n' roll hits with their crunching, stopped chords, he was just as much into the Chess artist's return to his R&B roots -which coincided with his arrest and prosecution for alleged pimping- under the racially motivated Mann Act.

Keith Richards' contribution to the Rolling Stones was crucial. He opened Brian Jones' eyes to the musical significance of Chuck Berry. And, in basing his own guitar technique on the St Louis man, Richards himself became the missing link at the start of a decade when Berry's imprisonment abruptly removed him from the scene.

Rock critics writing about Keith Richards and eager to depict him as an icon of snarling rebellion, would relish the fact that he'd been kicked out of school for bunking off. They brushed aside the fact that his head-master had provided his reference for art college.

It was true that Keith had given up on his studies after being stood down from the school choir when his voice broke. But Dartford Technical School was, as he saw it, a place of incarceration not education. Worse, he could only get there by riding his bike out of the huge and soulless Temple Hill council estate where he lived, running the gauntlet of teen-age gangs who resented anyone whose background seemed even slightly posher than theirs. Keith was a skinny boy, no good at sport, but he was a survivor, learning to defend himself from attack by lashing out with the spare bike chain he carried on him at all times.

The Richards family were certainly not unequivocally working-class. Although his dad, Bert, was a factory worker, he loved the middle-class sport of tennis and was a keen member of a tennis club himself. As to his mother, Doris, she was an office worker who became a bakery manager. Indeed a case could be made for the Richardses to be considered 'work-ing-class aristocracy' in that Keith's paternal grandmother, a dedicated socialist like her husband, had been mayor of Walthamstow. What's more,

Gus Dupree, to whom Keith was very close, was a professional enter-tainer, a guitarist, who took his grandson with him when visiting instru-ment repair shops in the heart of London.

Keith had made the unpardonable error of failing his 11plus exam. That shouldn't have ended his academic career. After all, the same thing hap-pened to Kinks' frontman Ray Davies who'd benefited from an excellent education at William Grimshaw Secondary Modern, becoming a prefect whose headmaster was delighted when he played blues guitar in school assembly. Dartford Tech was the exact opposite of William Grimshaw and such a place only made Keith the more determined to express his pent up anger in musical rebellion.

Despite what it says on the mythical plaque at Dartford Station, the band which Keith Richards helped form was not the Rolling Stones but the archly named Little Boy Blue and the Blue Boys. Richards had been staggered to witness Brian Jones' unprecedented expertise on slide gui-tar at the Ealing Club and he wanted in on Jones' new band. Sidcup Art College had seemed to him like a conveyor belt for jobs in advertising and he'd binned his portfolio in an outburst of defiance.

When he turned up to audition at the Bricklayers Arms in Soho, it opened Richards' eyes to another world. It seemed like Ian Stewart had scarcely noticed him at first. Stewart was in a world of his own, lost in a boogie-woogie rampage, his piano flush with the open window. He realised Stu knew he was there when he heard him exclaim "take a look at that!" and "I wouldn't mind wrapping myself round her!" as he clapped eyes on first one then another of the nubile girls strutting down Broadwick Street- strippers making their way from club to club.

Keith Richards joined the band in June 62 with Blue Boys bassist, Dick Taylor, and he was there when Brian Jones flushed out the hardline anti-Berry jazzers such as Geoff Bradford and Brian Knight with the words "fuck off, you stupid bastards, you're shit, I'll make it with these guys, not you!"

Richards was quick to realise that Brian Jones was an absolute girl magnet. He figured the Jones band would pull in more chicks than even its horny leader could cope with and that soon there'd be easy pickings for himself in an area where, till then, he hadn't had much success.

KEITH RICHARDS
"Shy, introverted, very appealing
and lacking in confidence" according
to his girlfriend, Linda Keith

By the late Summer of 62, Keith had quit the parental home in Dartford after an almighty row with his father – to whom he'd never been close – and moved in with Brian Jones at 102 Edith Grove in Fulham. Living from hand to mouth in the freezing winter which followed, he and Jones listened day after day to rhythm and blues records, playing along as a double guitar team, perfecting an interweaving style based on Hubert Sumlin and Freddie Robinson from Howlin Wolf's band. Not only that but when Jones took up the harmonica, bent on emulating Little Walter Jacobs and Walter Horton, Brian and Keith practised counterpoint between bluesharp and guitar.

Dedicated to their project, they emerged as a musicianly unit the like of which was unparalleled in British music. As for Keith Richards himself, Giorgio Gomelsky already had him down as "a great rhythm guitarist because he always gets on the right feel", adding "he's always at war, he's a rubbery kind of person because he bounces off anything, he always comes back, he's always there, he's great."

Standing next to Richards was another nineteen-year-old, a tall, gangling youth with a dad -style cardigan under his scarf and heavy overcoat. He was a business studies student in his second year at the London School of Economics, listed on their books as 'Jagger, Michael Philip.'

Although Jagger- at that time known to everyone as 'Mike'- was happy to try his hand in show business, his mind was on a political career. He was a limited musician who'd never bothered to do more than strum a guitar and who, as Bill Wyman put it, "could blow a bit of harmonica." On the other hand, he was already an extraordinary personality.

Almost everything was in Jagger's favour to become a Conservative MP within ten years. He'd grown up in the pleasant Kentish village of Wilmington on a secluded road known as 'The Close' at a detached house called 'Newlands.' It had a spacious garden where he and his younger brother played cricket under the supervision of their father, Basil Fanshawe Jagger, an administrator for the Central Council for Physical Recreation.

MICK JAGGER
Among his lyrics were ones inspired by reading
Baudelaire, Bulgakov and Carl Gustav Jung

Mike Jagger liked to stress that his mother was working class and this was true up to a point in that her own mum, brought home as a child from Australia after a marital breakup, had earned her living as a dressmaker. But the former Eva Scutts was a committed campaigner for the Conservative party. She'd noted that, even as a young boy, Mike had been fascinated with money. She'd been delighted when he started his business studies course and was proud her son was considering a political career.

At Dartford Grammar School, Mike had been noted for good conduct and sporting ability. He was intelligent but not in the slightest intellectual, scarcely reading a book beyond those prescribed. Well spoken and confident, Mike was promptly recommended for uni by his headmaster.

But there was one thing which, in the not too distant future, would have put off any Conservative parliamentary selection committee. The problem was his facial appearance which, in an age of pervasive racism, was held to be distinctly 'non-Aryan.'

Mike had already been the victim of vicious abuse on the streets of Dartford, catcalled with the N word ringing in his ears. In the eyes of those who jeered him, his lips were too full and his tongue too long.

This quasi -racial abuse led him to identify with African-American music, specifically rhythm and blues. He hadn't discovered it off his own bat, being guided there by his pal Dick Taylor, a working-class grammar school boy. Taylor was a plumber's son from Bexleyheath- and, along with Keith Richards, a guitarist in Little Boy Blue and the Blue Boys. Taylor would briefly play bass in the Rolling Stones but quickly got back to art school only to emerge later in another R&B band, the Pretty Things.

Till then Buddy Holly had been Mike's musical hero and he'd been to see the doomed Texan rock 'n' roller on his UK tour early in 58. Not long afterwards, however, Mike was getting blues records by mail order direct from Chess in Chicago. And he defiantly answered his father back after hearing him dismiss these as "jungle music."

Giorgio Gomelsky had no problem with Mike Jagger. This was more than could be said for Alexis Korner and the man who'd been at his side in the formation of Blues Incorporated and at the Ealing Club, Cyril

Davies. Alexis Korner had warned Brian Jones about taking on Jagger as his frontman while Davies, who broke from Korner to found his own band, the Rhythm and Blues All Stars, gave Jagger short shrift when he asked him how you bent notes on the harmonica. "You fuckin' blow it then you fuckin' suck it and the fuckin' sound comes out!" snapped the portly panel beater.

Korner made his warning more specific when he told Jones he could take on either Jagger or Richards but not both. But essentially they came as a pair, not just because they'd been bandmates in Little Boy Blue and the Blue Boys but because they'd been childhood chums at Wentworth Primary School. Although Richards sometimes made jokes about Jagger "living in Poshtown", there was little doubt he admired his friend's upward social mobility and envied his relaxed confidence.

Jagger had gained useful experience singing with Blues Incorporated but had never been Brian Jones' first choice as a singer with the Rolling Stones. After all, Jones' pal Paul Pond seemed just the guy to front the band. Paul was an excellent singer, a former chorister, technically accomplished, without blemishes and with sincere blues sensibility. Mike Jagger, by contrast, had an inherently harsh voice though he could put over a song in a powerful and compelling way.

Brian Jones never had to make the choice between Pond and Jagger. Whereas Jagger hadn't hesitated to join the Jones band along with Richards and Taylor, Paul Pond felt at that time there was no future in it. A year later, however, he changed his mind as well as his surname, becoming Paul Jones, frontman of Manfred Mann and steering that band towards rhythm and blues.

To make it as a rhythm and blues singer, it was of course essential to be able to sing earthy and sex -oriented songs with total conviction. At first that'd been a problem for Mike Jagger. In the early months of the Rolling Stones, he was coming to the end of an unsatisfactory relationship with a sixteen-year-old mixed race theatre arts student, Cleo Sylvestre. And it was around this time that Brian Jones' new girlfriend, Linda Lawrence, overheard Jagger seeking Jones' advice about how to bring a woman to orgasm. Shortly afterwards Jagger was in a flourishing relationship with the seventeen-year-old model, Chrissie Shrimpton and his confidence at the mic had clearly grown by leaps and bounds.

Neither Jagger nor Richards had played any part in naming the band. Jones had christened it on the spur of the moment when they were rehearsing at the Bricklayers Arms. He was asked over the phone by a booker what they were called. Spying a Muddy Waters record on the floor-'I'm a Rollin' Stone'- he shot back the answer. They took the stage under the name 'Rollin' Stones' on July 12 1962.

Ian Stewart wasn't happy with the moniker, strangely commenting that it made them seem like an Irish showband. But Mike Jagger and Keith Richards were all for it. Certainly the choice of name linked them perfectly with Chicago rhythm and blues. Musically it hit the nail right on the head in 1962 but it would come to have a crucial and controversial significance in the years to come.

Throughout 62 the Rolling Stones had been on the fringes of the Marquee Club, then located at 165 Oxford Street. Harold Pendleton, who ran it, was an accountant by profession, a solid but unadventurous business-man. He loved traditional jazz, was wary of rhythm and blues and had a total detestation of rock 'n' roll and what he described as "all those bloody awful leather jackets." Pendleton had little idea how to publicise his club with a young crowd, most of whom were made to feel distinctly ill at ease in the Marquee.

But that all changed with a brilliant stroke of publicity by Giorgio Gomelsky. He'd met Christine Keeler and Mandy Rice Davies in a Jamaican blue beat club. He chatted up the glamorous girls, the latter the eighteen-year-old mistress of wealthy slum landlord Peter Rachman, the former the twenty-year-old squeeze of none other than Tory War Minister, John Profumo. The momentous Profumo Affair was still six months away from breaking in the tabloids but Gomelsky knew full well what was going on. Describing Keeler and Rice Davies as "the hottest fucking things around", he didn't hesitate to invite them to the Marquee. The girls took him up on it, they became a sensation in clubland and attendances at the Marquee were rapidly boosted. The young Rolling Stones clocked all this and smilingly drew their own conclusions.

Brian Jones had at once become the leader of the Rolling Stones. He was not only their co-founder but their most complete musician. In terms of confidence, energy and determination to succeed he outshone Mike Jagger and was head and shoulders above Ian Stewart and Keith Richards. He was behind the ads which appeared in the trade press from September 62 inviting clubbers to 'A Shot of Rhythm and Blues with the Rolling Stones' every Saturday night at the Ealing Club.

The caption 'A Shot of Rhythm and Blues' was a clever reference to Arthur Alexander's song of that name, the B-side of 'You Better Move On', a hit on the Billboard chart in March 62. On the chorus Alexander had rhymed the phrases 'rhythm and blues' and 'a pair o' dancin' shoes', linking in "rock 'n'roll just for good measure" and echoing that with "have a lotta pleasure."

By alluding to Alexander's song Brian Jones was making it crystal clear that what the Rolling Stones played was not traditional blues but R&B tinged with rock 'n' roll, an up-to-the-minute music aimed at dancers and with sexual undertones.

Then there was his intellect and his analytical capacity. That shone out from a remarkable letter which was published in Jazz News on October 31 1962. In three paragraphs, the leader of the Rolling Stones set out to define rhythm and blues. This is what he wrote:

"It appears that there exists in this country a growing confusion as to what the term 'rhythm and blues' applies to. It also appears that there exists a movement here to promote what would be better called 'soul jazz' as rhythm and blues. Surely we must accept that R&B is the American city Negro's pop music – nothing more, nothing less.

Rhythm and blues can hardly be considered a form of jazz. It is not based on improvisation, as is the latter. The impact is, and can only be, emotional. It would be ludicrous if the same kind of pseudo-intellectual snobbery that one unfortunately finds contaminating the jazz scene would be applied to anything as basic and vital as rhythm and blues.

It must be apparent that rock 'n' roll has a far greater affinity for R&B than the latter has for jazz insofar as rock is a direct corruption of rhythm and blues whereas jazz is on a different plane, intellectually higher but emotionally less intense."

For all his academic intelligence Brian Jones was totally streetwise from the start. He knew the Rolling Stones would get nowhere without a hot rhythm section. As it happened, Cyril Davies – described by Ian Stewart as a "clapped out old jazzer"- had the very thing. When Davies had broken with Korner and set up his own band, the Rhythm and Blues All Stars, he'd quickly recruited a drummer and a bassist. They came from Screaming Lord Sutch's rock 'n' roll crew, the Savages. Jones tried to get hold of them them on a permanent basis. He received a brusque rebuff from Carlo Little and Ricky Brown – "fuck off, Brian! -we're earning ten times more than you with Cyril."

On December 2 1962 the Rolling Stones got a massive break. They auditioned a bassist called Bill Wyman. Wyman had heard from temporary drummer Tony Chapman that Dick Taylor had left. The audition was at the Wetherby Arms, World's End, Chelsea. This was where the full Rolling Stones band regularly rehearsed.

Bill Wyman was unhappy with the less than friendly welcome which he received from Keith Richards. Richards made little secret of the fact that he regarded Wyman as "a typical London Ernie", sneering at the bassist's brylcreemed hair and blue suede shoes. But the impact of his Vox AC 30 was undeniable. Still, as Ian Stewart would make crystal clear, Wyman hadn't been taken on thanks to his amp alone but because he was an excellent musician, adept at the walking bass. The first time Wyman played a gig with the band was on December 14, 1962 in the Ricky Tick Club at the Star and Garter in Windsor. It marked a crucial turning point in the career of the Rolling Stones.

Bill Wyman was far more than just a brilliant bassist. Rarely has there been a greater discrepancy between high intelligence and an education abruptly cut short. His birth name was William George Perks. One of five children, the son of a bricklayer, Bill had grown up in a humble terraced house on one of the roughest streets in Sydenham and endured a childhood which he would later describe as "scarred by poverty."

Bill had sailed through the 11 plus exam and went on to Beckenham and Penge Grammar School. All set for GCE success, he was pulled out of school early by a father who had no use for education. The height of old man Perks' ambition for his lad was to work as a bookie's clerk. So, when Bill Wyman, by then a storekeeper, auditioned for the Rolling Stones, his world was separated from theirs in several significant ways. First, unlike them, he hadn't escaped national service, an obligation which, when it was abolished in 1960, removed the shadow of institutionalisation from budding rhythm and blues musicians and upcoming rock'n'roll bands. Second, he was a married man, having taken a bride before the end of the Fifties.

Although Bill Wyman would turn his back on conventional Fifties morality, cheating on his wife by indulging himself on the groupie scene, there was still much of that decade about him. His reaction to the bohemian squalor in which Jones, Jagger and Richards lived in Edith Grove was much the same as the tabloids with their sensational articles about art students and "beatnik horror." Repelled by the filthy conditions in the flat, he visited as rarely as possible. Invariably conscientious at his workplace, he showed not the slightest hint of rebelliousness, reluctantly compromising his hairstyle only when he became, as he put it, "paid to look like this."

Bill was close to his mum and she'd encouraged him to take piano lessons from the age of ten. In that way he differed from the average working-class lad but, even more so, in the fact that he started keeping a diary from round about the same age, a habit he never dropped. At twenty-six, he was more mature than the others and, Jones apart, he outshone them in emotional intelligence.

Bill was a stranger to rhythm and blues when he first joined the band. Along with Tony Chapman, he'd played in the Cliftons, a strictly rock 'n' roll outfit, and his heroes had included Jerry Lee Lewis. Plied with blues and R&B records by Brian Jones, he not only discovered Elmore James' ringing guitar but came quickly to appreciate the Mississippi –born artist's raw blues poetry.

The Rolling Stones were delighted by the boost they got from Bill Wyman's bass. What they didn't yet realise was that he was keeping a meticulous record of their activities – musical and otherwise – which would serve as the leading primary source for their early history.

BILL WYMAN
Not content to rely on memory, he recorded
everything in his diary

CHAPTER 3

"Hitting Civilisation on the Head"

IN JANUARY 1963 the Rolling Stones got themselves a new drummer. They'd been fed up for months with Tony Chapman and were desperate to replace him. There were two possibilities. One was Carlo Little, of Screaming Lord Sutch and the Savages, and the other was Charlie Watts of Blues Incorporated.

Carlo Little was a fully pepped up rock 'n' roll drummer, something which Charlie Watts never wanted to be. Indeed Charlie detested rock 'n' roll. Aged twenty-one, he'd started on drums when he was fourteen, the year before rock 'n' roll hit the UK. Charlie couldn't have cared less. His musical world centred on jazz and his personal style reflected this. He wouldn't have been seen dead in a leather jacket, he was immaculately groomed and totally a product of the Fifties. Still living at home with his parents in Neasden, Charlie was going steady with his art student girl-friend, Shirley Sheppard, and he married her the following year. He would never show the slightest interest in the groupie scene and, although he'd relax with a spliff in a jazz club, he always steered well clear of hard drugs and hallucinogenics.

Charlie Watts wasn't academically gifted as Brian Jones was nor did he possess Bill Wyman's emotional intelligence. But he was a promis-ing graphic artist, highly thought of by the advertising agency for whom he worked. It took six months of constant persuasion from Brian Jones before he quit Blues Incorporated.

Although he disdained rock 'n' roll, Charlie Watts was prepared to give rhythm and blues a chance. As soon as they knew they had him on board, the others promptly sacked Tony Chapman and Watts made his full debut with the Rolling Stones at the Flamingo on January 12. He blended well with Bill Wyman. They were both working class lads, Charlie the son of a lorry driver.

Watts' playing style was totally different from Carlo Little. Where Carlo stomped the beat in all-out rock 'n' roll style, Charlie played lazily behind it like a good jazzman should. As Keith Richards put it –"he never hits 'em hard but his sound's more powerful than some guy ramming his fist through the drums."

With Watts on the skins, the Rolling Stones moved quickly forward as a dance band. Soon Brian Jones was plying the new boy with rhythm and blues records. Some were by Bo Diddley and they featured a marked Afro-Cuban rhythm, the clave, known in America as 'shave 'n' a haircut -- two bits.' Others were by the Jimmy Reed band resonating to Al Duncan's lazily sensual shoot-bop, shoot-bop drumbeat. It wasn't long before the new boy had mastered both.

Giorgio Gomelsky had fully clocked the advent of Charlie Watts in the Rolling Stones. He'd regarded Watts as the finest young drummer in London over the previous year and he realised at once the difference he was bound to make.

Barely into the new year, 1963, Gomelsky had launched his rhythm and blues club fifteen miles out of town in Richmond. It was no haphazard gamble.

Richmond was close by Kingston Art College and he'd sussed the link between an interest in modern art and an enthusiasm for new forms of music. It would come as no surprise to him that so many of the leading figures in what would soon become the British rhythm and blues movement had an art school background, not only Keith Richards and Charlie Watts within the Rolling Stones but also Eric Clapton and Jeff Beck within the Yardbirds, and many more. Selling art students as his potential clientele, he persuaded the pub manager at the Station Hotel to let him start up a Sunday night rhythm and blues club in a back room. From a personal point of view it suited him fine. He could be there soon enough –ten stops on the District line from his Kensington apartment at Lexham Gardens.

CHARLIE WATTS
The jazzman who became a great rhythm and blues drummer

When Brian Jones heard that Gomelsky's new venture was up and running, he set off for Richmond on February 6 to plead the cause of his newly augmented band. Their situation was desperate because they'd been playing intervals for Cyril Davies at the Marquee and packing them in. But when they'd asked the blues purist for a rise, at the end of January, he sacked them on the spot. Sneering to Harold Pendleton that "they're not authentic and they're not very good", Davies couldn't grasp the difference between blues and rhythm and blues.

That difference was absolutely vital in Brian Jones' eyes. It wasn't just that he was a young guy, not yet twenty-one years old. Most Englishmen of his age remained reluctant to get on the dancefloor, seeing it as little more than a necessary chore if they were going to chat a girl up. But not only was Jones an uninhibited dancer himself but his empathy with young women told him that danceable rhythms were what they most craved in any dynamic new music.

Jones was too astute to be sidetracked by cerebral arguments in specialist jazz journals. He'd also written to the down-to-earth chart pop mag, 'Disc', in which he'd given impresario Jack Good a proxy verbal bollocking for failing to distinguish between rock 'n' roll and rhythm and blues. As for R&B, he'd written a letter to the BBC, dated January 2 1963, asking for a Rolling Stones' audition on the Beeb's 'Jazz Club' programme. In that letter he'd defined the band's musical policy as being "to produce an authentic Chicago rhythm and blues sound based on the material of such R&B 'greats' as Muddy Waters, Howlin Wolf, Bo Diddley, Jimmy Reed and others."

When he met up with Gomelsky again, it hadn't taken Brian Jones long to get to his main point. "Why don't you come and see my band, Giorgio?" he urged, adding "they're the best band in London and they play only rhythm and blues." Gomelsky took him at his word and saw the Rolling Stones' gig at the Red Lion in Sutton, Surrey. Impressed, he'd gone back with them afterwards to Edith Grove, a neighbourhood he remembered well because he and an artist friend had rented a painter's studio there a few years earlier. Stifling his nausea at what he called "the abominable smell"- at its worst because Doris Richards hadn't yet made her weekly washing trip to collect her son and his mates' dirty clothes – he'd held forth on his problems with the Dave Hunt Band. They were, as he saw it, an outfit of doubtful reliability.

Brian Jones was on the case in an instant. "Look, Giorgio", he said "you can't count on a band if you can't be sure they're even going to turn up." Jones went on to make a remarkable offer -"we'll be there and we'll play for free." Gomelsky was unwilling to sack Hunt without good reason but when the erstwhile bandleader failed to show up next Sunday, that had put him straight on the phone to Ian Stewart the very next day.

The Rolling Stones' first show at the Station Hotel attracted only a handful of people. But, on subsequent Sundays, the numbers increased by leaps and bounds. Two factors accounted for that. For starters, the band made a huge impression and gained crucial word-of-mouth. The other thing was Giorgio Gomelsky's flair for publicity. Disadvantaged as he was by his written English – his board outside the pub misspelt 'rhythm and blues' as 'rhythm and bulse'- he still had a deep admiration for the English language. He took his cue from the popular TV programme, the 'Good Old Days ', presented in the style of the Victorian music hall, where compere Leonard Sachs revelled in polysyllabic presentation.

Soon Gomelsky was plastering ads all over the music press with precise instructions as to how to get out to Richmond via the Tube. His spelling was erratic but his meaning was crystal clear as he trumpeted the news that the Rolling Stones were "galvanic, intoxicating and incomparable." Attendances mushroomed from week to week, doubling to sixty, reaching a hundred then tripling that to three hundred.

The Rolling Stones were tentative the first night, when they were paid a pound a head and a share of the takings split between the six of them. But they soon got into their musical stride, boosted by Gomelsky ads in which he referred to them as "illustrious unknowns."

Gomelsky was quite clear he was promoting both a new genre and its foremost exponents. In naming that genre 'British Rhythm and Blues' he drew a bold line between the Rolling Stones and what Davies and Korner purveyed. It had all the intensity of blues but it was danceable. Not of course in the outdated jiving way of rock'n' roll nor in the stylised Twist but in the shape of 'the Push', the relaxed boogie birthed by the Jimmy Reed band.

In the first weeks the young clubbers loved the sound but scarcely knew how to react to it. So Gomelsky told his right-hand man, Hamish Grimes, to stand on a table and wave his arms above his head. Grimes did as he was asked and shouted the words "yeah, yeah, yeah!!!" The phrase owed nothing to the Beatles' 'She Loves You'-which wasn't released till six months later. It originated in Jimmy Reed's 'Baby What You Want Me To Do' which had reached #10 on the R&B chart three years earlier and was in the Rolling Stones' set.

During this time Giorgio Gomelsky was, as Bill Wyman would later phrase it, "steering us on a managerial level." Although no formal contract was signed, Gomelsky was finding them gigs at other venues. His motivation was threefold- "they were doing a great job for my club, I loved their music and I hated the insipid rubbish in the Top Twenty."

The Rolling Stones longed for the chance to make a record and Ian Stewart helped set this up. His best pal was Glyn Johns, who led an R&B band called the Presidents and was a recording engineer at IBC Studios in Portland Place. On March 11, the band laid down several tracks there. Johns passed them on to the studio owner who tried to place them with various record companies without success. The tracks included versions of Jimmy Reed's 'Bright Lights, Big City' and Bo Diddley's 'Road Runner.' As demos go, they were of a high standard.

Meanwhile, back at the Station Hotel, Gomelsky was facing the problem of what he called "typical English reserve." At the start of their residency the band had sat on battered old stools without turning full on to their audience. It was Giorgio who urged them to end the gig with what he called "a rave up", based on the number which had drawn the greatest audience reaction, Bo Diddley's 'Crawdad' - now extended to twenty minutes. Suddenly, as Bill Wyman would later recall, "their mouths would gape open." What's more, as Ian Stewart would in future recollect, "that got them off their backsides for the first time- they were literally swinging from the rafters." Giorgio Gomelsky had his own take on the transformation. Interviewed in the years to come, he said "I can't tell you the excitement there was at that place in that time. It seemed like we were hitting civilisation right on the head. It gave everyone energy for years and years."

These remarks fully reflected Gomelsky's attitude to society. As a relaxed, jocular and gregarious guy, he would never have the mindset of a political activist. Beyond that, he was deeply suspicious of Marxists preaching revolution. He was, after all, an entrepreneur himself, the man who opened the first coffee bar in London, the Olympia, off Sloane Square, in 1956. Yet, although he had no use for fanaticism, still less for violence, there was a definite strain of anarchism in his thinking. One of his favourite sayings was "when music changes, the city walls come tumbling down."

Brian Jones' interest in politics was peripheral – it had never gone much further than taking part in a couple of 'Ban the Bomb' demonstrations in Oxford. But, even in Cheltenham, he had a fierce resentment of conventional society and that had intensified in London as a result of his link with Gomelsky.

By April 63, events were moving at a fast accelerating pace. Gomelsky got vital positive press in the local newspaper, the Richmond and Twickenham Times in an article written by cub reporter, Barry Gay. Asked over the phone for the name of his club, Giorgio came up with a bit of spontaneous lateral thinking – mixed with a malapropism – and called it the 'Crawdaddy.' The exotic -sounding moniker ratcheted up interest still further.

In future years Giorgio Gomelsky's role would be glossed over by rock critics who believed he operated only on the margins of the jazz scene. This was anything but the case. Gomelsky had been in Hamburg getting to know the Beatles in the days before they were famous. Considering them a long-overdue exception to "insipid Top Twenty rubbish", he invited the high -riding Liverpool band to visit the Station Hotel and on April 14 they did just that.

After the gig all four Beatles, the entire Rolling Stones plus Giorgio Gomelsky went back to Edith Grove and talked music into the early hours. Although John Lennon bridled at any phrase containing the word 'blues', he knew a good thing when he heard one and George Harrison, for his part, was well impressed. The Rolling Stones' sound, as described by Harrison, had "a beat so solid it shook off the walls and seemed to move right inside your head." It was indelibly imprinted on George's mind as was the image of "a real rave- with the audience dancing on tables." Before long he would prove the vital link between the new rhythm and blues band and Decca Records.

Gomelsky's next move was unprecedented. Known for his imaginatively produced documentary on Chris Barber's Jazz Band, he was determined to turn his filmmaking skills to the advantage of the Rolling Stones. Recording a brief soundtrack at a cheap local studio in Morden, Surrey the day before, he filmed the band playing live at the Crawdaddy on Sunday, April 21, together with footage of the crowd outside on the pavement jostling to get in.

For two months solid Gomelsky had devoted himself "stock, lock and barrel"– as he phrased it -to the single-minded promotion of the Rolling Stones. Suddenly he was stopped in his tracks by a simple twist of fate.

C H A P T E R   4

—————— ♀ ——————

Entry of a Whizzkid

GIORGIO GOMELSKY HAD mixed feelings as he flew out of London airport on April 23. He'd been saddened to learn, the day before, the news of his father's death in Switzerland. But he was optimistic that his work on behalf of the Rolling Stones would soon bear fruit in terms of a recording contract. He expected to be away for three days, returning after the funeral. In fact his father's legacy was a complex one and it took him a couple of weeks to administrate it. In the meantime his seven minute film of the band playing live was in the safe hands of his devoted girlfriend, Enid Tidy.

Little did he know that, starting that very evening, a chain of events would unfold which would lead to his proto-managerial connection with the Rolling Stones being brusquely severed. A new visitor made his first visit to the Crawdaddy and, impressed with what he saw, he reported back to his prospective business partner. On the 28th the two of them were at the Station Hotel. They looked an odd pair.

Eric Easton seemed far too old to be visiting a rhythm and blues club. Aged thirty-five, he looked fifty, balding and bespectacled, clad in sports jacket and cavalry twill trousers, his pristine white shirt buttoned to the neck under a drab tie. Born in Lancashire, Easton had begun his show business career as a cinema organist. Then he set himself up in artist management. His firm, Eric Easton Ltd, was based originally in Preston. By dint of hard work and a genial personality, he'd gone from strength to strength and, in the Fifties, he moved to London and opened an office at 27 Regent Street, bearing the name of Radnor House.

Easton's companion, the guy who'd already taken a sneak preview five days earlier, was renting a room from him so he could operate as a freelance PR agent. In terms of his age no one gave him a second glance but the nineteen year old stood out from his peers in the crowd by the way he was dressed. They were in suede jackets, gaucho trousers and Chelsea boots but he was the height of trendy fashion sporting dark sunglasses and clad in tight fitting trousers and a shirt with a button-down collar. That was how he'd appeared a few weeks earlier in the fashion pages of the 'Evening Standard.' His name was Andrew Loog Oldham.

Tipped off by a contact in music journalism by the name of Pete Jones about a hot new band in Richmond, he made his way there to see what all the fuss was about. As he strode down a narrow alley by the side of the club, he encountered Mike Jagger having a blazing row with his new girlfriend, Chrissie Shrimpton. This was during the interval between the two halves of the band's set. Politely excusing himself, he pushed past the oblivious pair and made his way into the club by the back door. Amused at first by the incongruous potted palms and the cut out wooden quavers fixed to the wall, he was all eyes and ears when the band resumed, to the wild delight of the clubbers. But the image which remained uppermost in his mind was of Mike Jagger laying down the law to Chrissie Shrimpton on what was only their second date.

Many years later, in his published memoirs, Andrew Oldham penned his breathless prose-"they made an immediate impact on me and my reaction was – this is it! I felt they were magic. I saw that they had a unique style. The combination of music and sex was something I'd never encountered in any other group and the surprising thing was that you could take them as they were, without asking them to change a thing in clothes, hairstyle or anything else."

Oldham's preoccupation with sex came as a complete surprise to the band. Bill Wyman would recall their reaction. "Sex? It seemed amazing to us. Brian and Mick were keen on projecting the music. Selling themselves as sexy popstars had not crossed their minds."

Oldham had heard that Gomelsky was out of the country and he was soon satisfied there was no hint of a rival management deal. Eager as he was to become the Rolling Stones' manager, he was dependent on Eric Easton. It wasn't just a case of Oldham's youth. The key to his secondary status was that Easton was licensed by the London County Council and he wasn't. Without a licence, Oldham could still have booked gigs for the band but there was no way he'd have been able to set up a recording contract.

Reckoning he might have to work hard convincing the older man, Oldham was pleasantly surprised to hear Eric Easton enthusing, within a matter of minutes, about an atmosphere he described as "the most exciting I've ever witnessed in any club or ballroom." There was only one problem, as far as Easton saw it. He protested that Mike Jagger couldn't sing. Hoping the Rolling Stones' frontman could at least make a good impression face-to-face, Oldham called him over at the end of the gig and told him who the pair of them were. Articulate and eager to impress as he was, Jagger had to concede that Brian Jones was the leader of the band.

After a few minutes conversation with a clearly interested Jones, Oldham took a a contact number and said he'd phone him next day with a decision. As they drove back to the West End, Oldham and Easton decided to set themselves up as joint partners in a firm with only one purpose, the management and promotion of the Rolling Stones. Easton knew lawyers, he'd do the hard graft and Oldham would handle the publicity. Oldham thought up the firm's name then and there. No old-timey 'Limiteds' or anything like that, it'd be called Impact Sound.

When Andrew Oldham phoned, Brian Jones said he'd have to think things over and for two days he kept them waiting. Jones had no problem with Eric Easton. Indeed Eric seemed just the sort of chap Brian could have introduced to his parents, Fifties to the core, quietly spoken and undemonstrative. For his part, Easton had formed an excellent impression of Jones, noting his cultured accent and good manners.

Jones' hesitation centred on Andrew Oldham. Oldham had spoken about himself as a 'hustler', a term which had clear gangster resonance. Jones decided to make his own enquiries from contacts on the music scene. It was common knowledge that Oldham had worked as a doorman at Ronnie Scott's Jazz Club and as a waiter at the Flamingo. Before that he'd been a gopher for Mary Quant and he got to know Vidal Sassoon who was all the rage as a pioneering hairstylist.

What swung it for Jones was that Oldham had worked on behalf of Beatles' manager, Brian Epstein, for three months, starting in January 63 and had scored a notable coup by getting the Liverpool band featured in Vogue magazine.

Few knew Andrew Oldham's full background at that time. Born in January 1944, his father had died a few months before he was born, killed in action in the last year of the war. Andrew Loog was an American airman, born in Texas and raised in Louisiana, who'd come to England with the USAF. In London he formed a brief relationship with a WVS nurse named Cecilia Oldham. Celia had been born in Australia, her mother from Sydney and her father a Lithuanian Jewish immigrant named Militar Schatkowsky. They were never married and, when their relationship broke up, Celia moved to England.

Andrew's father's death left Celia Oldham a single mother who, when the war ended, got by as best she could, using relatives as babysitters while she tried to make ends meet working as a bookkeeper. She and her little son lived in humble circumstances in and around the Edgware Road.

But when Andrew was six years old, his life was transformed after his mother began a long lasting relationship with a much older married man by the name of Alec Morris. Morris was an immensely wealthy entrepreneur. He was East End Jewish by origin but had relocated to New York where he worked as a dance teacher. Returning to London he set himself up in a furniture business before becoming a banker. To all intents and purposes, Morris was Andrew's stepfather. He paid for the boy to attend prep school and later three exclusive public schools. What's more, the Oldhams, Celia and young Andrew, were wined and dined by Morris at some of the West End's most prestigious restaurants.

Living in Hampstead, Celia Oldham got to know many people in the theatre and cinema world. At the age of eleven, Andrew was taken to see Paul Scofield in 'Espresso Bongo'. Enthralled by theatreland, he struck out on his own at the age of thirteen when he started hanging around the 2'Is coffee bar in the heart of Soho.

Bored with academic work, Andrew bunked off more and more and he was expelled from Wellingborough when he was sixteen. After a short spell in the south of France in the tourist trade, he returned to London and found work as a window dresser with Mary Quant.

In contrast to Giorgio Gomelsky, Andrew Oldham leaned politically to the right. Although he giggled at the embarrassment of the Establishment over the Profumo Affair, he was instinctively at ease with wealth, he loved stretch limos and he found Labourites ugly.

By this time Gomelsky, still detained in Switzerland on family business, was fading fast in Brian Jones' mind. Jones was fed up with hearing about potential recording contracts. He wanted more than straws in the wind and Oldham had some very interesting news for him. If there was one man desperate to find an up-and-coming young guitar band, it was Dick Rowe, head of A&R at Decca Records. Rowe had become the laughing stock of the music business, notorious as "the man who turned down the Beatles."

As it happened, Dick Rowe had just been on Merseyside judging a beat group contest with none other than George Harrison. George reckoned Liverpool was a naff scene with the sole exception of the Road Runners, a sound R&B band. But he knew of an even better one. "They're right on your doorstep, Dick", he said, "you wanna get round to Richmond and sign 'em up." Rowe took him at his word and planned to visit the Crawdaddy as soon as he could.

At this stage Brian Jones was obliged to come clean and tell Oldham and Easton about the Rolling Stones' session at IBC. Indeed the band's tapes were still at Portland Place. Impact Sound had to counter this without delay. Those tapes had to be bought back. The cost would be £106 and a reason had to be given which wouldn't attract suspicion. Easton put up the cash and Oldham coached Jones in a plausible cover story.

Brian Jones was told to get back to IBC, pretending the band had realised they had no future in the entertainment world but would like their tapes back for sentimental reasons. Jones did a perfect job with the charade. IBC swallowed the story, hook line and sinker and Jones got the tapes back. They included the Rolling Stones' versions of 'Road Runner' and 'Bright Lights, Big City.' They would be suppressed for fifty years and there was nothing now standing in the way of a deal with Decca Records.

Easton's lawyers drew up two contracts. One dealt with management by Impact Sound and was ready for immediate signature. The other left the signature space blank. It was also with Impact Sound and it tied the Rolling Stones to a three year recording contract. There'd be a tape lease agreement between Impact Sound and Decca giving the recording company first option on the Rolling Stones' records and providing for a 6% royalty to each member of the band.

The second agreement remained provisional till Dick Rowe had time to see the Rolling Stones play live and report back to his company with a recommendation to proceed. Dick Rowe hadn't been to the Crawdaddy yet but Andrew Oldham was banking on his desperation and would be proved right.

On May 1 1963 Jones went round to Regent Street, read through the contracts, asked questions and got what he thought were satisfactory answers. Only one signature was needed to bind the band. Neither Mike Jagger nor Keith Richards could sign because they were both under twenty-one, the legal age of adulthood at that time. Of course any one of Ian Stewart, Bill Wyman or Charlie Watts would have been eligible to sign but all three were still in full-time employment and were at work on the day in question.

With the as yet unsigned contract in his hands, Jones nipped round to a Lyons tea shop where Jagger and Richards were waiting. He showed it to them and they nodded in agreement. He returned and put pen to paper.

That same evening the six Rolling Stones were on a high as they met at Edith Grove and set out, in Ian Stewart's van, for the first gig which Andrew Oldham had booked for them.

The venue was bizarre yet picturesque. The Eel Pie Island Hotel had been built in the nineteenth century on an island situated at a bend in the River Thames at Twickenham. From the late Fifties onwards its formerly immaculate ballroom resounded to traditional jazz but, by 1963, as the rhythm and blues movement gathered pace, that was a thing of the past.

The Rolling Stones parked their van on the mainland and carried their drums and amps with them as they walked across the tuppenny toll footbridge near the weeping willow trees. Little did they know they were crossing a musical Rubicon.

Andrew Oldham was waiting for them on the other side. Expecting to go promptly on stage, they were halted by a short address from their new manager. Thin as a rake, cold eyed and pale as death, he issued a diktat. Ian Stewart must stand down forthwith. Dismissing Stu as "your ivory thumper" he brusquely gave his reasons. Stewart looked wrong, he said, completely out of place and no good for the image.

The band were stunned and resentful but Oldham was insistent. Thinking fast on his feet as always, he offered a compromise to quell any hint of mutiny. Stewart could never go on stage again but he could play on records and he would become the band's road manager.

Stewart took his brutal demotion manfully – or so it seemed. As Keith Richards later put it, "I would have just told him 'fuck you!' but Stu had a very big heart." The show went on.

Andrew Oldham's secretary had known which way the wind was blowing. Her name was Cynthia Dillane and she was the well-educated daughter of a professor of paediatrics. Her taste in men was completely different from the mid-teen girls who loomed at the forefront of Oldham's thoughts. "Andrew loved the thin, pretty, long-haired boys" she would later say. And, by no stretch of the imagination could Ian Stewart be included in that category. Cynthia knew that Oldham had poked fun at what he called Stewart's 'Popeye torso' and joked about his protruding jaw.

Dillane soon got to know the band's new roadie. Indeed she fell in love with him and, four years later, they were married. Cynthia Stewart would recall "whatever anyone thought, Stu was deeply hurt by what happened. Not because he couldn't go on stage any more but because of the savage way he'd been kicked to one side." Although she would confirm that Oldham always treated her with the utmost respect, she knew full well that her man thought different. "Stu was contemptuous of Andrew" she would recall, politely refraining from adding his comment about Oldham – "I wouldn't piss on him if he was on fire!" That remark found its way back to the new Rolling Stones' manager but he laughed it off. He saw Stewart as no kind of threat. Thin was in and stout was out, end of story.

Andrew Oldham wasn't the only one Ian Stewart blamed for the Eel Pie Island decree. He was convinced that Brian Jones must have known about it in advance. As the burly Scot saw it, he'd been betrayed by the man with whom he'd founded the Rolling Stones almost twelve months to the day before.

But most on the music scene didn't buy it that Jones was in the know. Yes, he had form for a bad attitude to non-musicians and had treated his old Cheltenham pal, Dick Hattrell, like a dogsbody when Hattrell was sharing the flat at Edith Grove. Hattrell had risked arrest getting up before dawn to steal milk bottles from the float while the milkman's back was turned. Jones and Richards were quick to swill the milk down when they woke up but Hattrell got few thanks for that. Worse, he was actually the one to buy Jones his first fully electric guitar. It was a Harmony Stratotone from Lewington's in Soho but it didn't stop the good-natured Gloucestershire guy from being the constant target of jokes.

Yet it was a completely different Brian Jones who would be warmly remembered by his old bandmates. John Keene would recall how Jones would never let the side down, always ready to fill in at short notice if someone couldn't make a gig. And Paul Jones reflected – "I really liked him. First of all, he was a really good musician. But, although he was so good, he didn't rub your nose in it." And, where other musicians jealously guarded secrets of technique, Brian was always willing to share what he knew. He taught Paul the intricacies of cross-harping. Paul never forgot Brian's kindness, adding "he unlocked the secrets of the harmonica for me and I was off and running. It was as if he'd opened doors to an unseen kingdom and I would always like him for that."

It must surely have seemed to Keene and Paul Jones as it did to many others –jazzmen, rock'n'rollers, blues buffs, whatever- that Brian Jones' musical ideal was of a band of brothers who stuck together through thick and thin united by the common aim of producing cool sounds.

Within days of the Eel Pie Island gig, Giorgio Gomelsky was back in London, completely unaware of all that had happened during his absence. He promptly got in touch with the Rolling Stones and invited them to view the documentary film he'd shot of them at the Crawdaddy.

Curious as they were to see themselves playing live, this was of course the moment when they should have come clean. Yet they lost their nerve and the first inkling Gomelsky had that anything was wrong was when Brian Jones was the last to arrive, accompanied by someone Giorgio described as "a complete stranger, an odd young man called Andrew Loog." Jones introduced his companion as an old school friend from Cheltenham who happened to be in town for a couple of days.

It took Giorgio Gomelsky no more than a day to realise he'd been doublecrossed by Brian Jones. At first he could scarcely believe that someone he considered a friend, a fellow spirit in the cause of rhythm and blues, a truly gifted musician and a young man of high intellect could have behaved in such a way. Then his mind went back to the Beatles' show at the Royal Albert Hall on April 18.

The Beatles had invited the Rolling Stones to go backstage and, as Gomelsky and Jones were helping the roadie unload equipment, Brian had been spotted by gatecrashing teenage girls. Momentarily mistaking him for one of the 'Fab Four', they pounced on him with excitement and, even after realising their mistake, were still blowing him kisses. Jones was delighted. "This is what we want, Giorgio", he enthused – "this is what I want!" Gomelsky reassured him with a smile – "don't worry, Brian, you'll get it. But, after you've got it, you may not want it any more." The double meaning was obvious but Gomelsky underestimated the appeal of nubile girls to the twenty-one-year-old leader of the Rolling Stones. "He could never get enough of it" his erstwhile manager would later reflect.

Giorgio Gomelsky had hit on an explanation for what Brian Jones had done. But an explanation was not an excuse and he couldn't bring himself to forgive him. Yet Gomelsky took his time and considered the rest of the band.

He felt truly sorry for Ian Stewart. He'd always liked the shy guy from Sutton, the man he'd phoned to set up the Rolling Stones' breakthrough-only three months before but seeming now like a lifetime. As for Bill Wyman, he was anything but shy as far as women were concerned but Gomelsky saw him as a genuine bloke and an innovative but underrated instrumentalist.

Then there was Keith Richards, who'd been a key factor in the marriage of rhythm'n' blues and rock 'n' roll – which meant of course black rock 'n' roll à la Chuck Berry – which had built up the Rolling Stones.

At this stage the nineteen-year-old lead guitarist retained much of the idealism which had led him to turn his back on a career in advertising. Keith Richards later said "we got the message and we knew we were on the right track – and we weren't even looking for it – that wasn't the reason the band were put together. We were evangelists. It was a very pure, idealistic drive that did it. The money we needed to live on, we didn't give a damn about. That wasn't the point. The point was to spread the music. We were doing what we wanted. We had all these kids coming to clubs and we were spreading the music and doing what we wanted to do. It wasn't to make money. The money was a secondary thing – and we didn't see any for a year or two."

Richards' views chimed with Gomelsky's and that plus his loyalty to Stewart and Wyman made the ousted manager decide to cast aside his dismay at Jones' breach of trust. So he invited the Rolling Stones back to the Crawdaddy on May 12. Their audience received them with open arms just as they'd always done. Writing about Gomelsky many years later, Bill Wyman commented "he gave us more loyalty than we deserved."

There remained one obvious question to which no satisfactory answer was ever given. What happened to the film footage Gomelsky shot? Interviewed at his home in New York many years later, Gomelsky could only say "it was lost. No one knows where it is." On other occasions he seemed to hint that it might have been purloined by persons unknown who wished to deny him his crucial role in promoting the Rolling Stones. But he could never advance a shred of evidence as to their identity. The fact remains that, after Enid Tidy returned it to him, he was its sole custodian and could have kept it under lock and key had he been prudent enough to do so. The film was the most important primary source for the early history of the Rolling Stones, even more so than Bill Wyman's meticulous diary, and it was a shame that it wasn't preserved.

CHAPTER 5

Dancing in the Streets of Richmond

In May 1963, Carnaby Street had yet to become the world-famous fashion hub which it was three years later when it was referenced in the Kinks' iconic pop hit, 'Dedicated Follower of Fashion.' This was the song in which Ray Davies wittily lampooned a mod youth's cultural obsessions.

But Andrew Oldham was ahead of the game. Scarcely was the ink dry on the managerial contract than he had the five Rolling Stones over in Carnaby Street ready to be kitted out in black gear – jeans, rollneck sweaters and Cuban- heel boots. The homage to the Beatles was all too obvious- and a clear contradiction of what he said about not needing to change their style in clothes- but the band reluctantly acquiesced.

A week later Oldham opted for a variant but, when they saw photos of themselves in white houndstooth check jackets, they told him enough was enough and he had to change tack.

Yet their new manager never lost focus on his target audience, screaming midteen girls. The Rolling Stones might be in smart casuals at a gig in Battersea but when Oldham saw Brian Jones in front of cameras with his baby son, Julian, in his arms, he tore him off a strip. He promptly reminded the errant band leader that, in public, he must be seen to be 'available' to fantasising teens. These were the girls who devoured mags such as 'Boyfriend', 'Fabulous', 'Valentine' and 'Jackie' and soon photos of each band member were appearing in their pages along with titillating, spiced- up gossip.

As part of his deal with Decca, Andrew Oldham had crowned him-self record producer of the Rolling Stones. But, when they debuted at Olympic Studios in suburban Barnes on May 10, resident engineer Roger Savage was dumbfounded at the ignorance of their 'producer' about the most basic essentials of the recordmaking process. Oldham was blithely unconcerned but, though he clued up fast, he couldn't keep pace with Brian Jones in the learning process at the studio.

Oldham had already been told by his contact, Pete Jones, about his namesake's musical accomplishments and these were emphasised by his R&B specialist colleague on the Record Mirror, Norman Jopling. Pete Jones told Oldham-"Brian's the leader, the organiser, he lays down every musical move they make. He's got this great memory and he can tell you exactly where every single one of their songs comes from."

Now this was all very well for the likes of Pete Jones and Jopling but Oldham had sussed out only too well what these sources were and, as he saw it, there was no way any sort of bluesy stuff would ever get into the UK chart. Effectively he brokered a compromise. In the early Sixties, singles were still the name of the game and the album era was in its infancy. Oldham needed A sides and B sides but the Rolling Stones' rhythm and blues material would be shunted to the B sides.

There might be the odd item from the band's set which he'd okay as an A side. "Give me the most commercial song you've got" he told them. But neither he nor the band were satisfied with 'Come On', possibly the weakest song Chuck Berry ever wrote. Even though it only narrowly failed to make the Top Twenty, the band's version soon dropped out of the charts. A careful rethink was needed and, at least for a while, Oldham was prepared to bide his time.

The B side of 'Come On' was 'I Want To Be Loved ', the Rolling Stones' version of Muddy Waters' 1955 R&B track. It had been written by Willie Dixon, who was a fine stand-up bassist and the foremost blues songwriter ever. Around this time Dixon was in London as part of the American Folk Blues summer tour to Europe and the band were delighted to make his acquaintance when he looked in at Giorgio Gomelsky's flat, along with Sonny Boy Williamson II.

Sadly, Elmore James was not with them. He'd been lined up to make the tour but, on May 24 1963, he died of a heart attack in Chicago, aged only forty-five. Rhythm and blues had lost one of its greatest ever artists, the man whose ringing full octave slide guitar in 'Dust My Broom' had inspired Brian Jones and whose raw blues poetry in 'The Sky Is Crying' had impressed Bill Wyman.

Adjusting gradually to life in the recording studio, the Rolling Stones were back in their element at the Crawdaddy. That was until the evening of June16 when Giorgio Gomelsky greeted them with bad news. "Boys", he said "we've got to get out. I've been given notice to quit."

The problem lay with what had seemed like a rave review. Inde Coope, the brewers, had been shocked by an article from Patrick Doncaster, the pop writer of the Daily Mirror. Doncaster's article included the words "you could boil an egg in the atmosphere. Heads shake violently and feet stamp in tribal style with hands above heads, clapping in rhythm." Doncaster also wrote about "shaking figures above the rest, held aloft by their colleagues, thrashing and yelling, nobody seems to care."

Even worse, from the brewers' point of view, were the attendance figures, which Doncaster had given as 500. This was far in excess of the legal limit and Inde Coope moved to protect themselves without delay.

Never one to be disheartened for long, Giorgio Gomelsky sought to reassure the glum -faced band. They could scarcely believe their ears when he said "don't worry, I've got somewhere else in mind, just give me a couple of weeks to get it sorted."

Gomelsky was well aware that Harold Pendleton had established a National Jazz Festival, also in Richmond, in the grounds of the Richmond Athletic Association only a few hundred yards away from the Station Hotel. Pendleton's hostility to Gomelsky had abated as soon as the pro-moter ceased to threaten his fiefdom in the West End. When Hamish Grimes and Enid Tidy went to see him looking for help, he was more than obliging. The Crawdaddy would be resurrected in the Clubhouse of the Athletic Association and on June 30 the Rolling Stones kicked things off in their new home, taking hundreds of their fans with them. Soon Pendleton's jazz festival would be rechristened the National Jazz and Blues Festival.

Giorgio Gomelsky would always cherish the incredible atmosphere which the band had generated at the Station Hotel. Yet, viewed from another angle, their time at the relocated Crawdaddy in the Richmond

Clubhouse, where they played throughout July, August and most of September 63, brought a vibrant new focus. Although Barry Gay's article had spoken of "an irresistible urge to get up and dance", there'd never been much room to do that freely at the Station Hotel. And Gomelsky had conceded that "young guys were the main supporters of the Rolling Stones in those days."

But, underneath the Clubhouse Grandstand, in a huge bar area, there was ample space for hundreds of clubbers, many of them new fans of the band, to get up and dance. Soon it was estimated that at least eight hundred and possibly a thousand were dancing. It was now that girls came into their element, joyously dancing, sometimes with guys, sometimes together.

These girls were either in their early twenties or their late teens. Some were students, most worked in shops and offices. They had nothing in common with the Beatles' kids who figured so powerfully in Andrew Oldham's imagination. Contemptuous of teen pop, scorning 'Top of the Pops' and the very idea of boy bands, they were at the forefront of the British Rhythm and Blues movement. When the gig ended, they made their way happily to Richmond Tube station, singing the R&B songs the Rolling Stones had played, even dancing to the sounds they'd made. Guys were with them along the way but there was never a hint of the violence which had marked the advent of rock'n roll seven years before.

Among the girls who danced at the Richmond Clubhouse was Linda Lawrence. She was a sixteen-year-old hairdresser from Windsor who'd become Brian Jones' lover shortly after meeting him early in 63 after a Rolling Stones' gig at the Ricky Tick Club. By now the relationship between Jones and Pat Andrews had foundered and she remained with baby Julian in Cheltenham. Jones kept up child support for a short while, but, when he defaulted, Andrews went to court to obtain a paternity order against him.

In the late Summer of 63, Jones went to live with Lawrence and her parents in Windsor after Edith Grove was finally evacuated. The contrast between the filthy Fulham flat and the upscale residence of Linda's prosperous builder father- at 90 St. Leonard's Road- could scarcely have been greater.

It was in Windsor that Brian Jones began to cultivate what would become a revolutionary change in the male hairstyle and his locks would attract heavy media attention, most of it fiercely hostile, the following year. Not content with a Beatles-type mop top, he let his hair grow to lengths unprecedented within living memory.

During his time in Windsor, Brian seemed happier than he'd ever been before in his life. Linda was in love with him and he seemed to reciprocate. He was totally at ease with her parents and her brother, chatting freely with them over cooked breakfasts.

But as the band's schedule became increasingly hectic with TV appearances and gigs on the ballroom circuit, so his health began to weaken. The problem was asthma. It had started during his childhood when he'd been forced to drop out of school sports because of it. Although he detested rugby, he'd been a keen boy cricketer spending hours batting and bowling with his best friend. His father, pleased at his son's interest in what he considered an eminently respectable sport, had unhesitatingly moved his Wolseley off the drive so one boy could bowl towards the garage door while the other batted in front of it.

Now, on the brink of musical fame, he would be struck down again by asthmatic attacks. It was rare for him to miss a gig yet, in contrast to his bandmates who were all in good health, his weakness stood out. As Linda Lawrence soon realised, Brian would react to this by losing his self-esteem and blaming himself as a wheezing weakling. He tried to compensate with reckless behaviour and they were both incredibly lucky to escape with only scratches and bruises when he overturned his Jaguar E type at high speed. On another occasion, during a summer boating trip, he steered his motorboat towards fast flowing water near sluice gates-pulling away only when he heard his girlfriend scream. Asthma was the catalyst for Jones' increasing appetite for risks which, in the years to come, would drive him towards hallucinogenics.

At the same time as Jones quit Edith Grove for Windsor, Mike Jagger, Chrissie Shrimpton and Keith Richards went to live at a house in Hampstead, at 33 Mapesbury Road. Hampstead was Andrew Oldham's old stomping ground and he was delighted when Jagger told him he could move in to their new pad himself.

By this time Oldham had begun to install the Rolling Stones on the ballroom concert circuit where he hoped they'd draw increasing teen attention. This brought an end to the Crawdaddy residency which climaxed with an acclaimed farewell gig on September 22.

The Rolling Stones parted from Giorgio Gomelsky on good terms. Learning from his blunder earlier in the year, he had by now signed the Yardbirds to a formal managerial contract. The Yardbirds were a Surrey rhythm and blues band formed in May 63. Within a month of taking over the Rolling Stones' residency at the Crawdaddy, the Yardbirds acquired a new lead guitarist. He was an eighteen-year-old with cropped hair and a sullen stare. Slung out of art school for slacking, he was working on a building site. His name was Eric Clapton.

In future years Giorgio Gomelsky would be dismissed by Andrew Oldham as a clueless eccentric. Oldham scornfully cited his eventual sacking by the Yardbirds. It was certainly true that Gomelsky wasn't single-mindedly devoted to maximising revenue either for himself or the band and this was what led the Yardbirds to dispense with his services. Yet, whilst under Gomelsky's management, the Yardbirds had enjoyed huge chart success as well as artistic achievement. They were pioneers of progressive pop with such standout singles as 'For Your Love', 'Heart Full of Soul' and 'Evil Hearted You'/'Still I'm Sad.'

Giorgio Gomelsky's significance extended even beyond his promotion of the Rolling Stones and his discovery of the Yardbirds. He played a big part in the wider movement of British R&B and he was the organiser of the British Rhythm and Blues Festival in 1964. He was the first to realise that top-quality rhythm and blues bands could be found outside London. He spotted the Animals at the Club a Gogo in Newcastle and brought them to Richmond in a residency swap with the Yardbirds. He also clocked the Spencer Davis Group (with Stevie Winwood) in Birmingham and tried to sign them- only to be beaten to the punch once again by a whizzkid, this time the Anglo- Jamaican, Chris Blackwell. What's more, it was Giorgio Gomelsky who thought up the actual phrase 'British Rhythm and Blues' (BRB) and applied it to the hundreds of young British bands – stretching from Brighton to Belfast – who, after the Rolling Stones first broke through in 63, galvanised the jaded pop scene.

Until this time all five members of the Rolling Stones had carried on travelling to and from gigs in Ian Stewart's van. But, after their show at the Birmingham Plaza on September 14, Mike Jagger and Keith Richards returned to Hampstead in Andrew Oldham's limo. What might have seemed, at first glance, no more than a matter of logistics soon came to have a far wider significance.

This was the beginning of a split in the group about which Ian Stewart later commented "Keith and Mick were quite prepared to go along with anything Andrew said. They fed off each other. We had very little contact with them in those days. Edicts would just be issued from the Oldham office." This led Stewart to christen the new Oldham-Jagger-Richards axis 'The Unholy Trinity.'

Brian Jones considered there was no need for the Rolling Stones to write their own material because they could draw on a repertoire of eighty rhythm and blues songs in their set, Andrew Oldham thought differently. Taking the Beatles as his guiding light once again, he was impressed by massive media acclaim for Lennon and McCartney songs.

Mike Jagger, sensing imminent fame, had dropped out before the third year of his course began. Still, the ex-student must have developed a way with words, so Oldham figured, and could probably cobble up some sort of reasonable lyric. But he knew Jagger was a limited musician and that was where Keith Richards came in. If Keith could conjure up some neat tunes, a viable songwriting partnership would surely be up and running in next to no time. Of course Keith would have to get with it popwise and that led Oldham to excise the final 's' from his surname. It was now written exactly the same as teen idol Cliff Richard. Whatever Keith might have thought about it, he acquiesced.

Desperate for a hit single, Andrew Oldham solicited a song from Lennon and McCartney. Mike Jagger was highly impressed. By now he was beginning to develop a pseudo- Cockney estuarial drawl which, a couple of years later, he'd perfected. One generation on it would become standard pronunciation for words previously uttered as clipped pairs of consonants.

Jagger recalled in interview "Andrew braw Paul and John down to the re-'earsal. They said they 'ad this tune, they were really husserlers then. I mean, the way they used to husserl tunes was grea', like 'hey, Mick, we've got this grea' song. So they played it and we thought it was pretty com-mershiull, which was what we were lookin' for."

Suddenly two changes were in the air. First, the dreaded H word, one with which Andrew Oldham had always been at ease, could freely be used. Second, Jagger's abbreviated first name had altered. Hitherto known to his family and friends as 'Mike', he'd now become 'Mick.' As a PR man, Oldham was only too well aware of the significance of names. He'd savoured the similarity between 'jagged' and 'Jagger', a surname which conveniently rhymed with 'shagger.' As for 'Mick', any thirteen-year-old schoolboy knew what that rhymed with.

Before the name changes for frontman and lead guitarist, there'd been a slight but significant change regarding the way in which the name of the band was spelled. In its first year the word 'Rolling' was often printed as 'Rollin' When Andrew Oldham took over, that letter was brought back. It was more than the nonchalant elimination of a piffling apostrophe. Brian Jones, the originator of the name, frequently spelled the word as Chess Records wrote it on the label of Muddy Waters' 1950 blues song– 'Rollin' Stone.' But their new manager found links with ageing bluesmen dis-tinctly uncool. Significant though these alterations were, the most impor-tant change of the lot wouldn't come till January 65.

The number Lennon and McCartney came up with was 'I Wanna Be Your Man ', a fast-paced rock 'n' roll/Merseybeat effort. Bill Wyman would recall "we learnt it fast because there wasn't really much to learn." Then "Brian got his slide out and we turned it into something more rhythm and blues, more Rolling Stones, more Elmore James." Indeed, 'I Wanna Be Your Man' seizes the Lennon and McCartney number by the scruff of the neck and drags it from rock 'n' roll onto the cusp of rhythm and blues. Made by Jones' blistering bottleneck guitar, the track reached # 12 on the UK chart in November 63.

Andrew Oldham hadn't been present at the recording session, done at De Lane Lea Studios in Kingsway on October 7 with Eric Easton the nominal producer. In fact Brian Jones had taken charge of the session and had cranked up the amps as high as they'd go, bringing Bill Wyman's driving bass to the forefront of the track. Even though he'd skedaddled to Paris at the time in question, Oldham was delighted with the outcome-chartwise. So too were Decca Records.

Still one hurdle remained before the Rolling Stones would get the green light to record their eponymous first album. At this time Extended Plays were still a significant part of the British music business. The band had recorded a four track EP, mainly in November, consisting of light-weight tracks on the cusp of rock 'n' roll and R&B including one from Beatles' hero, Arthur Alexander. Their eponymously titled Extended Play began its steady climb to the top of the EP chart.

Preparations got underway for the recording of an eponymous album beginning on January 3 1964. The album cover photo would be a brilliantly innovative piece of work by Brian Jones' photographer friend, Nicholas Wright, who operated from the Dezo Hoffman studio in Chelsea. It bore neither title nor identifying information beyond the Decca logo, which appeared, almost in miniature, on the upper right hand side.

Nicholas Wright's photographic cover is a vital primary source for the early history of the Rolling Stones. It features all five band members standing sideways on to the camera against a black background. They're wearing smart casual jackets or, in Brian Jones' case, a sleeveless waistcoat. The photo appears to depict nothing more threatening than a group of earnest students preparing to go into an exam room.

Nevertheless it was found to be deeply offensive by the powers that be. The show business establishment was shocked rigid by the the band's demeanour. There was not the slightest hint of a smile between the five of them. The actual Establishment was horrified by the length of their hair. With the exception of Charlie Watts, they all wore it over their ears. The others had followed Brian Jones' example in this but even he hadn't yet let it grow to shoulder length.

The Rolling Stones' look may have been fully masculine in all respects bar hairstyle yet -to males over the age of thirty -it had disturbing connotations of effeminacy and gave rise to misconceptions about a supposed gay sexuality at a time when that was still four years from decriminalisation.

In addition to the absent smiles and abundant hair of the group as a whole, there was a third factor, applicable only to the frontman, which touched on a deep vein of prejudice. It wasn't apparent from Nicholas Wright's shadowy photograph, where none of the five was shown in close-up. But, as soon as the Rolling Stones began to appear on TV, in shows such as 'Thank Your Lucky Stars' and 'Ready Steady Go', the quasi - racist hostility to Mick Jagger – which he first suffered on the streets of Dartford – began to manifest itself more widely. In their belated reply to Brian Jones' request for an audition, the BBC had turned the band down and a producer had labelled Jagger's voice as "too black." Now another producer had buttonholed Andrew Oldham after a TV show with the advice that "if you want to get anywhere in the entertainment industry, you'd better get rid of that vile singer with the tyre tread lips!!"

The Rolling Stones' look was of course no problem whatever to Andrew Oldham. Its impact on teenage girls was all he cared about and they were soon screaming right on cue. Never a Svengali, deeply conformist, he'd sought to emulate the Beatles not to challenge them. It was the Rolling Stones themselves who'd bucked the trend and, contrary to the persistent rock myth that Oldham was the one responsible for their so-called 'bad boy' image, he merely jumped on the bandwaggon. Never the so-called 'architect of the Stones', he trivialised Gomelsky's anarchism into teen-oriented antics of outrage.

The next phase of the Rolling Stones' career would be defined not by appearances but by their recorded music and, above all, the contradiction between their commitment to rhythm and blues and Andrew Oldham's determination to establish them as a hitmaking unit.

Part 2: Revolution in Tin Pan Alley

CHAPTER 6

———— ⌘ ————

Marijuana, Stu and Nanker-Phelge

'I WANNA BE Your Man' hadn't been the only number recorded by the Rolling Stones on October 7 1963. Scarcely had the reserved recording engineers at 129 Kingsway recovered from its rousing rock 'n' roll strains than a rhythm and blues track was being laid down. 'Stoned' would not be included on the Rolling Stones' debut album but stylistically it's akin to it.

The nondescript Holborn studio had been set up after the war by French intelligence attache, Major Jacques de Lane Lea, ostensibly as a facility for dubbing foreign language films. Yet the bluesy melody of 'Stoned' and its fractured pseudo-lyric were more subversive than anything the spooky Major could ever have imagined.

Sensing that Andrew Oldham was encouraging his housemates, Jagger and Richards, to begin a songwriting partnership independent of the band, Brian Jones sought to counter this with instrumental tracks which would begin as pure jams and be credited to the group as a whole. Songwriting royalties would be equally shared among all six original members.

Asked for a collective publishing name, Jones cracked the others up with his zany suggestion of 'Nanker- Phelge.' It was another example of his thinking out of the box, combining their code word for po-faced jobsworths with the surname of his flatmate at 102 Edith Grove. Jimmy Phelge was a printer, a very down-to-earth Londoner indeed with a taste for crude practical jokes, a total disdain for personal hygiene and a propensity to piss wherever he pleased. Beyond the in-joke was a serious purpose – bonding the band as a brotherhood of musicians who would be one for all and all for one.

Ian Stewart's piano would be right at the heart of 'Stoned', just as it had always been before the Eel Pie Island decree. Convicted of corpulence by Andrew Oldham, it was not only Stu's burly frame which was displeasing in the sight of their maquillage-wearing manager. After all, a piano held no exploitable undertones. A pianist had to sit sedately on his stool, a world away from an electric guitarist thrusting out his instrument from the hip in phallic style or pointing it from the shoulder like a sniper. And Oldham was as fascinated with violence as he was with sex, surrounding himself with thuggish bodyguards. But now, hunkering down in Paris, he would be powerless to silence Stewart's Steinway.

'Stoned' is launched by Charlie Watts' crisp drum roll. Then he and Bill Wyman drive that pounding, sensual, hypnotic rhythm which had wowed the girls that summer as they danced in delight at the Richmond Clubhouse. Against the sinister backdrop of Brian Jones' haunting harp, Keith Richards seizes the track at fifty seconds to deliver a fantastic solo on his Harmony Meteor H70, stark and steely at first then tempered with Chuck Berry's Spanish tinge. Dedicated student of blues guitar from Charlie Patton to John Lee Hooker, he's suddenly on his own, delivering fresh sounds from his mind's ear.

As Keith ceases, Ian Stewart's jazzy tremolos ripple then recoil on themselves like cascades of water rebounding from rocks. 'Stoned' is a testament to teamwork yet, if any one musician shines even above the others, it's Stu. Here is a man whose face didn't fit but whose fingers roll majestically over the keyboard as his imagination takes flight.

Great as the Richards and Stewart solos are, the whole track unfolds in perfect counterpoint and the only pity is that it has to end as early as it does at two minutes and nine seconds, stopped short by another drum roll.

Rock critics would barely give the time of day to 'Stoned', brusquely dismissing it as derivative of Booker T and the MG's' 'Green Onions.' Sadly, Keith Richards would say the same ten years down the road when he'd become a different person from the idealistic nineteen-year-old who actually played on the track. Beyond the similarity of walking bass, the two instrumentals have little in common. 'Stoned' has a major toned blues melody and a slower shuffle.

The Rolling Stones had laid down a great track, the quintessence of danceable rhythm and blues. But it wouldn't remain a pure instrumental. Mick Jagger would flavour it with a series of interjections plus a burst of half -crazed laughter. The implications are unmistakable. The singer's a young guy high on marijuana, well out of it and not giving a damn.

Here were the Rolling Stones firing a shot across the bows of straight society and the conventional mores of the early Sixties. Ricky Brown of the Savages, who knew them from their earliest days in the Marquee, would later say "all they had in the beginning was orange juice and a packet of crisps." This was of course a figure of speech. But, in fifteen months, the band had travelled a huge distance from the boozy atmosphere of the moribund trad jazz clubs. After all, they'd played the Flamingo, haunt of ganja- loving Jamaicans, the place where Christine Keeler and Mandy Rice Davies had first sampled marijuana. And Eric Burdon, lead singer of the Animals, would soon speak of it – cryptically, as "Flamingo cigarettes"- in their version of Jimmy Reed's 'Bright Lights, Big City.' Certainly the Rolling Stones' acquaintance with cannabis came well before the Beatles were introduced to it by Bob Dylan in August 64.

The individual members of the band had differing attitudes to the drug. Ian Stewart wouldn't touch it but tolerantly shrugged his shoulders at what he thought were the silly antics of others. Charlie Watts liked to relax with the occasional spliff while Keith Richards bragged that he'd sauntered down Oxford Street carrying "a slab of hash as big as a skateboard."

It wasn't long before Brian Jones would follow suit. Stressed out by the band's hectic schedule and repeatedly laid low by bouts of asthma, his cannabis intake increased sharply early in 64. Mellow though he was on weed, his mood would change abruptly whenever he combined it with alcohol. Throwing caution to the winds from the earliest days of the Rolling Stones' American tours, he soaked himself in LSD. Busted by corrupt coppers, he was hauled before the courts for possession of cannabis and threatened with jail. He was quick to see himself as the victim of a vengeful Establishment but slow to realise that drug indulgence had sapped his creativity. Only in the last months of his short life did he divest himself of dope.

Many years later Mick Jagger, always more careful to protect himself than Richards and Jones, would recall with incredulity, when speaking of the late Sixties, "in those days there were people who seriously thought cocaine was good for you!"

In the 21st-century Keith Richards would be an object of fatuous veneration by ageing rock buffs as a raddled survivor of all manner of chemical indulgence. Yet although Richards' apparently iron constitution allowed him to defy his doctors' direst warnings, his creativity had deserted him decades earlier and certainly before he turned his back on heroin. And his musical revisionism would be curtly dismissed by his former flatmate, Jimmy Phelge, who said "Keith doesn't remember. It's the fuckin' drugs talking!"

Viewed from half a century later, 'Stoned', which was withdrawn as a B side in the U.S. "on moral grounds", has a tragic resonance. Even as its superbly sensual sound celebrates the carefree young women whose sheer joie de vivre had lit up the staid streets of Richmond, its tawdry vocal remains a befuddled paean to the stultifying substances which would contaminate a decade.

CHAPTER 7

Gasoline, Rubber and Route 66

ON JANUARY 3, 1964, a year and a day since Brian Jones had first written to the BBC pleading for the chance to be heard, the Rolling Stones arrived at Regent Sounds Studios at 4 Denmark Street to begin recording their eponymous debut album.

Denmark Street was the heart of 'Tin Pan Alley', the hub of the music business for half a century. Yet, by 64, sheet music publishers were already on the back foot, as were the big record companies, desperately seeking compromise arrangements with young guitar bands. Ray Davies of the Kinks had the likes of Decca's Dick Rowe in mind when he mocked these out of date operators in the song, 'Denmark Street.'

Determined to avoid big company studios such as Abbey Road, the Rolling Stones had opted for the cramped quarters of Regent Sounds, entered through a narrow shopfront door above which a wooden board proclaimed the name of the studio and, in smaller lettering, the words 'recording and phonographic studios Soho 379 6111.'

Regent Sounds was owned by James Cecil Baring, aged twenty-five, the Old Etonian younger son of Baron Revelstoke. Scion of a banking dynasty, Baring had turned his back on a career in the City for the cause of independent music and he operated as his own studio manager at 4 Denmark Street.

Andrew Oldham was of course keeping an eagle eye on proceedings. His confidence restored by the success of 'I Wanna Be Your Man' and buoyed by the imminent release of the Rolling Stones' EP (featuring a couple of safe rock 'n' roll covers plus commercially sound material by Berry Gordy and Arthur Alexander), he graciously consented to an album where the majority of the tracks would be rhythm and blues.

Bill Farley, the resident engineer at Regent Sounds, was staggered by the Rolling Stones' approach to recording. He said "when they arrived, there were no arrangements. They just busked it till they got the feel of the number, there was no dubbing, they just told me what they wanted as soon as the number had been worked out."

What they wanted would be best described by Bill Wyman who later wrote "on our first album we cut everything in mono because we always liked the mono sound of the original R&B records." He added "you don't have that polarity which you get with stereo that spreads out the sound, with stereo you lose a lot of the guts of the sound."

About the choice of tracks, Keith Richards would later say "our first album reflected what we played at the Crawdaddy, a regular diet of Jimmy Reed, Bo Diddley and Muddy Waters with some Slim Harpo-the album was basically the cream of the set." He went on "we cut the album in that tiny little room in Denmark Street, a room full of egg boxes with a two track Grundig. We'd sit round in playback going 'sounds good' or 'no, let's do it again' or 'yeah, that's it.'"

Bill Wyman summed up; "it was really just the show we did on stage recorded in one take – and that's how it should be!"

The Rolling Stones' inspired amateurism was obviously a high risk recording strategy. Yet on a London studio scene many years behind the great independent American studios such as Chess in Chicago and Sun in Memphis, it was a risk deemed well worth taking to avoid the glossy neo-classicism of the Beatles' George Martin at Abbey Road. A stunned Bill Farley would have to admit "how it worked out so well in the end I never really knew."

Three days into the new year, the Rolling Stones kicked things off with their take on Chuck Berry's 'Carol.' It was, as Andrew Oldham had been pleased to note, a specifically teen- oriented song, albeit the B-side of 'Johnny B Goode.' Valiantly though they tried, the band couldn't match Berry when it came to the all out rock 'n' roll of 'Carol'. But, when they turned to a number nearly twenty years old which he'd updated on his 61 album, 'New Juke Box Hits', it was a very different story. This was 'Route 66', composed by songwriter Bobby Troup in celebration of his relocation to Los Angeles at the start of the post-war recording boom.

'Route 66' would be the track to kick-off the Rolling Stones' debut album. It was a unique moment not only in their personal history but in the transformation of the musical scene which happened in the Sixties.

The impact of Route 66 is utterly breathtaking. Here's a young English band playing in absolutely perfect unison, pumped up with sheer joie de vivre, taking hold of a much recorded classic American number yet pulverising all the previous versions at a single stroke. Tackling a superficially bland lyric, Mick Jagger exudes confidence and zest, reflecting a real love of America's wide-open spaces – which, as yet, he'd visited only in his imagination.

The original 1946 version of 'Route 66' by the Nat King Cole Trio had featured in a 'soundie', a distant ancestor of MTV, a three-minute 16mm film used in the Forties to promote records. Nat Cole and the others presented themselves as the epitome of elegant respectability, all double-breasted suits and bland smiles. On first hearing, the music's nothing more than easy listening and that remains true of Cole's crooning vocal and the plunking upright bass. Yet Cole's piano playing and, in particular, the clever guitar work of Oscar Moore is modern jazz with more than a hint of rhythm and blues.

Four of the six Rolling Stones had a background in jazz. Jones, Stewart and Watts had played in jazz bands while Richards had absorbed the genre from his bandleader grandad, Gus Dupree. Jazz, for them all, was modern not trad. Indeed Brian Jones despised what he considered the shoddy musicianship of the trad bands and sought to overthrow them. Modern jazz, by contrast, was a music he deeply admired.

Chuck Berry had recorded his interpretation of 'Route 66' at a time when he was steering away from rock 'n' roll and back to the rhythm and blues with which he'd begun his recording career. Although Berry loved being at the wheel, his version of Bobby Troup's song has nothing in common with the bravado 'motorvating' he sang about in 'Maybellene' or the surreal automobile fantasy of 'You Can't Catch Me.' Instead the pace reflects the kind of leisurely journey which, in contrast to his actual trouble- freighted trips across the U.S., he must have longed to drive. Berry takes his time, enunciating with faultless diction and inserting carefully calculated guitar breaks.

In complete contrast, the Rolling Stones set a truly hectic pace, abrupt and insouciant. Yet skill would never be sacrificed to speed. Brian Jones totally respected the music of the swing era. He loved the Count Basie band and he clocked Duke Ellington's quip "it don't mean a thing if it ain't got that swing." What swing meant, in practice, was sophisticated and highly disciplined jazz musicians playing with real verve whilst maintaining perfect unison. Young, British and white though they were, Brian Jones and Keith Richards, as early as the Station Hotel, were the unacknowledged heirs of Basie and Ellington as they fired off intricately synchronised riffs without ever losing momentum.

Jones and Richards had perfected their interweaving guitars thanks to countless hours of practice, both together at Edith Grove and with the rest of the band at the rehearsal room in the Wetherby Arms. Returning home from unsatisfactory early gigs, Jones had said "that was crap! We've got to practice it over and over again till we get it absolutely right." And Richards was his partner in determination. They may have lived in what Dick Taylor called "the worst slum I ever saw" but they were anything but beatnik layabouts. Indeed their work ethic typified the Fifties and in any other context than youth music would have been praised by the Fleet Street bloodhounds who'd already begun to slag them off.

There are two other things about the Rolling Stones' version of 'Route 66' which transform a fine swing era song with a catchy melody, an arresting chorus and an inventive lyric into vibrant rhythm and blues. One is Bill Wyman's fully electrified bass of the kind which revolutionised music in the late Fifties, immediately rendering the upright bass obsolete. Wyman plays a blood-red, thin-necked Framus Star and pumps out a primal pulse from it.

Then there's Charlie Watts' drumming style and the way it's linked with Keith Richards' rhythm guitar. Watts would have nothing to do with heavy -hitting, hard -stomping rock drumming. He flicked his stick lightly on the snare and he even played the bass drum with his heel relaxed on the floor. And, whereas most rock bands would dutifully follow their drummer, the Rolling Stones followed the rhythm guitarist and there was always a slight but significant delay between Keith Richards and Charlie Watts. This produces, on 'Route 66', a wonderful, bounding, kinetic rhythm.

Mick Jagger would be in his element delivering the vocal. American-ophile since he entered his teens, he'd soaked up James Dean movies, he loved to play basketball and he admired the Harlem Globetrotters. Like many young Englishmen, he was fascinated with the romance of American place names – the likes of Amarillo, Flagstaff, Winona and San Bernardino- which pepper the lyric of 'Route 66.'

Rock critics would soon brush aside the perfectly swinging musician-ship of 'Route 66' because it had nothing to say about their pet themes – sex, drugs, fast cars and teenage angst – and it certainly wasn't rock 'n' roll.

As far as they were concerned it was just a boring travelogue with the singer no more than a tourist guide. Even worse, from their perspective, Mick Jagger, of all people, had urged his listeners to get their thrills on Route 66. That sounded suggestive yet the lyric yielded not the merest hint of a drug den or a whorehouse. The singer had never even men-tioned what make of car he was driving and his serene journey had not once been interrupted by a state trooper or any other law enforcement agent. Indeed he sounded more like a golf buff on vacation than a teen-ager stepping on the gas in his hot rod and eager to check out the chicks at the nearest truck stop.

American rock critics were baby boomers raised in the post-war era when the highway, Route 66, was promoted as a symbol of American get up and go. But, in the Depression era, it had been the badly kept surface along which the Okies- the dispossessed dustbowl migrants from Oklahoma in their beat-up Hudsons- had travelled, desperate to resettle in California. These were the poor folk celebrated in John Steinbeck's novel 'The Grapes of Wrath' and later in John Ford's film of the same name.

The Rolling Stones' 'Route 66' is far closer to Steinbeck's Tom Joad and his fellow travellers than it is to Chuck Berry's mythologised highway.

It smells of gasoline and reeks of rubber. The band were probably unaware of the less than blissful history of a road which ran two thousand miles from Chicago to L.A. Yet not only had their arrival at 4 Denmark Street transformed those ancient premises but they'd brilliantly saluted one of the finest of all American songs. Yet to set foot in the States, they were musically already there.

CHAPTER 8

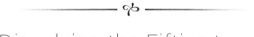

Dissolving the Fifties to an Exotic Dancer's Beat

BRIAN JONES WAS fifteen when, in the summer of 1957, he enrolled at the Gaumont School of Dance in Cheltenham. Eager as he was to learn a vital skill of the seducer's art- and quickly as he mastered the moves- he was soon bored stiff with the rigid rhythms of the waltz and the foxtrot. Even the brand-new jiving associated with rock 'n' roll left him cold.

Four months earlier, Bo Diddley cut the B-side of his seventh single, 'Mona.' Like the half dozen already laid down it featured a startling juba rhythm which had migrated from sub-Saharan Africa through Oriente province in Cuba, thence to New Orleans and finally to Chicago where Diddley first heard it. Making sure to collect his royalties under his real name, Ellas McDaniel, his thoughts turned to the woman who inspired the song.

Mona was an exotic dancer whom Diddley had seen in action at the Flame Show Bar in Detroit and, from the moment he first set eyes on her sensual gyrations, he was infatuated. The problem was that she was fifteen years older than him and, though he was twenty-seven, his boyish, gap-toothed grin made him seem a lot younger. As for Mona, age had not diminished her erotic allure.

Mainstream America had never been able adequately to describe the undulating clave-the beat Mona danced to- pervasive though it was in the Northern ghettos. 'Shave and a haircut – – two bits' was the feeble best they could do to render the irresistibly elastic rhythm in words.

Bo Diddley's records were issued on the Checker label and, when he recorded this one in the Chess studio in Chicago, he was backed by a drummer and his fiery maracas player, Jerome Green.

Surely seeing Mona in his mind's eye as he sang, Diddley's throat was constricted with unsatisfied lust as he frantically yelped the vocal. The first verse is surreal– he builds a house next door to Mona, the second all innocence–they blow kisses through the blinds. But by the third he's holding his dream woman tight and his heart's "goin' bumpety bump!" In those last two words the rhythm of the clave has become one and the same as the singer's raw desire. And the thrill of the embrace is signalled by the plunging tremolo of Bo Diddley's guitar.

Late in 1963, Bo Diddley and the Rolling Stones shared a bill, him on his first visit to the UK, them on their first nationwide tour. Bo was very impressed with Brian Jones' leadership of the band. He would vividly recall "the little dude that was pullin' 'em all together, he had 'em organised – he never took no mess." And he said to Keith Richards he'd never known anyone who'd worked out the secret to the beat the way Brian had.

That secret would be unfolded in the Regent Sounds studio on January 3 1964, the second track the Rolling Stones cut that day. Taking 'Mona' at a slower pace than Diddley had, Mick Jagger's vocal is solid but can't compare with the original. It doesn't matter. The lyric is only the surface and even the throbbing, insistent beat- laid down by Charlie Watts and Bill Wyman and augmented on tambourine by Brian Jones with Jagger himself on maracas- doesn't touch the heart of the matter.

Subtly murmuring in the opening bars, intensifying in the instrumental break, persistent in the protracted fadeout, the track's owned by the contrapuntal guitars of Brian Jones' gleaming green Gretsch Double Anniversary and Keith Richards' spruce top, maple neck, two tone sunburst Harmony Meteor. This is the clave, yes, but it's sky from a different planet, a shimmering, ethereal sound, interrupted only by a dazzling descent to the bottom of the scale on Jones' slide.

When the session was over, Keith Richards still had the Diddley beat in his head and, back home in Mapesbury Road, he tried it out playing along to Buddy Holly's 'Not Fade Away.' Holly was an artist admired by all the Rolling Stones, the only significant white songwriter of rock 'n' roll. This was not the Buddy Holly of rock legend but a young man who'd acknowledged his debt to rhythm and blues, as had his drummer, Jerry Allison. When Buddy Holly and the Crickets' 'Not Fade Away' was recorded in Clovis, New Mexico on May 27, 1957 – yet another significant event that year – Allison pounded out the Diddley beat, (which he and Holly knew as 'the hambone' in their native Texas) on a cardboard box. The track was scheduled as the B-side of the hit single, 'Oh, Boy!'

Overhearing Richards' improvisation, Andrew Oldham brought the band back into the studio a week later to record 'Not Fade Away.' On the forthcoming American release of the Rolling Stones' eponymous album – commercially titled 'England's Newest Hitmakers'- 'Mona' would be replaced by 'Not Fade Away.' Indeed their version of the Buddy Holly number would become the leadoff track. It's a really good piece of work, bright and breezy and catchy enough to give the Rolling Stones a # 3 hit when issued as a single in the UK. But it lacks the magic and mystery of 'Mona.'

Andrew Oldham, on the other hand, was delighted with 'Not Fade Away.' He later asserted that "although it was a Buddy Holly song, I considered it to be the first song Mick and Keith wrote. The way they arranged the whole Diddley thing was the beginning of them as songwriters." Bill Wyman refuted this claim, writing that "any musician would know that Holly's version had been built on the Diddley beat."

Far beyond such arguments, 'Mona' heralded a societal change. The likes of Sir Malcolm Sargent, Chief Conductor of the BBC Symphony Orchestra- and, for that matter, Basil Jagger- were doubtless disturbed by the primitivism of the Diddley rhythm which they dismissed as "jungle music." Yet, beyond the crude snobbery of such remarks, there lay another reality. Powerful as it was in its own right, the clave reached yet another level in the hands of Brian Jones and Keith Richards. Just as the Impressionists created a new reality by dissolving the norms of pictorial composition, so the Rolling Stones freed the dancefloor from the straitjacket of rigid rhythm.

Nothing had more typified the strictures on British youth in the Fifties than Saturday nights at the Mecca and the Locarno, which were constrained by traditional European dances while bandleaders such as Ted Heath condescended to teenagers with anodyne numbers such as 'Hot Toddy.' And dancing teachers all over the country carefully prepared young people as useful fodder for the dance hall scene. Belatedly adjusting to rock 'n' roll, they were quick to advertise themselves as instructors for what they called 'the jive.'

By the mid-Sixties, however, genteel dancing schools such as the Gaumont in Cheltenham, at which Brian Jones had enrolled a decade earlier, were struggling for business, dismissed as outmoded in the new era of open dancing.

As for the oscillating sound of the guitars on 'Mona', it would resonate with those indie bands of the Eighties who knew their musical history. Johnny Marr, guitarist and co-songwriter with the Smiths, had been a mere two months old at the time of the Rolling Stones' recording. In the course of time he would discover the clave for himself and he incorporated it in the Smiths' classy 1984 single, 'How Soon Is Now?' Marr belonged in the tradition of understated British guitar playing of which Brian Jones had been the original exponent. And the revolutionary rhythm and blues of Jones' Rolling Stones was still echoing twenty years on.

CHAPTER 9

You Must Be Joking- and Why Not!

In December 1963 a forty-six-year-old entertainer from Memphis named Rufus Thomas, hitherto little-known outside the black community, scored a Top Ten hit on the Billboard Hot 100. 'Walking the Dog' is a comedy number written by Thomas to a surreal lyric. Recorded on the Stax label, it features his powerful, exuberant voice with R&B brass backing over a highly danceable beat.

The Rolling Stones were so taken with 'Walking the Dog' that they adjusted their debut album schedule to fit in their own version and recorded it on January 4.

There's something inherently humorous in Rufus Thomas' voice as he effortlessly sparks a mood of spontaneous fun with zany words strung together for no other reason than rhyme. So Mary Mack's a girl who's dressed in black with silver buttons down her back. She walks on tiptoe, she's broken the needle and she can't sew. The singer leaves the meaning of the title phrase to the listener's imagination before resuming the good-humoured lunacy with the tale of an elephant jumping the fence and flying so high he doesn't get back till the Fourth of July.

There was a long tradition of earthy humour in R&B, very different from the contrived silliness of Fifties' novelty hits such as Patti Page's 'How Much is That Doggie in the Window?' and Rosemary Clooney's 'Where Will (the baby's) Dimple Be?' – the latter a record which Keith Richards particularly despised.

By contrast the Rolling Stones were cracked up when they heard Rufus Thomas' dog whistling as he promises his listeners he'd show them how to walk the dog! His backing band had opened the track with a solemn wedding fanfare which they brusquely subvert with crunching guitar chords, then rasping tenor sax and guttural baritone sax blasts. Thomas goes on to quote the 17th-century English nursery rhyme 'Mary, Mary, Quite Contrary', utters an ecstatic "oh-oh- uh-oh-oh!" and ends with a kind of jubilant stutter before finishing with the title words one more time.

Schoolboys over the years would gleefully surmise that the phrase 'walkin' the dog' had sexual implications while rock critics would simply ignore Rufus Thomas. Yet Thomas earned the respect of excellent music historian, Peter Guralnick, who said of him "his music brought a great deal of joy to the world but his personality brought even more, conveying a message of grit, determination, indomitability, above all a bottomless appreciation of the human comedy that left little room for the drab or the dreary in his presence."

Bringing in session saxophonists was never an option as far as the Rolling Stones' version was concerned. At the foundation of the band, Brian Jones had made clear to Ian Stewart that, much as he admired modern jazz saxophone, he found R&B sax crude and out of time. Now Jones rearranged 'Walking the Dog' on a basis of dual guitars, opening with a far crisper sound than Thomas' guitarists had achieved yet sparking into loud counterpoint in the middle before Keith Richards' brief but jumping solo. Charlie Watts lays down a chugging beat and, for the most part, Mick Jagger's vocal fits the bill. Yet Jagger goes drastically wrong when he opts to take the 'Mary, Mary' bit as a piece of spoken jive resulting in blurred mispronunciation and sheer muddle.

Although Jagger recovers on the stuttering break, his voice is inadequate to render the outstanding characteristic of Rufus Thomas' vocal-the humour. Jagger's own sense of humour was rarely spontaneous and usually depended on raising a laugh by piss-taking mimicry. Ian Stewart, on the other hand, was generous with his dry wit. But it was Brian Jones who really stood out. Dick Taylor would recall the early days, saying "Brian was a lot more worldly wise than the rest of us but he also had a great sense of humour. There was a hell of a lot of humour and that was why everyone got on so well."

On 'Walking the Dog' Jones' backing vocal doesn't really blend with Jagger who seems disinclined to let anyone else in. Jones' real contribution is the dog whistling, something which he puts over better than Rufus Thomas had. His whistling is like an additional instrument on the track and it has an intrinsically funny sound.

As time went by the friendly atmosphere remarked on by Dick Taylor would be dissipated and Keith Richards would let himself down badly when he retrospectively claimed that Brian Jones was trying to upstage Mick Jagger as a pop singer. Live footage of the Rolling Stones performing 'Walking the Dog' shows that, in truth, Jones was tentative with his singing yet he breaks into a confident grin after letting loose with the protracted dog whistle.

Dismissed in some quarters as a glum and hypersensitive dandy reluctant to ever let his meticulously shampooed hair down, Brian Jones actually loved earthy and sometimes juvenile humour. He was prone to gurning and racing around hotel corridors in the middle of the night clad only in his underpants. In those respects he resembled Mozart, revered genius of classical composition yet notorious for farting his head off and swearing like a trooper.

The Rolling Stones' version of Rufus Thomas' original is a remarkably good effort, a spicy contrast to what they brought to the eponymous album from their live set. The final track on the album, it stands as a reminder of the relaxed, easy-going humour which had characterised rhythm and blues but would soon be obliterated in the coming era of rock pomposity.

CHAPTER 10

Tall Tales of a Sexual Predator

ONE DAY IN 1960 Brian Jones saw Paul Oliver's newly published book, 'Blues Fell This Morning' on the shelves of a bookshop in Cheltenham. Its subtitle was 'Meaning in the Blues' and, as soon as he'd spotted it, he bought it. He read it from cover to cover, three hundred pages in full, the same day. Among the chapters which most intrigued him was 'I'm a Rooster, Baby', in which the author described bluesmen's fondness for comparing themselves to animals as a measure of their sexual prowess.

It was hardly surprising that Slim Harpo's 'I'm a King Bee' became one of Jones' favourite blues tracks and the Rolling Stones laid down their version of the Louisiana bluesman's 1957 recording on the Excello label. That was on January 10. In the meantime, Jones gritted his teeth as the band waxed a soul number, agreed between Andrew Oldham and Mick Jagger, which he found utterly boring. This was 'You Can Make It If You Try', a Gene Allison cover which was as earnest and sententious as its title. The track's sole redeeming feature was that Ian Stewart got to play organ on it.

Before turning to Slim Harpo, the Rolling Stones laid down their version of Jimmy Reed's 'Honest I Do'. Reed was a favourite with all the band yet their take on his R&B number was a disappointment. Mick Jagger was ill at ease on the slow love song. His vocal sounds as contrived as the letters he wrote to Cleo Sylvestre about the same time. Yet, early in his singing career, Jagger would be absolved from any imputations of insincerity by Robert Christgau, pompously styled 'dean of rock critics', who insisted that such notions betrayed a failure to understand irony.

Slim Harpo was the stage name taken by a New Orleans longshore-man, James Isaac Moore. Harpo recorded in the Crowley, Louisiana studio of his producer, JD Miller. They were an improbable partnership in that Miller held strong white supremacist views despite professing a love of the blues. That said, he was a skilful producer who did a good job on Slim Harpo recordings.

Slim Harpo himself was an outstanding bluesman and a clever lyricist capable of subtle changes of mood. 'I'm a King Bee', a cynical, almost amoral song, is the B-side of its polar opposite A, 'Got Love If You Want It.' On 'King Bee' Harpo rides roughshod over the entomological facts of life. He imagines that there exists in the insect world a creature of phenomenal power. more than a match for the Queen Bee – and he incarnates the King Bee. Driven on by drummer Clarence Etienne's remorseless slap beat, he tells the Queen that he's buzzing round her hive before demanding she let him "come inside!"

The second verse finds him bragging about his sexual potency, his ability to buzz all night long. No mere drone, he's equipped with the power to sting. And, by the third verse, he promises that, between the two of them, King and Queen, they can make honey like the world has never seen.

The final verse finds the singer returning to human form to finish his story with a sting in the tail. The lyric's unsheathed as an invitation to cuckoldry as he nonchalantly tells the woman he can buzz better when her man is gone.

In the hands of a lesser artist than Slim Harpo this flight of fancy would have fallen flat on its face yet he carries the whole thing off in a laconic, almost matter-of-fact tone which is all the more sinister for its restraint. The gentle beauty of the melody contrasts with the menacing lyric and, as on the A side, the minimalist bluesharp sounds almost poignant.

Despite the power of Etienne's drumming, the original version is let down by the other two players in the Harpo studio band, the Perrodine brothers – Gable on guitar and Fats on bass. Gable Perrodine makes a feeble attempt to mimic the buzzing and stinging of the King Bee and soon gives up. Yet Brian Jones would seize the chance to plug that gap on the Rolling Stones' reinterpretation and one verse of the lyric would be junked to free up space for his slide guitar.

Over a chugging beat, Mick Jagger sings a convincing vocal, somewhat lacking in character compared to Slim Harpo but very effective nonetheless while his concluding harmonica's more than adequate. The line "let me come inside!" has an obvious double meaning but rock critic Richie Unterberger's notion that Jagger sings it "with a suggestive leer" imputes the frontman's lascivious stage persona of the Stones' later years to a time when he still had a genuine concern for honesty of performance. Unterberger relishes what he calls "the Stones giving it a bit of updated rock raunch" but in fact the band were scrupulous in maintaining Harpo's understated style.

What transforms the track is Brian Jones' astonishing guitar solo, barely more than twenty seconds long, yet destined to linger in the mind's ear. Jones responds to Jagger's drawling "let's buzz awhile" by amplifying the humdrum sound of the everyday pollinator into the ominous growl of the mythical King Bee as he attacks his target. When Jagger calls out "sting it, then!", Jones answers with a fantastic burst of slide as this superpredator giant of the insect world penetrates his Queen. Brian Jones had launched himself on the London scene two years earlier as a dedicated student of the great Elmore James. Yet on 'King Bee' his virtuosity is on a level with the recently deceased Chicago master.

There would be a deplorable but significant postscript to 'I'm a King Bee', one of the absolute highlights of the Rolling Stones' eponymous album. Four years later Mick Jagger would casually remark "what's the point in listening to us doing 'I'm a King Bee' when you can listen to Slim Harpo doing it?" He went on to assert "why people should be turned on to blues by us is unbelievably stupid."

In making crass comments like these, Jagger's false modesty played right into the hands of the rock critics with their glib dismissal of the Rolling Stones' early tracks as "blues covers." They were nothing of the sort. They were the foremost works of the British Rhythm and Blues movement, a genre brushed aside by rock criticism as no more than the apprenticeship of stadium rock bands. What's more, tritely trotting out the banal phrase 'covers' ignores the possibility of total reinterpretation. The Rolling Stones' rhythm and blues band would be saluted by African-American musicians but would never get their due desserts from rock critics.

CHAPTER 11

— ❦ —

"All Right, Keith, Come On!"

THERE WAS A three-week hiatus during the album sessions while the Rolling Stones were touring the ballroom circuit. Brian Jones had mixed feelings about this – on the one hand relishing the adulation of teenage girl fans and all that went with it, on the other regretting the musical compromise involved in leaving the club scene and what he approvingly called its "diehard R&B fanatics." He was more than happy to return to the Regent Sounds studio on February 4. Of the seven tracks already recorded there, all but one had been in rhythm and blues style.

By the time the band reconvened, Andrew Oldham had added extra personnel. Phil Spector was a leading light on the US pop scene, then at the height of his fame as the producer of hit girl groups such as the Ronettes and the Crystals. His fellow –American, Gene Pitney, was a pop singer who'd just broken through on the UK chart. Spector was in London for a party thrown in his honour by Decca Records and Oldham was full of admiration for him. As for Pitney, he'd just arrived to start a UK tour.

Gene Pitney would later give an account of the February 4 session emphasising that he arrived with a bottle of cognac, shared it with the band and, as a result, "we had a helluva session." That may well be right as far as it goes but the singer's claim to have played on 'Not Fade Away' is of course untrue since that track had already been recorded on January 10. Pitney's fib was a cover for Andrew Oldham's false press release which, as Bill Wyman noted in his diary, was put out purely to generate publicity for an imminent single. It also casts doubt on the alleged reason for inviting Pitney, which the American said was because of a bad atmosphere in the "little dinky studio in Denmark Street." He implied that Oldham sought his genial presence– plus booze- to lighten up the mood because "the boys hated each other that day and he couldn't get them to do anything."

Pitney went on to claim that he and Spector "played on the flip side which was 'Little by Little'"– himself on piano and Spector by "clicking the empty cognac bottle with half a dollar."

Andrew Oldham's own account of the composition of 'Little by Little ', given to the media in 64, had "Phil and Mick disappearing for about five minutes then returning to play us the number they'd just written in the corridor outside." The Spector-Jagger effort was so good, Oldham asserted, that he decided to use it as the B side of 'Not Fade Away.' Referring to those who actually played on the track, he picked out Jagger on harmonica plus Spector on maracas and said that Pitney and "the Stones' road manager, Ian Stewart, sat down at the same piano."

The Oldham-Pitney account of the February 4 session reeks of show business hype replete with personality clashes, bottles of booze and a piece of instant songwriting done ten times quicker than those masters of spontaneity, Lennon and McCartney, could ever achieve. The contributions of Charlie Watts, Bill Wyman and Brian Jones are brushed aside and even Keith Richards' wonderful solo on 'Little by Little' is ignored. The piano's far too good to be other than the work of Ian Stewart and, at the most, Pitney may have been on the keyboard with a couple of suggestions.

Oddly there's no mention at all of the presence of Graham Nash and Allan Clarke, members of the stylish Manchester group, The Hollies, who, as noted by Bill Wyman, shared tambourine and maracas. Gene Pitney's contribution was probably no more significant than Nash and Clarke's – although doubtless more colourful. And, despite Phil Spector's alleged moments of incredible inspiration in the corridor, he was obliged to share songwriting credit with Nanker-Phelge, the Rolling Stones' alias for the band's collectively composed work. Even this may have been more than he deserved since 'Little by Little' was- like 'Now I've Got a Witness' later that day- as Bill Wyman put it, "a song we invented on the spot."

Andrew Oldham was, at this time, clearly desperate to promote Mick Jagger as the true leader of the Rolling Stones. From his manager's point of view, Jagger had much to commend him. Oldham had sussed the frontman's essentially theatrical persona. What's more, Jagger had a protean voice and could adapt easily to a wide variety of genres. Jagger wasn't intellectual but was more than savvy enough to pick up on changing trends in the arts. His commitment to the blues was transient and he was eager to try his hand singing soul and writing teen pop. And, although Jagger's style at the mic was still relatively restrained at this stage, his manager had been quick to discern a camp sensibility which would chime with the coming heyday of 'Swinging London.'

Brian Jones, on the other hand, although his popularity with teenage girls in the Rolling Stones' fan club made him, in his manager's eyes, a big commercial asset, was equally a significant threat. He was cleverer than Andrew Oldham and suspiciously intellectual. He had an almost ideological commitment to rhythm and blues, a genre which Oldham neither liked nor understood.

Andrew Oldham was also eager to emphasise his own links with prominent young American showbiz figures, notably Phil Spector who currently commanded umpteen column inches in the US trade press. Another advantage, from Oldham's point of view, in emphasising the presence of Spector and Pitney would doubtless have been to deflect attention from the names of Bo Diddley, Jimmy Reed and Slim Harpo, true rhythm and blues artists, who would have to be mentioned in the album songwriting credits.

Bill Wyman's comment about 'Little by Little' is unintentionally misleading. The number is a pastiche of Jimmy Reed's 'Shame Shame Shame' which had been released the previous year. The Rolling Stones' track keeps the Reed band's melody and rhythm while Mick Jagger plays harmonica à la Reed. Yet the lyric's entirely different and the sound's enriched by meshing guitars, by Ian Stewart's rolling piano and, above all, by Keith Richards' incendiary solo.

Jimmy Reed had never wanted to be labelled a bluesman. "I never called my songs no blues" he insisted "I always felt good behind 'em." Anyone hearing his exultant "yeah-yeah-yeah"(soon lifted by the Beatles) on 'Baby, What You Want Me To Do' would've been in no doubt about that. Essentially Reed was at the heart of the transition from blues to rhythm and blues, scoring hit after hit on the R&B chart. On harmonica he began by copying the piercing squall of John Lee 'Sonny Boy' Williamson but modified the sound to make it closer to a relaxed, easy-on-the ear-whistle. His band included such stellar performers as Eddie Taylor on guitar plus Earl Phillips on drums and their loose- swinging shuffle was dancer- friendly. Indeed the band pioneered the change to open dancing when they promoted the Push in Dallas and Houston. It was a far more significant dance than the vaunted Twist, favoured by high society elements in New York.

'Shame Shame Shame' seemed to some like a reversion to old-style blues lyrics with its bitterness against a stop -out woman. Yet the rhythm was entirely novel. Prompted by his wife, Mary Lou, who was worried about his drinking, Jimmy Reed had got rid of his brilliant but boozy drummer, Earl Phillips, and brought in jazz sticksman Al Duncan. What's more, their son, Jimmy Reed Jr, an excellent electric bassist, had been deputed by Mary Lou to keep an eye on his dad and make sure he stayed off the licquor. Between them Duncan and Jimmy Junior generated a fast-paced, rolling rhythm which galvanised the dancefloor. Brian Jones was very impressed with the beat of 'Shame Shame Shame' and urged Charlie Watts to learn it. Charlie did more than that-he mastered it in double quick time.

On 'Little by Little' Charlie Watts' snare rings out crisply on the two and four and he leaves tantalising hi hat space. This establishes a skipping, girl-oriented, dancer-friendly rhythm which is filled out by Bill Wyman's bass and Ian Stewart's piano. Mick Jagger's in fine vocal form as he tells the tale of a suspicious young guy who tries to trail his girlfriend by car, quickly admitting he slipped up because he was scared of what he was looking for. As a result, he slowly but surely loses his love for her when he realises she's been cheating on him.

The naive lyric blends perfectly with Jagger's shout to his Dartford pal – "all right, Keith, come on!" Responding to that cry, Richards delivers a blistering solo on his Harmony Meteor. Rock critics would claim he recycled blues licks mixed with Chuck Berry chords but a pedantic search for influences can never recapture the sheer verve of Richards' playing, the raw delight with which he sparks his guitar into life -alternately pounding it, briefly blending it with Brian Jones' Gretsch then making it sing.

Just turned twenty, it was only five years since Keith had brought tears of joy to his mother's eyes when she heard what she thought was a guitar on the radio from the floor above her head only to see her son walking downstairs still playing the same melody on his instrument. Doris Richards had been the first to witness Keith's innate gift starting to flourish after hours of devoted practice. Now his dedication was being fully vindicated in the Denmark Street studio.

Determined not to be outdone, the more modestly talented but more confident Jagger abruptly shuts down the guitar solo with the words "my turn!" before mimicking Jimmy Reed's whistling harp. Then the rest of the band return with the bouncing dancefloor beat before Richards, Jones and Wyman play descending chords in perfect unison. Jagger returns with the muddled second verse of the lyric before calling time on the proceedings with his shout of "let's get out o' here, come on!" duly triggering the fadeout.

'Little by Little' is a dazzling piece of work, an implicit tribute to the blues- derived artistry of Jimmy Reed on the one hand and a brilliant example of BRB on the other. The twenty-year-old Mick Jagger's youthful enthusiasm permeates the track and the contrast between that and the sinister persona he cultivated in the late Sixties matches that between early Sixties rhythm and blues and the overblown rock which would blot it out before the end of the decade.

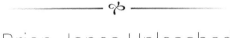

Brian Jones Unleashed

ONE MORNING IN 63, at Edith Grove, Keith Richards told Brian Jones he had to be out all day dealing with urgent personal business. Guitar practice would have to be suspended but Jones was undaunted. Richards left him hunched over his new harmonica, his pride and joy, a Hohner Echo Super Vamper, wrestling with the techniques of tongue blocking and fluttering which he needed to master if he was to become a true blues harpist.

When Richards returned, late in the evening, Jones greeted him with triumphant shouts of "I've got it! I've got it!" Their double guitar drill would be resumed next day but, from then on, Jones had his harmonica in his pocket wherever he went.

Although there was no single moment of epiphany such as when Brian first heard Elmore James' slide guitar, he'd become gradually drawn to the sound of blues harp and learned it by playing along to records. Little Walter was his exemplar. Born in Louisiana, Walter Jacobs had moved to Chicago in his teens where he amplified the mouth organ by cupping it in his hand with a miniature mic plugged into a guitar amp. It was Walter's fierce solos on Muddy Waters' records which Brian Jones listened to first and then his jaunty number one hit singles on the R&B chart. Backing his own voice on tracks such as 'Juke' and 'My Babe', Walter's harp took flight in more lyrical mode.

There was something about the intensely raw and earthy sound of the blues harp which deeply appealed to Brian Jones. Whilst he made no attempt to modify his cultured speaking voice, the humble mouth organ was a means of acquiring street credibility at a time when kitchen sink drama was ousting polite comedy and the Beatles' Liverpool accents had become all the rage.

Jones was acutely conscious of the difference between his own speech and the London accents of his bandmates. Jimmy Phelge would vividly recall an incident at Edith Grove when he happened to notice an official document with his flatmate's full name on it. "So it's 'Lewis Brian HOPKINS Jones', is it?" he laughed, putting the emphasis on the 'Hopkins.' Jones reacted angrily, fixing Phelge with a baleful stare and snarling "do me a favour, Phelge, never mention that name!" Then he changed abruptly to a more conciliatory tone, almost pleading as he muttered the words "you know how people will take the piss."

It wasn't long before Jimmy Phelge became the first witness from outside the band to Brian Jones' mastery of the harmonica. But, next year, on February 4, there would be two others, musicians themselves, who would be witnesses to his virtuosity, this time in the recording studio. The last track recorded that day, 'Now I've Got A Witness', is quintessential rhythm and blues, an instrumental originating in a spontaneous jam and credited to Nanker Phelge.

This track makes an oblique reference to the presence of Phil Spector and Gene Pitney in Regent Sounds. Its subtitle, listed in brackets, is 'Like Uncle Phil and Uncle Gene.' Whilst there was no hint of hostility between the band and their two American visitors, the use of the word 'uncle' seems like a light-hearted dig. Spector and Pitney had been brought in by Andrew Oldham, supposedly to lighten the mood, but they'd both witnessed, in 'Little by Little', and now in this instrumental, a display of R&B potency way beyond the capacity of any white American musicians. What's more, in between recording their rhythm and blues originals, the Rolling Stones had covered Marvin Gaye's soul song, 'Can I Get A Witness.'

With the Beatles making a big impact on the Billboard Hot 100 and about to leave for their first American tour, Andrew Oldham was eager to promote a Rolling Stones' tour of the States as soon as the band could make a chart impression there. Picking up on the news that soul was not only displacing R&B as the preferred music of black Americans but was crossing over into the mainstream market, he urged the Rolling Stones to record a Motown song. They chose 'Can I Get A Witness', a number Mick

Jagger had been raving about. 'Can I Get A Witness' had been recorded in Detroit in July 63 and issued on the Tamla label. It was the best soul song yet waxed. Marvin Gaye's vocal renders anguished sentiments with tremendous emotive power in one of music's most stirring renditions -albeit one at variance with the irrepressible jubilation of the rhythm.

There are aspects of the Rolling Stones' cover (an appropriate critical phrase in that there's no attempt whatever to reinterpret the original) which improve on the track laid down in the Hitsville studio. Ian Stewart's boogie piano is even better than Earl van Dyke's and Charlie Watts' crisp drumming has a jazzy flavour. But Mick Jagger's vocal is a poor effort indeed compared to Marvin Gaye. His rasping tones are particularly harsh on the key word "witness" and he seems to be having trouble with breath control.

Andrew Oldham would try to distract attention from that with a tale that Jagger had forgotten the words to the lyric and had to rush over to a sheet music publisher to jolt his memory, returning to 4 Denmark Street with the lyric sheet in hand. It was a scarcely credible story anyway and, even if accurate, recording could easily have been delayed till Jagger had got his breath back. It was regrettable indeed that musicians of the calibre of Stewart and Watts should have been wasted on such a spurious piece of work as this.

With the Motown cover out of the way, the band could relax and joyfully let off steam in 'Now I've Got A Witness.' Bass and drums lay down a kinetic R&B rhythm augmented by Mick Jagger's tambourine whilst Stu at last has the instrument he'd craved right at his fingertips. It's a Vox Continental rather than a Hammond but the organ sound not only blends with the beat but becomes a vital instrument in its own right, suffusing the track with its powerful sonority.

Yet the most distinctive feature of 'Witness' is the astonishing fluidity of Brian Jones' Hohner which can be heard almost uninterrupted for most of its two and a half minutes length. Indeed time almost stands still as he lets rip with a cascade of sound, sometimes crowing, sometimes piping, ranging high then delving low to explore bluesharp canyons, accelerating then veering off into a razzle-dazzle bypass. Something long suppressed is now vented in the Regent Sounds studio; here, for sure, is the songbird never allowed to sing in Hatherley Road, here too the rooster banished from Cheltenham.

For all his technical expertise, Jones had no time for egocentric soloing- as he'd made clear in a letter written to the band's fan club secretary, Doreen Pettifer, the previous May. He'd said "unlike in most forms of jazz the accent in R&B should not be on soloists but on an overall integrated group sound." Totally in keeping with that, the counterpoint between Ian Stewart and himself perfectly meshes the contrasting sonorities of harmonica and organ.

Suddenly a staccato burst from Jones announces the entry of a third player. Keith Richards' pounding tremolo seizes the track. Yet never for a moment does he disrupt the tone. Far from it, he boosts it with a staccato outburst before an elemental yelp and there's a slice of edgy counterpoint between guitar and bluesharp. Then Brian resumes, with Keith content to herald the fadeout with biting twang.

Exactly what Spector and Pitney made of it is unimportant. They should have counted themselves lucky to have witnessed at first hand the beautiful integrated group sound of the Rolling Stones rhythm and blues band at its very best.

CHAPTER 13

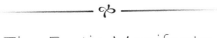

The Erotic Manifesto

THE FINEST TRACK on the Rolling Stones' eponymous album is 'I Just Want To Make Love To You', recorded at the final session on February 25. This is a reinterpretation of Muddy Waters' original, cut in the Chess studio in Chicago on April 13 1954.

Chess Records' role in the development of electric blues with a strong dance beat, was crucial. Its actual history– as opposed to the fiction peddled in the Hollywood travesty, 'Cadillac Records'– centred on the partnership between the Chess brothers, Leonard and Philip, blues song-writer and arranger Willie Dixon and vocalist, guitarist and bandleader, Muddy Waters.

The Chess brothers were Polish Jewish immigrants who arrived in the US as boys. Having established themselves in the nightclub business, they set up the label which bore their name in 1950. Chicago was the ideal base for a record company specialising in blues. This was due to the mass migration of African-Americans from the segregationist South to the 'Windy City'. With Phil concentrating on business, Leonard was free to scout blues talent and to bring it to fruition in the recording studio.

Willie Dixon was a man of many talents and strongly held views. 6'6" tall, he'd been a professional heavyweight boxer in his twenties, a spar-ring partner for world champion, Joe Louis. He refused military service in World War II, a conscientious objector protesting against institutionalised racism. Beginning a career in music he became an in- demand session exponent of double bass. Keenly interested in poetry, his flair for words found an outlet in songwriting. In Delta blues lyrics were of traditional origin but in Chicago R&B they were, for the most part, written by Dixon.

By 1953 the full Muddy Waters band had been brought into the Chess studio and these were the musicians who laid down 'I Just Want To Make Love ToYou': Little Walter on harmonica; Jimmie Rogers on second guitar; Otis Spann on piano; Elgin Evans on drums; Willie Dixon on bass and Waters himself with his unique voice which combined effortless power with purity of tone, as melodic as it was fierce.

In 'I Just Want To Make Love To You' the singer's consumed with desire for a woman who's with someone else. He salutes her sensuality, her voluptuous walk and the loving way she treats her man. But he pours scorn on her existing relationship, contrasting it with his assertion of unbridled longing. He doesn't want to enslave her and make her work all day washing clothes, cooking and suchlike tasks. He isn't after her money and doesn't need her to cure his sorrows. He'll free her from domestic chores but he'll go far further than that, promising sexual passion enjoyed as long as possible to the ultimate moment of orgasm.

Muddy Waters, ex-cottonfield stud turned smooth-tongued Chicagoan seducer, was ideally suited to deliver Dixon's lines and he does so with enormous force, deliberately and with his words clearly enunciated. Behind him Otis Spann's brusque, teetering piano and Willie Dixon's ominous bass grind out a remorseless riff. But it's Little Walter's magnificent harmonica solo which lifts the lid right off– a sustained high which resolves into a bloodcurdling swoop, obliterating the conjugal cosiness of the woman's existing relationship with its edge of envious anger and substituting blind erotic ecstasy.

In taking on a Chicago classic, Brian Jones ensured the Rolling Stones' re-interpretation would emphasise youth and all-out pace. With Mick Jagger racing through the lyric and Charlie Watts powering a breakneck beat, the new version is complete at two minutes and sixteen seconds, fully half a minute faster than the Waters band-vibrant, pulsating yet nervous. Brian Jones' mid-track harmonica trembles on the cusp of dementia and there's only a brief respite with Keith Richards' brilliant, sparkbright solo. Tambourine and handclaps are thrown into the mix and the effect is of exuberant lads gleefully celebrating the sexual command which their new-found fame has given them. Where Waters, turned forty, incarnated the experienced womaniser, Jagger, just twenty, comes over as a young man delighting in his ability to have the pick of available girls and eager for constant gratification.

The first time he took on a Dixon-Waters number, 'I Want To Be Loved'– the B side of the band's first single –Mick Jagger couldn't go beyond slavish imitation. Yet now, with his confidence immensely boosted as the frontman of a touring band, he delivers the title words a capella with almost savage relish. All told, it wasn't surprising that Muddy Waters hailed the track, released as the B side of the band's first US single, with the words "I like their version of 'I Just Want To Make Love To You' – they're my boys!"

The difference between the Waters band original and The Rolling Stones' re-interpretation is not a difference in genre. Though the song would remain in the Stones' set for decades, it's not rock. It's rhythm and blues, but an R&B of London not Chicago, of a new decade, speeded up, younger and with Bill Wyman's electrified lines superseding the out-moded stand-up bass. As for Mick Jagger, his ruthless assertion of sex-ual priorities strikes a blow at the bourgeois foundations of the Fifties. Giorgio Gomelsky had been right on the money when he drew excited crowds to the Crawdaddy Club with the phrase "UNREPRESSED rhythm and blues" and 'I Just Want To Make Love To You' is the epitome of that.

What's more, Willie Dixon's lyric may well have had personal significance as far as Brian Jones was concerned. Graham Ride was a former bandmate of his in Cheltenham. After Jones jilted Val Corbett, Ride married her. Speaking about his wife's former boyfriend, he said "Brian was a very instant person, he lived in the here and now. So if he wanted to make love, that's what he would do. He never thought about the consequences."

Without doubt Brian Jones had an aura about him which led many women to feel an instantaneous rapport. Pat Andrews spoke about being awestruck from the moment she first set eyes on him and Linda Lawrence, recalling their first meeting, said "I instantly felt close to him. He was so calm and so deep."

Yet Jones would never be satisfied with individual relationships. He craved casual sex and, in the two years after the Rolling Stones achieved fame, he satisfied himself to the hilt on the groupie scene. Bill Wyman, himself no slouch in these matters, roomed with Jones when the band was touring and, as Wyman saw it, Jones genuinely looked to mutual satisfaction and not just the gratification of his own lust.

Beyond that, Eric Burdon, frontman of the Animals, who got to know Jones well in the musicians' hangout, the Bag o' Nails, would later say "he seemed obsessed with hookers", something which would be reflected in testimony about Jones' use of Berber prostitutes whilst in Morocco. In Cheltenham, during his late teens, he'd frequented the Queens Hotel. Behind its genteel facade, it was a haven for high-class call girls who profited from the high-stakes gamblers descending on the town during Races week. There's no evidence that the youthful Jones honed his sexual skills with escorts but he certainly had ample opportunity to do so.

If the February 25 session had finished with the recording of 'I Just Want To Make Love To You', it would, from Brian Jones' point of view, have been a fitting end to what had been an essentially rhythm and blues album, an achievement of which he was justifiably proud. Yet, as Andrew Oldham saw it, the most important business of the day had be left for the finale. That would be the songwriting debut of Mick Jagger and Keith Richards. True, the session had actually begun with a Jagger-Richards number called 'Good Times, Bad Times.' But that had been written in the style of a traditional blues, a form which, as Jagger would confirm, Oldham didn't understand. 'Good Times, Bad Times' would be held over to the Rolling Stones' second album, '12×5', while the band's energies were focused on a pop song.

'Tell Me' lasts almost four minutes, much of which is consumed by uttering a line containing the title phrase no fewer than twenty-four times. Upset by his girlfriend's rejection, the singer's a teenage boy who insists she must change her mind right now. Andrew Oldham was delighted with a scenario which perfectly reflected the preoccupations of the girls who read 'Valentine' and 'Jackie.' He was equally chuffed with the sound of the song- melodramatic chord changes, Mick Jagger's deliberately adolescent tone, Jagger and Richards' male voices in harmony and dollops of "whoa-oh" and "oh yeah." The whole thing was an all –too- obvious attempt to follow in the footsteps of Lennon and McCartney and it has the saccharine flavour of the early Beatles' weaker work.

The chart fate of 'Tell Me' was all that interested Andrew Oldham but he was to be disappointed when it failed to reach the Billboard Top Twenty. The number pales into insignificance compared to 'I Just Want To Make Love To You.'

Regardless of whether Willie Dixon's lyric served as a kind of erotic manifesto for the likes of Muddy Waters and Brian Jones, it remains a great song. A target of carping criticism over the years by politically correct feminists of both sexes, the actual lyrics are completely free of misogyny and don't objectify women. Indeed it's been covered, with certain words altered to fit the gender of the singer, by female artists from Etta James to Norah Jones, incarnating women more than happy to respond to a man promising the ultimate in love-making.

Andrew Oldham scheduled release of the eponymous album for April 16 1964. He was duly gratified when it quickly reached number one on the UK album chart and remained there for no less than twelve weeks. A month and a half after British release, the album was issued in America with the subtitle 'England's Newest Hitmakers.' It narrowly failed to reach the Billboard Top Ten.

Beyond these commercial successes, the debut album was a great artistic achievement. Fuelled by sheer self belief, the Rolling Stones had shown they could reinterpret classic R&B tracks, never failing to do them justice and, in some cases, transcending them.

The whole album remains stark and vibrant to this day. Its fierce power was without precedent in England but it was never raw– like punk would be– just practised and polished, reflecting countless hours of sheer hard work.

Part 3: Welcome to Chicago- The Chess Sessions

CHAPTER 14

'It's All Over Now'- Time to Man Up

THE ROLLING STONES set off for a three-week tour of America on June 1 1964. In business terms it was a total flop. They had no US hit record to promote, their potential fanbase was not properly tapped and they were left open to insult by hostile showbiz elements who preferred the distinctly unsubtle approach of the Dave Clark Five, the drum-banging, sax-rasping, boot-stomping, perma-grinning Tottenham rock'n'rollers.

The band did, however, realise a cherished ambition, namely to record in the capital of rhythm and blues, at the Chess Studios in Chicago. Benefiting from the superb sound facilities at Chess, they laid down a series of outstanding tracks, continuing their reinterpretations of R&B classics. The Rolling Stones' Chess Sessions contained more than enough material for a great album but, due to Andrew Oldham's insistence on promoting the songwriting partnership of Mick Jagger and Keith Richards, this would never happen. Some of the tracks remained unreleased while others were dispersed across albums which were filled up with soul and pop numbers.

Even before their debut album was completed, the Rolling Stones felt that, as Bill Wyman later put it, "our best move was to get to America as quickly as possible and record there." The reasons were obvious –"in England the studio acoustics were bad because you couldn't play loud." Chess Records were already impressed by increased sales in the wake of the band's eponymous album and were more than happy to to welcome them to their home at 2120 South Michigan Avenue in Chicago. There they would be warmly greeted by various R&B artists, above all Muddy Waters and Willie Dixon.

Although Andrew Oldham would be listed as the producer for the Rolling Stones Chess Sessions, it was experienced sound engineer Ron Malo who was effectively in charge. Bill Wyman would recall that "Ron Malo knew exactly what we wanted and got it almost immediately. We knew what numbers we wanted to get in the can and the atmosphere was so marvellous that we got through them in double quick time."

On the first day, June 10, four tracks were recorded. The first of these was 'It's All Over Now.' This number had already been waxed by Cleveland R&B group, the Valentinos, on SAR Records and was ready for release. DJ Murray the K had stepped in to alert the Rolling Stones to a song which, as he put it, was "right up your alley." The band agreed with him and hastened to record it, beating the Valentinos' version to the punch.

Although the lyric of 'It's All Over Now', written by Valentinos' lead singer Bobby Womack and his sister-in-law Shirley Womack, stands out, the group's performance doesn't go beyond a jaunty beat and a gruff Bobby Womack vocal. The Rolling Stones' version outclasses it. It would give them their first UK number one but, in the States, though it squelched the Valentinos' version, it failed to reach the Billboard Top Twenty.

The key to the Rolling Stones' reinterpretation is the dual guitars of Brian Jones and Keith Richards: the gentle introduction; the sweet, minimalist harmonies punctuating the vocal; the sublime central counterpoint triggering Richards' brief but sparkling solo and, at the close, the stately diminuendo.

The Valentinos' original lyric describes the collapse of a relationship. There's not the slightest hint of misogyny in it, scarcely surprising in view of the fact that the joint songwriter was a woman, Shirley Womack.

In the song, the female partner's heavily at fault because she's been a promiscuous stopout. But the gal wasn't always like that. The singer has to admit that she'd often soothed his worries. What's more, he himself had been a weakling and he admits he shed pitiful tears when she kicked him out.

In essence the singer badly needed to man up and now he does just that! The chorus is powerfully delivered with Jones and Richards backing Mick Jagger's voice. It contrasts the way the singer used to love his woman with his realisation that their affair's finished. The woman hurt his feelings but opened his eyes and she's the one who's weeping now. Certainly there's an implication of revenge sex but there's a lot more to the story than just that. The words "used to" recur throughout the lyric, poignantly emphasising the collapse of a once happy relationship.

Although he was careful not to criticise a bandmate, Brian Jones was almost certainly referring to the vocal when he admitted "I'm not that keen on the record. I don't know – there's just something." Yet, while Mick Jagger's tone is technically raw, he's certainly not overly emphatic.

What remains in the mind's ear is neither lyric nor vocal but the absolute sonic beauty of the interweaving guitars. Despite assertions to the contrary by American critics, there's no hint of country in the sound. As to Keith Richards' solo, he would reveal in 'Life 'that John Lennon had taken him to task over it. By contrast, Bruce Springsteen, only fifteen when he first heard it, would always consider it a truly inspired break and was right to do so.

The real heart of 'It's All Over Now' only reveals itself in the protracted finale where the plangent chords coming out of one guitar contrast with the glittering sounds issuing from the other, reflecting the mixed feelings of the singer- shaken by the betrayal yet determined to reassert himself.

'It's All Over Now' was the vehicle for the Rolling Stones to deliver one of their finest live performances– on French TV in 64. In marked contrast to the hysterical atmosphere cooked up on the TAMI show filmed at Santa Monica, California where Mick Jagger responded to the screams of teenage girls by dancing without restraint, here he's almost inhibited. With the glossy facade of Andrew Oldham's adolescent faux outrage discarded, the band were free to perform as they really were.

Uploaded to YouTube by Leonard Nosferatu in October 2013 (and matched by Ruudtes two months later), the Rolling Stones' superb musicianship on that day is totally recaptured. It doesn't matter that Jagger's less than dominant. In fact his almost nervous rendition brings out the true meaning of the song. The singer' isn't merely "a jilted lover let loose on the town", as claimed by rock critic, Richie Unterberger. Still less is he "revenging a two-timer with spiteful venom" as Unterberger insists. He's a young guy mistreated by a woman who wronged him but opened his eyes. Regretting his initial reaction, he mans up, puts his failed love affair behind him and gets on with his life.

Whilst Charlie Watts' effortlessly relaxed drumming is a vital ingredient, the heart of the matter is the three-man wall of guitar sound. The comradeship between Brian Jones and Bill Wyman, standing side-by-side shouldering their instruments, is obvious. On the other side of Mick Jagger stands Keith Richards, perfectly together with his two bandmates, as impeccably in unison as classical musicians.

Whereas, in future years, impatient DJs would typically shut off the fadeout, here it's unveiled in all its majesty. And in the mid-track instrumental break Keith Richards' face lights up as he delivers his brief but wonderful solo.

American critics, reared on duelling banjos and suchlike, misheard the sound as country. In fact it springs from the confluence of Anglo-Irish folk with rhythm and blues, a synthesis beyond the grasp of white Americans in the early Sixties, with the sole exception of Bob Dylan. Whilst the Valentinos certainly deserve recognition for their clever lyric, their version is utterly transcended by the Rolling Stones. Never was rock critics' facile use of the term 'cover' more inappropriate.

CHAPTER 15

'I Can't Be Satisfied'

WITH THE HOT- off -the presses 'It's All Over Now' in the can, the Rolling Stones switched abruptly to an ancient blues source. 'I Can't Be Satisfied' had been recorded by Muddy Waters only sixteen years earlier. But the verses stemmed from more than one Delta blues song which Waters had heard when growing up in Mississippi.

The choice of material clearly indicates Brian Jones' continuing leadership of the band at this stage. The distinctive feature of 'I Can't Be Satisfied' was Muddy Waters' fierce bottleneck guitar and Jones was confident that he could do more than emulate it. By contrast Mick Jagger would sound tentative in the vocal, as if daunted by comparison with Chess' greatest star, even though the original was recorded at another studio before the move to South Michigan Avenue in the mid-Fifties.

Waters' version, released in 1948 on the Aristocrat label, featured him backed only by stand-up bassist, Big Crawford. He sings in tones of subdued menace, occasionally bursting into a kind of snarling yelp. The apparently disconnected traditional blues verses include an invitation – "goin' back down south, child, do you wanna come?" and a murderous threat – "feel like snappin' pistol in your face, let some graveyard be your restin' place", the apparently confused thoughts of a singer who admits "woman, I'm troubled, I be all worried mind", adding "I jus' can't keep from cryin.'"

The title of the song bears an obvious resemblance to the Stones' '(I Can't Get No) Satisfaction' which they would record nearly twelve months later. Yet the Waters' lyric contains no overt sexual references. Still, it was certainly perceived by Waters' female fans as implicitly erotic in terms of their own reactions to the bluesman's deep, resonant voice. It was this

103

that fired up sales of the record, leading to a #11 hit on the R&B chart and breaking Muddy as a star- much to the delight of his producer, Leonard Chess, who'd been wary of grim blues lyrics only to find them overridden by Waters' appeal to women.

The Rolling Stones' version hinges on a tour de force of slide guitar from Brian Jones with two lyrical solos, the second culminating in a striking run- ascending, descending and rising again. Bill Wyman is another significant player, his electric bass far more expressive than Crawford's plodding stand-up. On the other hand, while Mick Jagger's vocal is good in terms of disciplined performance, it's lacking in character, hinting at spite without ever conveying menace. He misheard "can't keep from cryin'" as "can't keep on cryin'" and cannot get anywhere near Muddy Waters.

For all the breathtaking brilliance of Jones' slide, 'I Can't Be Satisfied' doesn't compare with the great tracks on the eponymous album. Essentially it's bogged down in an out of time sensibility. Blues historians would romanticise the sinister aspects of Delta blues while giving short shrift to the innovative songwriting of rhythm and blues, whose lyrics lit up the Fifties and were meat and drink for the early Rolling Stones.

Whether it was the surrealism of Slim Harpo and Bo Diddley, the playful humour of Rufus Thomas, the reproachful weariness of Jimmy Reed or the brutally honest eroticism of Willie Dixon, these were the solid foundations on which the Rolling Stones built their musical reinterpretations. Songs such as 'Mona', 'Walking the Dog', 'I'm a King Bee' and 'I Just Want To Make Love To You' sounded vibrant and modern whereas 'I Can't Be Satisfied' sounded bleakly ancient.

Usually Brian Jones had been careful to place clear blue water between the Rolling Stones and bands such as Blues Incorporated or John Mayall's Blues Breakers. These were bands which appealed to blues purists of the kind who frequented the Marquee before it relocated to Wardour Street And, if Brian ever lost sight of the distinction, there was always Keith Richards there to remind him.

However valiantly the other instrumentalists play on 'I Can't Be Satisfied', the track remains in a musical no man's land, Jones' guitar too sophisticated for a Mississippi blues yet the overall ambience far too glum for rhythm 'n' blues. It was shunted onto the album 'The Rolling Stones No. 2' where it stood out like a sore thumb amidst various soul and pop numbers.

CHAPTER 16

— ❧ —

2120 South Michigan Avenue

At the time of the Rolling' Stones arrival at the Chess Studio in the spring of 1964, they remained essentially the same rhythm and blues band which had been founded by Brian Jones and Ian Stewart two years before. They wanted to reinterpret classic R&B tracks and to branch out with self-composed material which would be credited to Nanker Phelge. These aims contrasted with Andrew Oldham's wish to boost the songwriting partnership of Mick Jagger and Keith Richards. That partnership was still in its infancy, however, and certainly Richards and, for the most part, Jagger remained committed to the collective ideal.

The studio at 2120 South Michigan Avenue was perfectly suited to instrumental jams. From his earliest days as a producer, Leonard Chess had loved sonic experimentation, placing mics in bathrooms and corridors to come up with daring effects. As Chess prospered, so he and his brother, Phil, had a Chicago engineering firm construct a custom-built echo chamber. What's more, engineers such as Ron Malo had adjustable panels at their disposal which enabled them to control resonance and isolate instruments so there'd be no leakage. This was an ideal environment for the Rolling Stones' instrumentalists, one which they entered into with unrestrained delight. They were greeted in a friendly and respectful manner by Chess recording artists such as Willie Dixon (whom they'd already met in London), Buddy Guy and Muddy Waters -who joined Ian Stewart in carrying instruments into the studio.

Stu was in his absolute element at Chess. By now he'd put behind him his resentment at demotion by Oldham. More relaxed than the others because he could keep in the background during showbiz promotional activities, he played on a number of important tracks during the group's time in Chicago and, at least for a while, was fully reintegrated into the band which he'd jointly founded.

The first instrumental laid down at Chess was done on the first day, the last of only three completed tracks. It was entitled 'Stewed and Keefed' in appreciation of the work of Ian Stewart and Keith Richards. Its alternative title was 'Brian's Blues.' In fact Brian Jones didn't play on it. He was feeling unwell and needed to rest. This strongly suggests a psychosomatic reaction after the stress of recording 'I Can't Be Satisfied.' Happily, he'd fully recovered the following day and was totally involved in the eleven tracks that would be laid down on June 11.

'Stewed and Keefed' begins with Stewart's piano tremolo in subdued, jazzy style. As he starts to embroider the phrases, he evokes the atmosphere of a smoke-filled jazz club. But this is definitely not pre-war Kansas City. Soon Keith Richards enters with pounding, bluesy guitar. The instrumental voices mesh perfectly reflecting the empathy between the two buddies from Broadwick Street. Still, Richards pulls no punches, hitting home hard with yelping chords. The track is impeccable if slightly soporific. The Rolling Stones' purist detractors would scarcely recognise them from it. Probably the same would have applied equally to the fans and it was no surprise that it would remain an unreleased gem.

In contrast to 'Stewed and Keefed', 'Empty Heart' is distinctly upbeat with an unusual and highly sensual rhythm. It sounds like an instrumental, although there is a lyric, albeit a feeble one without chorus or bridge, consisting of the title words plus a repeated phrase about wanting his lover back. It comes across as an uninspired piece of last-minute improvisation.

That said, 'Empty Heart' is a glittering track, linking organ, harmonica and guitar to striking effect over a stop -start guitar riff. Basically it's aimed at dancers, something the girls who danced at the Richmond Clubhouse would have loved. In the pre-video age, it still cried out for a dance-oriented promotional film. In 2011 Andy Glass paid a belated tribute to it by uploading footage of Sixties dancers to YouTube across the track. Including black and white shots of a girl in a miniskirt and thigh boots swaying voluptuously, a blonde highkicking and cavorting on her bed plus a half-crazed go-go dancer whirling her hair behind a glass screen, it captured the spirit of the mid-Sixties yet it's notched up 107,000 views.

Andy Glass' video's a far better tribute to the timeless track than the dreadful 1972 version by MC5, a maelstrom of cacophonous sound which only points up the superb, disciplined musicianship of the Rolling Stones.

The final track recorded in Chicago was entitled '2120 South Michigan Avenue' – the very address from which the fifteen-year-old Mick Jagger had obtained blues records by mail order.

A superb jam which is the quintessence of danceable R&B, it begins from Bill Wyman's bass riff over ultra-fast Charlie Watts drums. Ian Stewart, Brian Jones and Keith Richards take turns in the spotlight. Stewart's organ bites and rampages before Jones comes in on bluesharp, really fired up. This was a period when he preferred to play harmonica rather than guitar and he delivers a glorious solo. Yet his skill would never be acknowledged by blues buffs who ignored him in their haste to acclaim the likes of Paul Butterfield, Charlie Musselwhite and Jerry Portnoy. Even the technically limited Bob Dylan would be referenced ahead of a virtuoso such as Brian Jones.

After a neat diminuendo, Keith Richards announces himself with pounding guitar. On his own at first, he's soon blending with Stewart's resurgent organ before he in turn fades down yielding to a brief, final blast from Jones. In terms of artistry, membership of an ensemble, being a player steeped in teamwork and not seeking to show off, Richards is musically well ahead of such as Hendrix, Clapton and Jimmy Page despite not possessing their technical proficiency.

It was not Keith Richards' fault but, in the coming age of rock, the guitar, like some pernicious, all- consuming weed, overgrew the musical garden and such marvellously expressive instruments as the Hammond would be relegated while the harmonica would be shamefully silenced.

As for '2120 South Michigan Avenue', it would be released in a short-ened version first on the '5× 5' EP and then-together with 'Empty Heart'-on the '12×5' album. It could be heard in full only on a West German LP. It had been under consideration as the title track of a putative R&B album which in fact never materialised. The excellent work done by the band at Chess would be dissipated by Andrew Oldham, never grouped on the same album, truncated and, in some cases, left to gather dust.

CHAPTER 17

— ❧ —

Chicken Fried in Bacon Grease

ON THE ROLLING Stones' second morning at Chess, Chuck Berry sauntered into the studio while they were recording his song, 'Around and Around.' After a brief chat about amps, he left them with the words "swing on, gentlemen, you are sounding most well, if I may say so." His condescending tone via the use of formal UK English was of course not lost on the Rolling Stones and contrasted with the genuine friendliness of Muddy Waters and Willie Dixon.

'Around and Around' was in fact one of Berry's weaker tracks, a lacklustre B-side to his greatest hit, 'Johnny B. Goode.' It was relatively easy for the Rolling Stones to surpass a feeble vocal and a formulaic lyric and, although they were making money for him, Berry doubtless had his reasons to be on edge at a time when he was not long out of prison and desperate to relaunch his career.

By the time Chess' foremost rock 'n' roll artist returned, he let down his guard, exclaiming "wow, you guys are really getting it on!" This time he was listening to the Englishmen's version of 'Down the Road Apiece' and his praise was fully justified. He'd recorded the number himself and it had appeared on his 1960 album, 'Rocking at the Hops.'

Rock critics would assume the Rolling Stones had learnt the song from Berry's version. Yet in fact his recording was the seventh cover of a prewar boogie-woogie number, originally recorded by the Will Bradley Trio (one of whose members, Don Raye, was the writer). What Chuck Berry did was to transpose boogie piano figures to guitar thus revamping 'Down the Road Apiece' in rock 'n' roll style.

Ian Stewart knew and loved what was by far the best version of the song, that waxed by Amos Milburn in 1946. Milburn was a brilliantly gifted pianist who effortlessly rolled out sparkling boogie while confidently accompanying himself on vocal. He was a vital link in the chain stretching from pre-war boogie-woogie through rhythm and blues to rock 'n' roll. His style was upbeat and extrovert and he crossed over to white audiences who'd recoiled from the grimness of Delta blues.

The Rolling Stones would not be the only British rhythm and blues band to be offering a reinterpretation of 'Down the Road Apiece.' As Brian Jones knew from his friend Paul Jones, Manfred Mann were about to record their version. A highly musicianly outfit with Paul Jones himself an excellent lead singer, it looked for a while as if they might offer significant competition as far as British Invasion bands were concerned. The Rolling Stones were thus well and truly on their mettle. Yet, impressive as Manfred Mann's record is, it lacks the uninhibited verve of the Rolling Stones.

'Down the Road Apiece' salutes an all-night diner, famed for its spicy food – notably chicken fried in bacon grease. The lyric's a paean to America's remote roadhouses, the dives and joints straddling county lines where law enforcement was less than rigorous and illicit pleasures beckoned.

'Down the Road Apiece' suited Mick Jagger down to the ground. His voice was perfectly adapted to belt out a fast-moving rock 'n' roll vocal and he sounds totally convincing as he conjures up hedonistic images of a joint where a guy can do as he pleases. After Keith Richards opens the track with a straight Chuck Berry lift, the three-man rhythm section of Stewart, Wyman and Watts incarnate an imaginary combo which had an old piano, a knockout bass and a drummer named Charlie McCoy.

Yet the most striking feature of the track is the fantastic instrumental fadeout which lasts almost a minute and a half, a boiling synthesis of contrasting riffs, some tumbling, others brusque while sustained throughout by Stu's delicately embroidered boogie-woogie piano figures.

Archive footage of the Rolling Stones performing 'Down the Road Apiece' reveals a tremendous boost to their onstage confidence over the twelve month period between their low-key arrival in the United States and their subsequent acclaim as a British Invasion group second only to the legendary Beatles. Initially a nervously smiling Mick Jagger had cast worried sidelong glances, tentatively trying out foot movements as he desperately tried to personify the lyric's 'rubber- legged boy.' By May 65, however, four months after the track appeared on 'The Rolling Stones No.2', he was treating the screaming Shindig audience as no more than worshipful fodder.

Jagger lacked the incredible natural athleticism of Chuck Berry and his astounding 'duck walk' but his frontman antics took the focus off Keith Richards and enabled him to conquer his earlier shyness. On the Rolling Stones' finest live rendition of the number- a 'Top Gear' clip uploaded to YouTube by ruudtes in July 2013- Keith's face lights up with sheer delight as he fires off the licks while Brian Jones smiles, temporarily lost in the sheer joie de vivre of a great performance. Even the gaunt Bill Wyman gives his face a holiday as he bathes in the boogie. The Rolling Stones had built on Don Raye, Amos Milburn and Chuck Berry to take the wonderful boogie-woogie heritage to an even higher musical level.

CHAPTER 18

High Heel Sneakers and Old Crow Licquor

As the June 11 session wore on, the pace began to tell on the Rolling Stones. They'd already outclassed Chuck Berry on 'Around and Around', they'd done a fine job on an old blues- 'Confessin' the Blues'- they'd laid down two fiery tracks in 'Down the Road Apiece' and 'Empty Heart' and they'd done their best with 'Down in the Bottom'-which wasn't one of Willie Dixon's finest songs.

The problem lay in the preposterously tight schedule with which they'd been lumbered. Another day would have been more than welcome and would doubtless have suited Marshall Chess, Leonard's son, who was the same age as the band and was revelling in his role as their guide to Chicago. But Andrew Oldham had other priorities, namely their appearance at Big Reggie's Ballroom in Minneapolis the following day. He'd been willing to let them indulge their R&B craving up to a point but his patience was becoming exhausted.

From their manager's point of view, there was the consolation of a soul number, a genre which he could relate to and which, he was convinced, would be their stepping stone to chart success. The track was Wilson Pickett's 'If You Need Me.' Here Ian Stewart could prove really useful. Organ figured prominently in soul and the portly road manager was lined up to get weaving on Hammond.

Before turning their attention to Pickett's song, the Rolling Stones were eager to record their version of a recent big hit, namely Tommy Tucker's 'Hi- Heel Sneakers' which had topped the R&B chart and had narrowly failed to reach the Billboard Top Ten. It was a track which had everything: superb counterpoint between Tucker on organ and the woefully underrated guitarist, Weldon Young; a wonderfully danceable beat laid down by Johnny Williams on drums and female bassist, Brenda Jones; and a strikingly different and inventive lyric by Tucker himself, credited under his real name, Robert Higginbotham. The musicians came from Newark, New Jersey but had recorded in Chicago for Chess subsidiary, Checker.

Tucker had structured his song as a twelve bar blues and, handling the vocal, he begins with the singer conventionally advising his girlfriend to wear a red dress on their night out. Then everything changes. Aware that the couple will soon be the centre of attention, some of it hostile, he warns her to wear boxing gloves.

Switching to 'what the hell' mood, the singer urges his girl to wear bizarre gear – high heel sneakers and a wig hat. Yet this is a poor working-class couple who can barely afford a night on the town. The singer will have to make do with cheap booze- Old Crow licquor. The downmarket Kentucky bourbon is all he can afford because bootleg whiskey costs much more than he can stand.

The only weakness in the original is Tucker's slurred diction. Mick Jagger clearly hadn't deciphered the verse about Old Crow liquor and time was running out for him to listen and learn. It was decided to junk that verse and, in doing so, much of the originality was lost.

What shouldn't have been a problem was counterpoint. If ever two bandmates were suited to tackling that it would've been Keith Richards and Ian Stewart. But it was not to be. By this time Jagger had almost given up and he can barely suppress his laughter at the image of the high heel sneakers and wig hat before he incongruously shouts "better do some!" It's left to Brian Jones to try and redeem the track with bone-chilling Little Walter-style blues harp but, good as his solo is, the band fail overall.

The track would never be officially released. Consigned to bootleg, it eventually revealed itself as a competent piece of work which fell below the high standard the Rolling Stones had set in their reinterpretation of R&B classics. Hundreds of performers, including Elvis Presley, would take on 'Hi- Heel Sneakers' over the years, only underlining the great opportunity that had been lost. As for Tommy Tucker, he became rapidly disillusioned with the music business and quit a few years later to set himself up in real estate.

CHAPTER 19

—— ❦ ——

Sex Marathon

CHUCK BERRY MADE his mind up on a career in music when, as a fifteen-year-old boy, he sneaked into the Rhumboogie Club in Chicago to hear bluesman Joe Turner. Among the songs Turner sang that night was 'Around the Clock Blues.' It tells the tale of a marathon sex session lasting from one o'clock in the morning to midday. Except for hourly glances at the clock and a brief bathroom break, the singer and his woman begin in bed and, after breaking the springs, continue on the floor. Explicit as the song obviously is, Turner delivered it in a light-hearted style and stressed his capacity to satisfy his girlfriend. It typified the attitude to sex in rhythm and blues. In easy listening music, the slightest hint of sex was taboo whereas in rock it would become an obsession. In R&B it was simply a fact of life.

Joe Turner got to record 'Around the Clock Blues' five years later. But he'd been beaten to the punch by R&B singer Wynonie Harris. Harris recounts a similar episode, singing in a relaxed style and prefacing his story with the words "sometimes I will then again I think I won't – sometimes I do then again I think I don't." Although the singer's not always in the mood for hours of continuous sex, he emphasises that the goal is mutual satisfaction, enquiring of his woman "Mama, is your daddy thrillin' you?" Humour is brought in as the singer declares "it's like Maxwell house coffee – good to the last drop."

Chuck Berry had longed to deliver his own version of the round the clock theme. But Leonard Chess made it unmistakably clear that Berry's audience was high school kids and that DJs would keep any explicit number right off the radio. So, in 'Reelin' and Rockin', the flipside of his innocently titled 'Sweet Little Sixteen', he substitutes a rock 'n' roll dance for copulation and casual glances at his wristwatch for clock watching. Yet

Berry was determined to hint at the real context for his fast-paced rocking song. For starters he lifts Harris' preface word for word. Then he sets a brief timeframe of alleged dancing which leaves him shouting that he doesn't know if he's dead or alive. That apart, 'Reelin' and Rockin' is little more than harmless fun, with Berry's highly talented boogie-woogie pianist, Lafayette Leake, complaining that his thumbnail was nearly torn off as a result of Leonard Chess' insistence on sweeping glissandos on take after take.

The Rolling Stones decided to tackle 'Reelin' and Rockin' by slowing the rhythm down to voluptuous R&B. Doubtless this was at the instigation of Brian Jones who, in his letters to the jazz press, had argued that rock 'n' roll was "a corruption of rhythm and blues." At the same time, they junked three verses of Berry's lyric with the result that they clocked in at three minutes thirty-six, less than twenty seconds longer than Berry's version. The verses cut included incongruously innocent ones about a dancing ballerina and holding hands.

After a brief intro of plunging guitar chords, Mick Jagger snarls the preface. The wristwatch- related verses get far less emphasis than the chorus where, over a menacing guitar riff, the emphasis is on the word "rollin.'"

Although Chuck Berry had been Keith Richards' earliest guitar hero, the chords Richards plays in his lengthy mid-track solo are savagely bluesy not crunching and double stopped. And, as far as the verses go, Jagger's emphasis is on 'dead or alive' and the size of the woman the singer's with. No one could be left in the slightest doubt that it's an adult sexual encounter that's being referred to not a rock 'n' roll hop for jiving teens.

This was yet another significant reinterpretation by the Rolling Stones. Yet it would remain unreleased, possibly because American kids went overboard for British Invasion band, the Dave Clark Five and their so-called 'Tottenham Sound.' Clark's crass, hysterical version of 'Reelin' and Rockin' was a Cashbox Top Twenty hit in the States the following year. Yet musically it was on the same level as the Bill Haley material which Brian Jones had scorned at the age of fourteen.

Eventually Chuck Berry would get to record 'Reelin' and Rockin' in the manner he'd always wanted. His live version of the song, recorded in England at Coventry in 1972, found him delivering possibly the most lewd vocal ever, egged on by wildly yelling English teens. It was a Top Twenty UK hit, reflecting the sexual obsession of white rockers emerging from decades of repression and contrasting utterly with the light-hearted delight in mutual satisfaction which characterised the Joe Turner number Berry had heard in his own teenage years.

The Rolling Stones had completed a Chicago blues, Muddy Waters' 'Look What You've Done' before turning to 'Reelin' and Rockin' and, after it, they recorded a traditional blues, Bill Broonzy's 'Tell Me, Baby' before finishing a momentous day's work with '2120 South Michigan Avenue.'

The material recorded by the Rolling Stones at the Chess studio in Chicago would never remotely get the recognition it deserved. Completed in the mere two days Andrew Oldham's rigid touring schedule allowed, it was a superb performance under pressure. Yet it didn't suit Oldham's primary purpose, that of promoting the songwriting team of Mick Jagger and Keith Richards. None of the songs recorded in Chicago was a Jagger-Richards original and, from their manager's point of view, it was only slight consolation that a couple of commercially oriented soul numbers, 'Time Is On My Side' and 'If You Need Me' had been waxed.

There was ample material from the Chess Sessions for a great rhythm and blues album but it would never see the light of day. This was all grist to the mill for rock critics whose agenda was to ignore BRB. Whether it was wonderfully danceable material such as '2120 South Michigan Avenue' or brilliant reinterpretations such as 'Down The Road Apiece', R&B makeovers of a rock 'n' roll song such as 'Reelin' and Rockin' or an instant classic such as 'It's All Over Now', the whole lot would be swept under the carpet even though they comprised some of the Rolling Stones' finest performances.

Part 4: Farewell to Rhythm and Blues

CHAPTER 20

— ♭ —

Diversion into Soul

SHORTLY AFTER RETURNING from their first American tour, the Rolling Stones recorded a soul number at Regent Sounds. Andrew Oldham, who'd put up with enough rhythm and blues to last him a lifetime, had noted for himself, whilst in the US, that black record purchasers were turning in droves from R&B to soul. Eager for hits, he had little difficulty in persuading Mick Jagger to record 'Time Is on My Side.' Jagger saw himself as a protean vocalist, able to switch styles at the drop of a hat and deliver a telling rendition of any song- blues, R&B, pop or soul.

'Time Is on My Side' had an odd history. Danish- born jazz trombonist Kai Winding was eager to try his hand with something more rhythm- oriented and commercial. Songwriter Jerry Ragovoy came up with the tune and Winding recorded it. Ragovoy had used the pseudonym Norman Meade (which he thought sounded more ethnic) to credit his lyric- which was little more than a scrap before it was extended by black songwriter Jimmy Norman.

'Time Is on My Side' was then recorded by New Orleans soul singer, Irma Thomas, who delivered an over the top vocal, shouty and screechy, which was the B-side of her hit single 'Anyone Who Knows What Love Is.' The song thus had slight commercial legs and this left a gap which Oldham was determined to exploit.

Recorded in London on June 24, 1964 with Ian Stewart's sonorous, churchy organ intro limited to a few seconds, the Rolling Stones' original version was released in the US three months later and it gave the band their first Top Ten hit on the Billboard Hot 100. Jagger's vocal's better than Thomases despite a tendency to over-emphasis. Yet it was not until a re- recording at Chess in November 64 that 'Time Is on My Side' received a truly classy treatment. This was thanks to Keith Richards' peal-ing twenty-second guitar intro and, even more, his beautiful mid-track solo. It was released in the UK in January 65 on the album 'The Rolling Stones No.2.'

When the song was debuted on the Ed Sullivan Show, however, Mick Jagger's vocal was directed straight at the screaming teenage girls while Brian Jones looked glumly on, absorbing the price of his fame-driven Faustian pact with Oldham. Though Jagger commented in interview that the Ragovoy/Thomas song was "the epitome of the sort of music we like", he was speaking for himself and Keith Richards rather than Wyman and Watts and certainly not for Brian Jones.

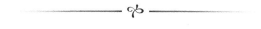

CHAPTER 21

The Little Red Rooster and
the Strange Kin People

DURING THE COURSE of 1964, events in Brian Jones' personal life caused trouble between him and Andrew Oldham. Oldham was concerned about Jones' deepening involvement with Linda Lawrence. During the band's American tour, Brian had written her romantic letters on a regular basis. Linda was in the last stages of her pregnancy at the time and their son, Julian, was born in July.

Linda hoped– and her parents certainly expected– that marriage would promptly follow. But though Andrew Oldham didn't bat an an eyelid at the shock-worthy serial shagging of groupies– in which all band members, except the happily married Watts, indulged- fatherhood was a different story. The Rolling Stones' co-manager was worried that, if Brian and Linda were to marry or even to live openly together, Jones' huge fan club of teenage girls would desert in droves, resulting in a substantial drop in the band's record sales.

Under pressure from Oldham, Jones drew the line at marriage and Linda Lawrence's father told him to get out of his house. Relieved that Jones and Lawrence had split up and the child had been adopted, Oldham was staggered to be told, four months later, by Dawn Molloy that she was carrying Jones' child. Molloy was an aspiring model, a beautiful nineteen year old who lived at Chesham Place in upscale Belgravia where her father was a property manager. Though she'd followed the Rolling Stones since they debuted in Richmond, she now lived only a couple of blocks from Jones' new flat.

Recovering swiftly from the setback, Oldham brokered a deal, which Jagger witnessed, whereby she was paid £700 for her silence. The child, a boy named Paul, was born in March 65 and immediately adopted without press or public knowing a word about it. And, by acquiescing in Oldham's diktat that both women must be shucked off, Jones sealed himself even further into the hustler's fame-driven Faustian pact.

Neither Linda Lawrence nor Dawn Molloy had deluded themselves about Brian Jones' infidelity. But, decades later, when both were free to speak, they countered the image of him as a callous womaniser. Certainly, his sex drive was unrestrained and he was prone to jealous outbursts. Yet he was capable of great tenderness, a skilled and patient lover who sought satisfaction for his partner as well as himself. Still, he'd been compromised by the Molloy deal and Oldham was free to promote the band with Jagger as its undisputed leader.

Gratified though Oldham was that Jagger could now compete for attention with Jones among teenage girls in the band's fan club, there was also the crucial matter of songwriting royalties. It was vital, from his point of view, that Jagger and Keith Richards should establish a profitable writing partnership which in turn would ensure a lucrative producer's royalty for himself.

Anticipating the first fruits of their writing partnership, Oldham was stunned to learn that the Rolling Stones' next UK single was going to be 'The Red Rooster', a blues song written by Willie Dixon and recorded by Howlin Wolf. He protested the plan, demanding its replacement by a salesworthy poppy song. But, with Jagger insistent as well as Jones, he had to give way. The band cut the song at Regent in September 64 but, dissatisfied with the Regent sound, they didn't complete their version till their return to Chess in early November on the next American tour.

By 1961, the year of recording 'The Red Rooster', Howlin Wolf's band had become even more popular than Muddy Waters. Wolf himself had completed the transition from the Mississippi Delta via Memphis to Chicago. His inimitable voice was a colossal foghorn yet it had a distinctive pain-wracked quality emanating from Wolf's wretched youth when he was cast adrift by his blues–hating, religious fanatic mother. In his private life Howlin Wolf was a devoted husband and stepfather yet his lewd stage antics would be copied years later by cock-rocking white vocalists too feeble to emulate his impassioned singing.

In Willie Dixon's 'The Red Rooster', the singer laments the loss of a fowl dismissed by some as a lazy, dry-throated bird. Yet this rooster's the sentinel of the farm and, in his absence on the prowl, dogs bark and hounds howl. There's a sense here of chaos descended but also a stated warning to strange kin people who are urged to watch out. The last verse urges any finder to seize the rooster and bring him back home. That's the only way peace can be restored to the farmyard.

There's a strong sense of regret in Dixon's blues and Wolf's tone is anguished. His voice is an immense, groaning, hyper-melismatic shout, a vast lament not, in any sense, a roar of exultation. On 'The Red Rooster', Wolf gives a fantastic performance, hurling himself utterly into the lyrics, his voice roaring off the grooves with immense power and sonority. And, throughout the track, the rhythm section of Willie Dixon and Sam Lay is relatively subdued but the guitar accompaniment is one of rare beauty, Wolf's slide blended perfectly with Hubert Sumlin's murmuring lead.

Exactly what Dixon intended to convey by these enigmatic lyrics is unclear. The fierce intensity of Wolf's voice makes it plain this is no mere farmyard fantasy. Nor is it some sort of sex epic replete with double meanings. Dixon was a politically aware man, an ex-conscientious objector, who, in the years before the civil rights movement gained momentum, may have opted for metaphor in his warning to strange kin people.

Two years later, Sam Cooke had altered the title to 'Little Red Rooster' and had a Top Ten R&B hit with it. Cooke's voice, so effective in the emerging soul idiom, is unsuited to the song, which he plays for laughs and, with the exception of Billy Preston on Hammond, the backing's silly. But, with white teenagers chortling over puerile sexual double meanings, the record rose to #11 on the Billboard chart.

The Rolling Stones used Sam Cooke's title not Howlin Wolf's and the first line of the lyric's entirely different – where Wolf had sung about owning a prize fowl, Jagger boldly asserts that he IS the rooster! This gives the track a sexual twist à la Sam Cooke but without the slightest hint of the puerility on the Cooke version. Indeed, in the final verse, the rooster's once again referred to in the third person.

'Rooster' would be rightly acclaimed as Brian Jones' finest hour. Yet in truth the entire band combine to give a beautiful rendition. Jagger's vocal is possibly his finest yet - clear, emphatic and compelling. And there's a sensual, danceable beat with Charlie Watts' clipped stickswork and Bill Wyman's thudding bass.

Yet Brian Jones' performance is an absolute tour de force. He punctuates the lines with exquisite shivering slide, mimicking the gruff bark of the dogs and the eerie howling of the hounds and adding minimalist harmonies from time to time. And, in the final half minute, Jones' bold bluesharp's layered in.

Many years later Bill Wyman would wisely observe that "it realised Brian's cherished ambition to put blues music at the top of the charts and meant his guilt at having sold out to pop fame was diminished."

As with the band's cover of Waters' 'I Just Want To Make Love To You', the two versions are in the same rhythm and blues continuum but with the Rolling Stones' reinterpretation speeded up compared to Wolf in proportion to their youth and their Englishness. Though the band were on the first peak of their personal popularity at the time, it was still a remarkable feat to take a song whose antecedents lay in the Mississippi Delta right to the very top of the UK chart. But, with most American radio stations uncomfortable with possible sexual implications, it was never released as a single in the US.

The negative American reaction was not the only downside to the story of 'Rooster.' Brian Jones had arrived at the Regent studio, together with Ian Stewart (who wasn't scheduled to play) in the belief that he'd be joining the rest of the band there. When they arrived, none of the others were present but there was a brusque written message for Jones telling him at which points on the track he should play his slide. The others had recorded their parts in advance.

As Stu witnessed, Jones was deeply upset by the duplicity, for which he blamed Oldham and Jagger. Yet he composed himself to deliver a fine performance. Still, it was only when the band broke off their second American tour to revisit Chess that the track was completed.

The reasons behind their hostility were principally personal dislike, in the case of Oldham, and, for Jagger, his determination to oust Jones from the leadership of the band. Yet the others had gone along with the insult, something for which Bill Wyman would always reproach himself. There were additional factors such as the extra fiver a week in wages which Jones had negotiated for himself with Eric Easton. And Jones' susceptibility to illness. Jagger and Richards put him down as a hypochondriac, someone who was always taking medication – if not for his back then for his legs and feet and even his ears. Had the phrase 'Sicknote' already been in vogue, they'd doubtless have used it.

Bill Wyman, more emotionally intelligent than Jagger and Richards, never indulged in such mockery. He was well aware that Brian Jones was undermined by asthma. Yet there was probably more to Jones' ill health than even that, serious as it was.

Many years after Jones' death, Bill Wyman traced his daughter (by Angeline), Carol, who'd been born on August 4, 1960 but whom he never knew. Carol disclosed her own troubled medical history and that she'd been diagnosed with temporal lobe epilepsy. Wyman told Carol that her father had been permanently worried about his health, that he suffered sudden depressions and swings of mood, that he could be okay one minute and then switch off from the conversation. Carol concurred that these were exactly her symptoms. Yes, her medication was controlling it but there was no cure.

In retrospect Bill Wyman came to believe that Brian Jones may well have been an undiagnosed epileptic. Even during Brian's lifetime, Bill wondered whether Jones' ill health had made him think the struggle for power against Oldham and Jagger wasn't worth fighting.

Brian Jones had been fascinated with the role of the Rooster in blues mythology ever since reading 'Blues Fell This Morning.' Although Mick Jagger had incarnated the prowling bird in song, Jones was the linchpin of the band just as the rooster was the sentinel of the farm. As he became estranged from his bandmates, so the Rolling Stones rhythm and blues band began to split. Jones had hoped for a musical band of brothers but Mick Jagger and Keith Richards were starting to become strange kin people.

CHAPTER 22

—— ❧ ——

What a Shame - About Keith Richards

THE JAGGER/RICHARDS COMPOSITION 'Heart of Stone' was the first fruit of their new songwriting partnership. It has a mournful melody and an obnoxious lyric where the singer boasts of his emotional invulnerability. Glad to get away from the Chess scene where he never felt at home, Andrew Oldham turned to RCA Studios in Hollywood which boasted a highly accomplished and experienced engineer in Dave Hassinger.

There, in November 64, the band's previously crisp guitars were supplanted by a murky drone over which Jagger warbled words as petulant as they're nauseating. 'Heart of Stone', cynically dismissed by Keith Richards as "a puerile ballad", duly gave the band a Billboard Top Twenty hit at the close of 64.

Dire as 'Heart of Stone' is, the B-side, 'What a Shame', recorded by Ron Malo at Chess, is a triumph, albeit one unheralded by rock critics doubtless because, although rightfully credited to Jagger and Richards, it's in rhythm and blues style. Indeed it combines a lyric with an A-A-B blues pattern with an irresistibly danceable beat. Charlie Watts' rat -tat -tat drums combine with Bill Wyman's slurping bass and Stu's piano imparts a tremendous bounce.

Jagger's in good form on the vocal but, when he shouts "all right!", what follows is far more than that. Keith Richards' lead interweaves with Brian Jones' vibrato-heavy slide in a marvellous resurgence of the meshing technique they developed at Edith Grove. Then there's the fantastic, protracted outro, lasting a minute and twenty seconds; the Rolling Stones at their most relaxed with Mick Jagger, his vocal over, contributing good harmonica.

What's also significant is the lyric. It may seem trivial on first hearing. The singer bemoans the way things are turning out in his life before adding the title phrase. And the second verse simply refers to pugnacious people. But the lines which jump out are those about slumbering in a shelter scared stiff.

The shelter in question can hardly be a nuclear fallout shelter but may well be an Anderson shelter of the kind in which the Richards family took refuge during the V2 campaign in the last year of the Second World War when Keith was a babe in arms. In his autobiography, he would state that he has memories of wailing air raid sirens and the terror they induced.

As a boy he detested the gang warfare which prevailed in Dartford on the Temple Hill estate. His mother, Doris, described Keith as a shy lad who, whilst he would certainly stand up for himself if attacked, preferred to avoid confrontation. When Keith Richards first became a professional musician, he suffered stage fright in front of audiences and, at the Station Hotel in Richmond, he got by only by turning his back on them.

As the Rolling Stones became more and more popular, their confidence stretched even to him. Nevertheless, in a highly revealing interview which he gave to the magazine 'Beat Instrumental', in 1964, he disclosed that, for a long time, he "used to wish I could have a screen between me and the audience." He added that he "just wanted to play not put on any showmanship." In time, however, he "realised people like to watch something as well as listen."

When Mick Jagger developed his flamboyant antics at the mic, he became the cynosure of all eyes as far as the fans were concerned. In effect, Keith Richards had gained a human screen between himself and the audience. He could play to his heart's content out of the limelight while Jagger cavorted in front of hordes of teenage girls.

Whereas Keith, as a lad, had resorted to lashing out with his bike chain as the Temple Hill gangsters tried to knock him off his Raleigh, he had to restrain himself when confronted by verbally aggressive journos and paparazzi bombarding the Rolling Stones with all manner of hostile questioning.

It's highly likely that Keith Richards wrote the words as well as the music to 'What a Shame.' The line about sleeping in the shelter all night may well have been a flashback to his early childhood. And the mention of constant fighting is probably a reference to journo scrums. Yet, whether or not that was the case, his desire for a human screen whilst on stage would certainly be a powerful additional motivation for throwing in his lot with Mick Jagger, who was, in any case, his boyhood friend and with whom he obviously savoured the prospect of writing lucrative hits.

By contrast, Brian Jones, his fellow guitarist and natural musical partner, would have seemed, due to his persistent ill-health, a source of weakness whereas the athletic and hyper-confident Jagger would certainly have been a tower of strength as far as Richards was concerned. These considerations assisted Andrew Oldham in his aim of detaching Richards from Jones and promoting him as co-writer with Jagger.

In time Keith Richards would need more to sustain him than just the fans focusing on the frontman, Jagger. Before the end of the Sixties he'd become a heroin addict. To his credit, he kicked smack in 1978 but it had done much to negate his creativity. Though hailed by rock critics as 'The Human Riff', he would never be the same wonderfully inventive guitarist as he'd been in the Sixties. He was a truly outstanding musician who made a vital contribution to the Rolling Stones and his decline was indeed a great shame.

CHAPTER 23

'The Last Time' : First Progressive Pop Hit

EARLY IN 1965 events began to move against Brian Jones both in terms of his previously undisputed leadership of the band and also regarding his preference for rhythm and blues. Their third American album, 'The Rolling Stones, Now!', was released in mid -February and comprised a mix of genres, pop and soul as well as R&B. Amid the furore engendered by Andrew Oldham's liner notes, something more significant was missed. Bent on shock, Oldham had urged prospective buyers to "cast deep in your pockets for the loot to buy this disc... if you don't have the bread, see that blind man, knock him on the head, steal his wallet and low and behold you have the loot, if you put in the boot, good, another one sold!"

Beyond this nonsensical nastiness, Oldham had announced "this is THE STONES new disc within." At a stroke he'd shortened the name of the band by removing the word 'Rolling.' Although their name would continue to be rendered as 'the Rolling Stones' for official purposes, they would be 'the Stones' from then on in everyday speech. There were those who considered any consideration of the difference to be pedantic.

They were mistaken. 'Rolling Stones' was the original name chosen by Brian Jones with reference to Muddy Waters' blues single, 'I'm a Rollin' Stone.' By blurring the first word of the name, Oldham severed the link with the world of blues and R&B and at the same time got in a dig against Jones.

For over a year Mick Jagger and Keith Richards had struggled to deliver the hit songs which Oldham had demanded. In future years Jagger would have little or nothing to say about this period whereas Richards was remarkably open. He said "when you first start writing, the first batch of songs is almost always puerile ballads for some reason – I think they're just easier to write. Writing a good rock 'n' roll song is one of the hardest things because it has to be stripped down so simple, to that same basic format shared by rock 'n' roll, rhythm and blues and Irish folk. It's a very simple form and yet you have to find a certain element that still lives, that isn't just a rehash. It can remind you – and probably will – of something else but it must still have something new, a certain freshness and individuality about it."

Specifically Keith Richards was alluding to accusations that 'The Last Time' (recorded at RCA on January11-12 1965 and released in the UK on February 26) had ripped off the Staple Singers' gospel song entitled 'This May Be The Last Time.' He commented "we were basically adapting a traditional gospel song that had been sung by the Staple Singers but luckily the song itself goes back into the mists of time." He added "I was trying to learn it on the guitar, just to get the chords, playing along to the record. At least we put our stamp on it which was something the Staple Singers and others had done." That was an indirect reference to James Brown's soulful cover of the traditional gospel song.

This is an honest enough account of the origin of the song – as far as it goes. Although the Rolling Stones' chorus in 'The Last Time' borrows the Staple Singers' words, the melody is speeded up in keeping with the verses which deal with a sexual relationship not the religious concerns of the Chicago gospel group's stark and impassioned song. Indeed the first verse blames the singer's girlfriend for not getting her act together sexwise. In later verses he repeats his final warning that he'll be gone for good unless she changes her ways.

What Richards omits to mention is that the track is made by by Brian Jones' sublime obbligato which haunts the grooves, mesmeric and melancholy, strangely alienated from the lyrical ultimatum. It comprises the insistent intro, punctuates the lines of the verses and resumes even before the jangling accompaniment to the chorus is complete.

The mid-track break contains two brilliant solo bursts by Keith Richards which complement the riff which Jones himself had written. The outro's marred by Jagger's silly pseudo- soul shrieking where it almost sounds as if he's trying to shout down Jones' guitar.

At this stage in the band's history, Mick Jagger was not the equal of Keith Richards and Brian Jones in terms of musical contribution despite being the focus of showbiz attention. As a singer, he had yet to deliver a vocal without strain and his lyrics lacked the depth which they subsequently achieved.

'The Last Time' owes much to Keith Richards in terms of melodic adaptation and his brief but sparkling solo. Nevertheless it's the sound of Brian Jones' Vox Mark III which lingers longest in the listener's memory. Visually as well as aurally iconic, the glistening white 'Teardrop' was especially designed for him and remained his preferred make from mid-64 to the late summer of 65.

Jones' wonderful contribution to 'The Last Time' indicated that, though his days as the leader of an exclusively rhythm and blues-oriented band were over, his musicianship was of such a high quality as to make him indispensable if the Rolling Stones were to go down the route of progressive pop.

'The Last Time' would be the band's third consecutive UK number one and was a Top Ten hit in the US. It's a very significant milestone in the history of the Rolling Stones because it's essentially their first hit in iconic pop style, soon to be their preferred mode after a brief flirtation with rock.

To illustrate 'The Last Time', ihadadreamcrazydream uploaded a brilliant montage of Brian Jones shots to YouTube in May 2010. It captures the complexity of his personality: sometimes deadly serious, absorbed in the music as he plays dulcimer and recorder; at other times fooling around, standing on his head and gurning; often immaculately clad in dandy-style gear; yet occasionally careless of his appearance as he shins up a fire escape or rides a clapped out old bike in the street. There's also a significant contrast between his world-weary demeanour in the late Sixties and the boundless energy which typified him before then and which found a triumphant outlet in his contribution to 'The Last Time.'

CHAPTER 24

—— ℺ ——

Satisfaction- for Some!

THE CHART SUCCESS of 'The Last Time ' prompted Andrew Oldham to consider ousting Brian Jones from the band. His patience with the posh -talking, blues- loving, little provincial was exhausted. Oldham had put up with Jones for two full years for the sake of the teenage girls who read 'Jackie 'and 'Fabulous', who bought records by the truckload and who- infuriatingly- adored someone Oldham himself habitually referred to as "the cunt."

After all it was, his co-manager was sure, a given that Jones was no songwriter. He heard Mick Jagger put down Jones with the words "you? write songs? YOU can't write songs!" and Ian Stewart had described Jones' attempts as sounding "like some bloody old Welsh hymn." The comments were inaccurate. Brian Jones had actually written two songs as early as 63-4, 'Sure I Do' and 'I Want You To Know', the acetates of which are believed to have disappeared. Tony Calder, Oldham's PR business partner, thought them good enough and he recommended them to Oldham only to be told to "fuck off!"

Asked, many years later, to account for Oldham's hostility to Jones, Calder observed that "Andrew only had eyes for Mick" and "he fancied Mick more than he did everybody else." Oldham's attitude contrasted with that of Brian Epstein who, although fascinated with John Lennon, was careful to maintain the Beatles as a partnership of equals and to encourage George Harrison as a songwriter.

While Jimmy Phelge had faded from the Rolling Stones' circle after the move from Edith Grove, there was by this time another close non-musician witness to the unfolding of events. This was Dave Thompson, a Scottish student of textile design who'd got to know Shirley Watts, Charlie's wife, at art school. Thompson had infiltrated the band's entourage and heard Oldham persistently slagging off Jones even to the extent of saying "we must get rid of him." When Thompson asked Keith Richards if he wanted Jones out of the band, Richards emphatically denied it.

Jagger's reaction to Thompson's question was different. He merely shrugged his shoulders. It wasn't that he had any personal antipathy to Jones. But Jagger was a politician manque and, like most politicians, wished to exercise power as fully as possible and hold onto it as long as he could. He wasn't prepared to play second fiddle to anyone.

Brian Jones knew full well which way the wind blew. With Charlie Watts neutral, his only ally within the band was Bill Wyman. Yet he had one key ally outside it. Jones' relationship with Eric Easton still flourished and, while Oldham took the limelight, Easton, as co-manager, did much valuable work behind the scenes.

By the time of the Rolling Stones' third North American tour, beginning in April 65, Brian Jones was in turmoil. Supposedly unwell, he cried off a gig in Toronto and met up with a friend of his, the DJ, Scott Ross, in New York. As they walked around Central Park, Jones unburdened his dissatisfaction with the drift away from rhythm and blues. When Ross asked him whether he wanted to quit the band, Jones couldn't bring himself to give a clear answer. He was clearly tempted by the prospect of starting up a new band which would cleave to his own original vision of R&B.

By this time the British rhythm and blues movement was in full swing and Jones had friends in other bands for whom he had a high respect as musicians. There was not only his old pal, vocalist Paul Jones from Manfred Mann but also the likes of harpist Keith Relf from the Yardbirds, guitarist Hilton Valentine from the Animals and the prodigiously gifted Stevie Winwood from the Spencer Davis Group. If at least a couple of these could be persuaded to join him, a new band could be up and running. Against that, however, Jones was very reluctant to quit the band which he'd founded and the bandmates he always regarded as musical brothers. He decided to let matters rest.

May 6 1965 was a significant date in the history of the Rolling Stones. Whilst they were staying at a motel in Clearwater, Florida, Jones was accused by a groupie of attacking her after they had sex. What wasn't clear at Clearwater was whether there was any substance to her allegation or whether it was a trumped up charge. Yet rough justice was summarily dispensed by Mike Dorsey, the band's American roadie, who battered the alleged offender.

Meanwhile, Keith Richards dreamt up the key riff of his career. It formed the basis of the Stones' first massive hit, 'Satisfaction.' Ironically, Richards and Jagger, composer and lyricist, considered it no more than a B side or an album track. They were outvoted by the other three who were on for it as the band's next single.

Events moved fast. On May 10, just after their Chicago concert at the Arie Crown Theater, the band went to Chess and cut a version featuring Brian Jones on harmonica. Yet the very next day, after they'd flown to California, with a three-day break scheduled before their next gig, they adjourned to the RCA Studios in Hollywood and laid down the record which would launch their worldwide fame. Its outstanding feature was the riff which Keith Richards played through a Gibson Maestro Fuzz Box.

On May 20 'Satisfaction' was debuted on Shindig. It was a time of mixed emotions for Brian Jones. Televiewers could contrast his glum demeanour while the song was being performed with his evident joy at introducing Howlin Wolf to a mass audience of young white Americans. Asked by interviewer Jimmy O'Neill for a few words of introduction, Jones replied in his usual serious and courteous manner- "Howlin Wolf was one of our greatest heroes when we were starting to play rhythm and blues." When O'Neill asked Mick Jagger for additional comment, Jones grinned as he cut him short with the words "it's about time we shut up and let Howlin Wolf play." And, when Wolf launched into a titanic rendi-tion of 'How Many More Years ', Brian Jones' face lit up as he watched the veteran bluesman, hitherto virtually unknown outside the R&B world, stun the teens in the TV studio into awestruck applause.

'Satisfaction' would go on to be a huge number one hit in both the US and the UK.Its rhythms are wonderfully kinetic, played in perfect lockstep by Charlie Watts and Bill Wyman while the melody, staccato and insistent, harks back to rock 'n' roll. But it's the aggressive riff which Keith

Richards blasts through the Fuzz Box which signifies the coming of rock. Arguably the genre had been inaugurated the previous year when, during the Kinks' recording of 'You Really Got Me', Dave Davies had slashed the speaker cone with a knife but, technically, of course, Richards was far ahead of Davies.

The other distinctive elements in the Stones' 'Satisfaction' are the vocal tone and the lyric itself. For the first time Mick Jagger adopts a leering, insinuating voice to accompany words on what would become two characteristic rock themes-the petty vexations of life on the road for a touring band and the disposability of available females. There's also petulant whining about useless information and TV ads for soap powder. But the worst's saved for the last verse and the singer's complaint that, when he's hoping to have it off with a girl, she refuses him, saying she's on a losing streak.

With such a lyric the Stones were clearly entering a different world from that of rhythm and blues whose songs had an open and relaxed attitude to sex – in total contrast to its taboo status in easy listening music – but never descended to the sexual obsession of a singer bleating about the nuisance of menstruation when he'd lined up a girl for a shag.

'Satisfaction' delighted the budding rock critics, young guys who remembered their disgraced boyhood heroes such as Little Richard and Jerry Lee Lewis, pined for such songs as 'Tutti Frutti' and 'Great Balls of Fire' and saw the Stones taking innuendo over the line into the explicit. They revelled in Jagger's sarcastic vocal contrasts and, as they saw it, the stage was now set not merely for the obliteration of uptight easy listening but also for the eclipse of relaxed rhythm and blues.

Andrew Oldham, Mick Jagger and Keith Richards were utterly satisfied with the massive sales of 'Satisfaction.' That meant little to Brian Jones. He came to detest the song which, when he participated in its debut on Shindig, marked a symbolic juxtaposition. His only satisfaction that night was in listening to Howlin Wolf. Now his beloved rhythm and blues was being superseded by proto-rock.

Coming closer than he ever would -before the final weeks of his life-to quitting the Stones, Jones liaised with Eric Easton to line up interviews with sympathetic journalists to whom he disclosed that he might set himself up as a producer, working independently of the band.

What Eric Easton didn't realise was that his days as co-manager were numbered. Andrew Oldham intended to bring a new face in. This was Allen Klein, an accountant from New Jersey whom he'd just met at the Columbia Records Convention in Miami. The antithesis of a stereotypical accountant, Klein was an aggressive even bullying operator in the world of American showbiz, renowned for his ruthlessness in securing better record company deals for the entertainers he represented.

Oldham was convinced that Klein was the very man to confront the record labels on behalf of himself and the Stones and to maximise their marketing potential. Just as he shucked off Giorgio Gomelsky in 63, he intended to kick out Easton, even though his co-manager's status had been legally established.

While still in America, Oldham sent Klein letters of authority empowering him to negotiate for a new recording agreement and consenting to pay him 20% of the gross compensation paid pursuant to the agreement entered into. Oldham referred to Easton in a few brief words, stating that he'd be informed.

On his return to London, Oldham met Mick Jagger and Keith Richards to brief them on the deal. When the whole band was convened en route to meet Allen Klein in his suite at the Hilton, Jagger and Richards were all for it, with only Wyman urging caution. Watts and Jones acquiesced and the deal was almost in place.

It was at this stage that the band first learned that, since May 1963, Impact Sound had been receiving a 14% royalty from Decca on Rolling Stones records but were only paying the band 6% to share between them. Of that 6%, Andrew Oldham and Eric Easton were also taking a 25% management fee-a move which left the band trailing far behind the managers in their share of Decca loot.

By coming clean about what had happened two years earlier and promising a vastly improved deal, Andrew Oldham came up smelling of roses while Eric Easton, still being kept in the dark, looked like the bad guy.

Allen Klein then drew up two letters of agreement for all members of the band to sign in the presence of the chairman of Decca Records. The first stated that in appreciation of "your phenomenal success in the recording business" all royalties on future record sales would be divided equally between the band and their producer.

The second letter referred back to the agreement dated May 9 1963 between Andrew Oldham, Eric Easton and Brian Jones acting on behalf of the Rolling Stones. It specifically indicated the paragraph in that agreement regarding the commission of 25% of all record royalties. That portion of the agreement was now eliminated.

The only clear loser under the new agreement was Eric Easton. As anticipated, he began legal proceedings as soon as he learnt of his effective dismissal. But in the end he accepted an out of court settlement.

At the signing of the new deal in Decca House, each member of the Stones was presented with a hefty cheque. While Mick Jagger, Keith Richards and Charlie Watts departed utterly satisfied at the turn of events, their joy was not shared by the other two. Fat cheques were fine and dandy, of course, but Wyman and Jones were uneasy about the astounding speed with which Oldham had acted and about the remorseless way in which Easton had been ousted. What's more, they both had reservations about Klein's grandstanding manner.

Mick Jagger essentially pulled rank on the dissenters, contrasting himself, as a former student at the London School of Economics, with the business naivete of Brian Jones who'd signed the 63 agreement without apparently scrutinising its clauses.

The new agreement between Andrew Oldham, Allen Klein, the band and Decca was dated July 30 1965. It was in effect the business corollary to the massive record sales which 'Satisfaction' was bringing in at that time. But there was scant cause for satisfaction as far as Brian Jones was concerned. The Rolling Stones had begun under his leadership as a dedicated rhythm and blues band. Yet now he'd been usurped and, while the original name remained in official documents, the effectively renamed 'Stones' were free to pursue a musical policy to be decided by the Jagger-Richards songwriting team.

Part 5: The Rolling Stones' Peak of Progressive Pop

CHAPTER 25

A Rolling Stone from Howard City, Michigan

THE WORLDWIDE SUCCESS of 'Satisfaction' spelled the end of the Rolling Stones as a band dedicated to rhythm and blues. But, despite the insistence of various critics to the contrary, the Stones would make no immediate transition to rock. Indeed the term 'rock' was not yet in widespread use and the highly influential school of American rock criticism did not come into existence until the years 1967-9.

In actual fact, during 1965 and 1966- crucial years during which the whole future of music was at stake- the Rolling Stones would be at their zenith, climbing a peak of progressive pop. In the album, 'Aftermath', and in several sparkling singles recorded around the same time, the band reached their apogee.

Delighted as he was with the success of 'Satisfaction', and its raucous follow-up,'Get Off My Cloud', Andrew Oldham reckoned much more was needed before the songwriting partnership of Mick Jagger and Keith Richards could be promoted in the same breath as Lennon and McCartney. In particular, the album 'Out of Our Heads' had proved a commercial disappointment.

Looming large in Andrew Oldham's mind were, as always, the Beatles. In October and November 65, they were recording the album, 'Rubber Soul', and the word from Abbey Road was of a quantum leap forward in terms of songwriting quality. 'Rubber Soul' was scheduled for release in the UK on December 3 and it would be issued in the US three days later.

Planning for the new album, Andrew Oldham knew that, with the Stones' reputation on the line, it had to be got right. He remained their nominal producer but he was only a producer in the Hollywood movie sense i.e. the person in charge of logistics and recruitment. He swiftly made key decisions. Recording would take place at RCA Studios in Hollywood and plenty of time would be allocated so there'd be no question of a rush job.

RCA Studios was located at 6363 Sunset Boulevard in Los Angeles. The Rolling Stones had already worked there and taken a liking to it. Many years later Mick Jagger would describe Studio B as "a great studio with a lovely big room." In charge was the engineer, Dave Hassinger, a man in whom the band had full confidence. Although Hassinger was a thirty-seven-year-old World War II veteran, he'd been quick to see through the manufactured showbiz hostility to the Stones stemming from what he called "the countless jibes of mediocre comedians all over the world." He praised the band as "real professionals, extremely exhilarating to work with." The appreciation was mutual with Bill Wyman saying that Hassinger had "a really good ear for sounds and we could get a really good take with three or four shots at a song." Wyman also praised the freedom in a studio where "we could experiment for the first time ever and pick up any instrument that was there."

In addition to a technically accomplished engineer like Hassinger, Oldham saw that a gifted arranger was vitally needed, someone who could flesh out the basic rock 'n' roll instruments of electric guitar, bass and drums with contributions from instruments which figured in other genres. Yet, unlike George Martin's work with the Beatles, those would't come from the classical orchestra.

The man he brought in to fulfil this crucial role was someone with an uncommon appreciation of the Rolling Stones' musicianship. This was twenty-seven-year-old Jack Nitzsche, who'd risen to prominence in Hollywood as Phil Spector's arranger. Andrew Oldham was, of course, a huge Spector fan.

Nitzsche was a distinctly unorthodox figure on the West Coast music scene. Raised on a farm near Howard City, Michigan, the son of German immigrants, he fell in love with cool jazz as a teenager and schooled himself as a saxophonist. He'd also seen James Dean in the movie, 'Rebel Without a Cause' and he admired Dean's anti-authority attitude. Armed only with a mail order music diploma, he jumped on a Greyhound bound for California.

Finding employment copying music scores, he joined forces with Sonny Bono and wrote the hit song, 'Needles and Pins.' This brought him to Phil Spector's attention and he made a name for himself arranging Spector's 'Wall of Sound.' Lean and pallid, small-faced but sporting massive shades, Jack Nitzsche loved to smoke dark green marijuana.

Nitzsche was thunderstruck when he first met the Rolling Stones in 64. At first it was just a matter of their appearance and attitude. He described their impact like this: "the first time I met them was when they walked into RCA Studios and everyone just stopped because no one had ever seen anyone who looked like that. I'd never met anyone British before and they had these funny accents."

It didn't take Nitzsche long to realise that the Rolling Stones had far more to them than just long hair and what he thought was exotic speech. He commented "the Rolling Stones were the first rock 'n' roll band I met who were intelligent. They could make conversation with anyone." He observed that "the Stones stood for something and I thought they were going to be leaders of change. They were telling record executives to go fuck themselves and not cracking under any of the social pressure and not doing it the way other people would've done it." Clearly, for Jack Nitzsche, the Rolling Stones combined the rebelliousness of James Dean with a distinctive approach to making music.

Originally the upcoming album was intended as a soundtrack to a movie which would've been directed by Nicholas Ray, who'd filmed James Dean in 'Rebel Without a Cause.' But the deal had fallen through. Yet the Rolling Stones remained, for Nitzsche, rebels with a cause – that of high quality popular music.

Nitzsche first got to know the Rolling Stones when he played harpsichord on 'Play with Fire', the B side of 'The Last Time.' He was a friendly and hospitable guy and, after Charlie and Shirley Watts stayed with him and his wife, Gracia, his house became a home from home for other members of the band whenever they took solo holidays in California.

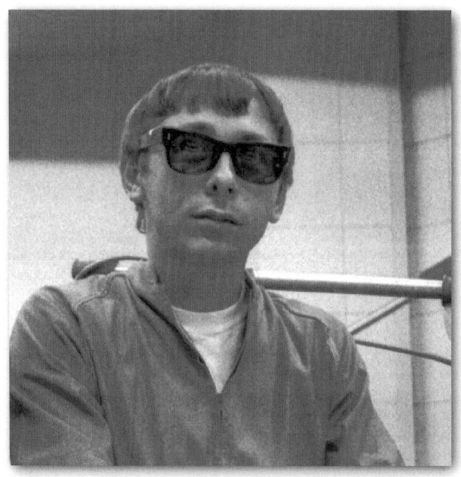

JACK NITZSCHE
He arranged the 'Aftermath' sessions at RCA Studios in Hollywood

Jack Nitzsche soon got to know Brian Jones well. They shared a disdain for Hollywood celebrity culture and a preference for mixing with members of the artists' colony at Topanga Canyon, ranging from singer-songwriter Toni Basil to assemblage painter, Wallace Berman. And they both dug the folk singing duo, Richard and Mimi Farina, whose album, 'Reflections in a Crystal Wind', featured Richard playing Appalachian -type music on a dulcimer. Brian Jones was so impressed that he promptly bought himself a dulcimer and soon mastered it.

Although Jack Nitzsche made clear to the Rolling Stones that he was an arranger not a session musician per se, they knew him as a skilful keyboardist in his own right. Responding to their invitation to join them on their forthcoming album not only as arranger but also as a pianist and harpsichordist, he became a significant influence on 'Aftermath.' That suited Andrew Oldham. Nitzsche was a modest and unassuming man, for all his gifts. He would help maintain the fiction that Oldham was the producer of the upcoming album. In fact Nitzsche took on the role and acted as the band's equivalent of George Martin—without the neo-classical flourishes!

The first series of sessions took place at RCA through December 3-8 1965. A total of nine tracks was recorded, seven earmarked for the album and another two for the Stones' upcoming single and its B-side. Three cuts were teen pop, intended to keep fanbase girls on board. Of these, 'Take It Or Leave It' and 'Think' are routine while 'Sad Day' is pathetic.

'Doncha Bother Me' is a pleasant, inconsequential, country- tinged number and 'Going Home' a beautifully played blues jam let down by a simple, repetitive lyric and unwisely prolonged to a full eleven minutes. But the remaining four were truly memorable tracks combining fine melodies, insightful lyrics and striking tone colours. They had much to say about the rapidly changing world in which the Rolling Stones moved and about the band members themselves.

CHAPTER 26

Gypsy Tunes, Frozen Steak and Valium

IT WAS DOUBTLESS around Belvedere Marshes when the boy Keith first heard gypsy music. Only three miles from his home in Dartford lay the biggest gypsy camp in England where up to a couple of thousand travellers congregated in the years after the war. Their lives were disrupted when the Thames was flooded in 1953 and, as mechanisation and herbicides made their livelihood as hop pickers in Kent redundant, their community dispersed.

As a lad, Keith and his mates had roamed the marshes, intrigued by the outsiders who gathered there –tramps, deserters and Romanies. While many adults were hostile, the young Richards was fascinated by the sights he saw and the music he heard. And, long before he heeded the clarion call of rock 'n' roll when he entered his teens, these sounds had lodged themselves in his mind's ear.

Talking about 'Mother's Little Helper' years later, Keith Richards said "it's a semi-gypsy melody" and he added "I had that song pretty well set up when I brought it into the studio and I had the main riff." He soon found the instrument he wanted to "add some nice bite to it, something to make it twang."

The superbly appointed RCA Studio was a musical candy shop for inventive musicians such as the Rolling Stones. Keith Richards recalled that "someone walked in and said 'look- an electric twelve string!" He went on "it was some gashed up job – no name on it, no one knows where it came from or where it went. I put it together with a bottleneck. Then we had a riff that tied the whole thing together." With these typically down-to-earth words, Richards perfectly nailed the flair for improvisation which typified the Rolling Stones in December 65.

Musically gifted though he was, Keith Richards remained ill at ease in the world of words. A tongue -tied twenty-two-year-old, he hid behind Mick Jagger and Brian Jones when the band was collectively interviewed. As far as song lyrics were concerned, he was more than happy to rely on Jagger. Their way of working was fundamentally different from that of Lennon and McCartney and, as Richards put it, "in those days Mick and I were in a solid words-music bag, unless I thought of something outstanding which could be put into the title."

Mick Jagger had always seen himself as a protean vocalist, able to switch his voice readily from blues to R&B and from soul to pop. As a lyricist, he'd been perfectly content to churn out teen trifles but, from late 65 onwards, he was increasingly ready to "get inspiration from things that are happening around me – from everyday life as I see it." Jagger's maturation as a songwriter was a crucial development in the history of the Rolling Stones. Yes, he had his finger on the pulse of society but, more than that, his suddenly revealed gift for wordplay lit up track after track in sparkling style.

Jagger made sure to keep across every available media outlet- press, radio and TV. He noted the rapid spread of prescription drugs, in particular tranquillisers, since the launch of Valium by Hoffman LaRoche in 1963. Well aware of growing middle-aged resentment against the perceived hedonism of pop stars, he was pissed off with what he saw as tabloid hypocrisy. In short, young musicians were fair game for rumours about illegal drug use yet the dependence of suburban housewives on prescriptions to relieve anxiety was strictly off-limits.

Such was the core of 'Mother's Little Helper' which took its title from the slang term for Valium, and other anxiolytics, which were also known– regardless of the actual colour of the tablets prescribed– as 'little yellow pills.'

The lyric of 'Mother's Little Helper' is a subtle one in which the narrator alternates between quoting a housewife who laments the pressures of the modern world and chastising her for running to the doctor for pharmaceutical comfort.

Despite beginning with a sneer about the drag of ageing, the singer tries to see the woman's point of view. A mother's nerves need to be soothed because of annoying children and impatient husbands.

The singer's empathy is strictly momentary. The mother's to blame for her laziness and her all -too -easy resort to junk food. That's why she buys instant cake and burns frozen steak. The chorus lambasts the housewife for seeking shelter in her 'little helper.' And, in the bridge, she's pilloried for pleading with her doctor for more pills before gulping down the handful she's still got on her as soon as his door's closed. What's more, the core of the lyric-the link between Big Pharma and the facile diagnosis of anxiety is anatomised in one deft dart of a line about unreal ills and yellow pills. The singer adds a stern warning to the housewife about the danger of an overdose while the final chorus is a stark comment on her drug-related dying day.

Jagger sings in a London accent, dropping the aitches off "helper" and thus accentuating the music hall tone. He finishes with a shout of "oi!", a well-known Cockney interjection(suggested by Bill Wyman) often used as a wake-up call.

It wouldn't be long before the Rolling Stones would be accused of callousness in their attitude to a weak-willed woman whom many might have pitied. The combination of sarcastic words with a jaunty, Romany-derived tune and a bouncy beat was too much for some to take, not least that final "oi!"

The target of 'Mother's Little Helper' was plainly a suburbanite, a very different type of woman from the likes of Doris Richards and Molly Perks, Doris who vigorously combined household chores with a career and Molly, Bill Wyman's mum, who never caved into self-pity in the struggle against poverty. And, in adopting a quasi-Cockney accent, Jagger seemed to be aligning himself with the music hall tradition of working-class London.

The lyric of the song is very wide-ranging, taking in the the use of tranquillisers as an instant fix for society's ills and the complicity of NHS doctors in their widespread use. Ray Davies would soon be rightly praised for the socially observant lyrics he wrote for the Kinks but, at least as far as 'Mother's Little Helper' is concerned, he had nothing on Jagger.

From a commercial point of view, Andrew Oldham was keen to publicise the song, which had already been earmarked as the leadoff track on the forthcoming album. What's more, it was intended for release as a single in the US. To draw attention to this, he hit on the idea of claiming that the Stones' new music was so novel that a completely new instrument had been invented for it. This was the so-called 'nitschephone', which derived from a misspelling of Jack Nitzsche's surname. In actual fact, Nitzsche had simply added subtle colour to the track by using a differently mic-ed organ.

In June 66, 'Mother's Little Helper' reached # 8 on the Billboard Hot 100. Though its subject matter applied even more to the United States than to the UK, the music was distinctively British and it was a brilliant achievement by the band to have put it across so convincingly in America.

CHAPTER 27

Trying to Re-arrange Her Mind

THE NEXT TRACK the Stones set down on Sunset starts with a riff. Played by Brian Jones, it's uncannily similar to the one from 'Diddley Daddy'– which the band let loose in their unreleased demo at IBC nearly three years earlier. It heralds Keith Richards' riproaring, piledriving tune, as kinetic as anything Chuck Berry might have played in his prime. Soon Richards blasts out another riff, gruff, menacing and fiercely fuzz tone. Driven by a pounding beat from Charlie Watts and Ian Stewart on piano, the dual electric guitars blaze brilliantly and there's clever counterpoint between Jones and Bill Wyman's bass. Then Wyman wraps things up with a dive-bombing bass run à la Bo Diddley.

It was no wonder Brian Jones was smiling happily as the band per-formed the song on the Ed Sullivan Show. This was the Rolling Stones playing in unison with incredible verve, much as they had in the early days, albeit in ebullient rock 'n' roll style rather than rhythm and blues.

But the lyric Mick Jagger conjures up is at the opposite pole from Bo Diddley's happy tale of a humble Chicago woman acclaiming her "natural born man." It's complex, perceptive, brilliantly observed– and ruthlessly dismissive of a high society girl who's on the verge of her 'Nineteenth Nervous Breakdown.'

The subject of the song is introduced in the first line as someone who frequents dreary social gatherings. Only later, in a bridge, is her female gender made clear. In the summer of 65, Jagger had met the Californian heiress and New York model, Edie Sedgwick, at a Manhattan nightclub. Sedgwick's short life was a desperately unhappy one, sadly featuring teenage anorexia, committal to a mental hospital, abortion, drug abuse and, by 1971, death by barbiturate overdose.

Edie Sedgwick speculated that the lyric of 'Nineteenth Nervous Breakdown' was about her. This is highly unlikely. Yet it may well be an imaginary composite portrait, linking common aspects of her family's history. Her father, the rancher and sculptor, Francis Sedgwick, had suffered two nervous breakdowns and her oldest brother, Francis Jnr, had sustained several.

In the first verses of 'Nineteenth Nervous Breakdown' the narrator treats the subject with seeming sympathy while he unfurls a dazzling display of devices- including alliteration, internal rhyme and paradox -to outline her background, one which includes being neglected by her mother. And her father's eccentricity is summed up in a line about sealing wax as bizarre as anything Bob Dylan might have conjured up.

But the sympathy's only skin deep. Having sung along with the chorus' brusque words telling her to stop and look round, Keith Richards puts the boot in with his menacing, mocking riff. In the third verse comes a startling revelation. The narrator turned himself into the girl's psychiatrist while they were tripping on drugs. He tried in vain to rearrange her mind and ended up washing his hands of her.

Throughout the track music and words are brilliantly fused with weirdly descending high harmonies echoing the subject's neurosis. The tick-tock Diddley riff suggests it's only a matter of time before she'll be stricken yet again and the final bass run signals her ultimate collapse. Over the years various critics would denounce what they saw as the lyric's cruel mockery of an afflicted person. Certainly the narrator is harshly unsympathetic yet his attitude seems to stem from a fear that he might be dragged down along with the girl herself. His crass attempt to turn himself into her shrink while high on dope rebounded on him and he found himself hastily pushing her off the psychiatrist's couch on which he ought never to have placed her.

'Nineteenth Nervous Breakdown' was successful commercially, reaching # 2 on both the UK chart and the Billboard Hot 100. Yet Mick Jagger seemed immediately ill at ease with the critics' response. "We're not Bob Dylan, you know"-he shrugged –"it's not supposed to mean anything, it's just about a neurotic bird, that's all." And, many years later, a middle-aged Jagger brushed the song aside with the words "it's just not very good."

Mick Jagger was mistaken in resiling from the brilliant lyric of 'Nineteenth Nervous Breakdown.' He was twenty-two when he wrote it, two years younger than Dylan, who was already a hero of the intelligentsia and soon-to-be acclaimed by rock critics for songs such as 'Like a Rolling Stone' and 'Leopardskin Pillbox Hat' – the latter a clear dig at Edie Sedgwick's offbeat fashion sense. Unlike Dylan, Jagger had never been involved in the folk music scene where lyrics were typically focused on ahead of melodies and rigorously critiqued by the Greenwich Village crowd. His style would be succinct rather than surrealistic but it was highly effective just the same.

Mick Jagger was a multifaceted personality whose blatant showmanship existed alongside a flair for words which he'd fully demonstrated in 'Nineteenth Nervous Breakdown'- together with the sparkling musicianship of Brian Jones and Bill Wyman- while Keith Richards' skill in composition was really starting to flourish.

CHAPTER 28

'Ride On, Baby' – a Girl from an FBI File

As THE 'AFTERMATH' sessions got under way, Brian Jones' mood was one of elation. The soul-searching of the summer was over and he'd decided to stay with the Stones. Now, in RCA Studio B, he feasted his eyes on an instrumental smorgasbord the like of which exceeded his wildest dreams.

As with his musical career, so with his personal life. Three months earlier, thousands of miles away, in Germany, he'd found the woman he thought was the love of his life. She was Anita Pallenberg. Pallenberg was a twenty-two-year-old model, Italian by nationality, German by upbringing, multilingual and an ex- medical student who'd turned to graphic design. Her blonde good looks were striking and her features seemed to those who knew them both like the feminine equivalent of Brian Jones.

When she knew the Rolling Stones were in Munich, Pallenberg hastened to their concert at the Cirkus Krone. When she saw Brian Jones in the flesh, she determined to have him. When the gig was over, she blagged her way backstage and accosted him in fluent English. The same night they became lovers. The following year, she relocated to London, installed as his mistress in their trendy South Kensington apartment.

Meanwhile, over in Hollywood, Keith Richards had written a simple tune, as punchy as it was pretty, one with a real lilt to it. It's the basis for 'Ride On, Baby.'

'Ride On, Baby' is a track which has Brian Jones all over it, bringing out the harmonies, first with one instrument, then with another, finally a third. A pianist since he was a boy of six, he takes to the harpsichord, its ancient predecessor, as to the manner born. Next he configures the marimbas (the pride of Central America, the national instrument of Guatemala) mallet in hand, striking the rosewood bars. Then he edges in a sound which appears in some session records as a Japanese koto and in others as a classical harp.

It was of course common knowledge, by the time of their second US tour, that the Rolling Stones, with the solitary exception of the happily married Charlie Watts, were taking full advantage of the American groupie scene. It carried with it dangers, against which the band had to be on their guard. Before the English Establishment ever attacked them over drugs, hostile elements in the US mulled over the possibility of bringing them down over sex with underage girls – if such could be proved- and by entrapment, if need be.

The British Sunday tabloids familiar to the Stones were as nothing compared to sleazy American mags. The 'National Enquirer' was in its heyday and 'Whisper' was salacious in the extreme. Among its 1965 front pages- which anyone could see displayed on newsstands- was one captioned 'my mother sold me to 500 men', accompanied by a picture of a skanky teenage girl. The likes of these so-called news features provided the fuel for Mick Jagger's lyric in 'Ride On, Baby.'

Talking from the perspective of a young guy confronted by a suspect girl, the singer speaks his cynical thoughts about the girl's fake smile, her phony shyness and exactly what the giveaway was which made him suss she was sexually experienced beyond her years.

In the chorus she's brusquely rebuffed with the title phrase then sneered at with the dig that her face would stand out in an FBI file. As he banishes the girl from his presence, the singer turns the screw with the taunt that, by the time she's thirty, she'll look fifty-five. Then he repeats his message with the title phrase drummed home by being repeated nine times.

This is a lyric which, at best, is ruthlessly honest and, at worst, a piece of cheap sarcasm. Yet it scarcely detracts from the memorable band performance of which the obvious highlight is Brian Jones' multi-instrumental virtuosity. In addition, Charlie Watts adds flavour by playing Cuban congas as well as his usual drums while Jack Nitzsche's rolling left hand piano emphasises the girl being sent brusquely packing.

Brian Jones' artistry, which he would continue on track after track in Hollywood, would be almost universally admired. Even Andrew Oldham, who personally disliked Jones, saluted his performances on Sunset in 1965-6. "Brian's contribution can be heard on every one of those tracks at RCA" he said, adding "what that guy didn't know, he went out and learned. You can hear his colour all over songs like 'Lady Jane' and 'Paint It Black.' In some instances it was more than a decorative effect. Sometimes Brian pulled the whole record together."

Yet Keith Richards would have decidedly mixed feelings about the guy who'd stood side-by-side with him on the dual guitars of 'Nineteenth Nervous Breakdown.' On the one hand, Richards could only acknowledge what he called "Brian being incredibly inventive." On the other, he would vent his dismay, which would become more bitter as the years passed. He complained "sure, I was mad! I did all the parts on half the album which Brian normally would have done." "It threw a lot of the pressure on me" he added, before piling on harsh words which would resonate through the years, leading to divisions among Stones fans- "Brian was becoming a deadweight."

In the Sixties and Seventies, Mick Jagger made sure to stand by his pal, Keith. Many years later, however, he summed up the impending schism between Jones and Richards in more measured words. He concluded "at this point I don't think Brian was necessarily shying away from guitar. He enjoyed being a colourist and that was very effective. His guitar playing was good when he played slide guitar – that was his strength. But he wasn't much of a rock player really. Keith could do the other parts and Brian wasn't really that needed. So he was more interested in playing the sitar or the recorder. Brian was more like an all-around musician rather than a specialist guitar player." These comments by Jagger are controversial in themselves but there's not the slightest hint of personal nastiness contained in them.

Although the first signs of the split between the two great Rolling Stones guitarists appeared when 'Ride On, Baby' was laid down, it was ironic that the track itself was shelved for eighteen months, belatedly resurfacing only on a compilation album, 'Flowers', released in the US alone. The song would never be performed on stage.

'Ride On, Baby' remains to this day a virtually unknown item in the Stones' canon, accumulating no more than 20,000 YouTube views. Andrew Oldham kept the number for his protégé, Chris Farlowe, who recorded it on Oldham's Immediate label. North London soul singer Farlowe would bleed every last ounce of subtlety out of it with an over-emphatic vocal accompanied by boring, conventional strings. He got no further with it commercially than a feeble #31 slot on the UK chart.

By contrast, the original Rolling Stones' version of 'Ride On, Baby' remains a hidden gem, deserving a far wider audience.

CHAPTER 29

Living in Sin and Loving It

THE MODEST TUNE which Mick Jagger solicited from his pal Keith, while the Stones were touring Ireland a couple of months earlier, survived as the core of 'Sittin' on a Fence.' But it would yield pride of place to the unusually brilliant melody which Brian Jones plucked out of the Californian air in the final RCA session. That was something so startling that many listeners were misled into thinking it was played on a mandolin.

By this time Jones was well on his way to mastering the dulcimer yet 'Sittin' on a Fence' would remain as a piece for two acoustic guitars, with Brian playing lead. As he immersed himself in Appalachian music, he was struck by its resemblance to the early classical style which he'd always loved.

Thus inspired, Brian Jones' part is joyful and percussive and climaxes with a marvellous flourish which hints at the work of English baroque composers such as Purcell and Jeremiah Clarke. Sadly he wasn't given time to correct one flubbed note but nothing could distract from the beauty of his performance. As for Keith Richards, his subdued and velvety tone perfectly complements Jones.

Mick Jagger's lyric falls below the level of Jones and Richards. Still, the middle verse contains an insight which was rare for 1965. Reflecting how all his fellow students had settled down the singer adds ten stunningly cynical words about wedlock. With these devastating lines, Jagger punctures the cosy petit-bourgeois consensus of the early Sixties and claims a young man's right to live his life in defiance of convention.

In the chorus the singer explains his dilemma about committing to a marriage- and the horryfying prospect of having to decide At that time Mick Jagger was under parental pressure to wed his girlfriend, Chrissie

Shrimpton. His old lady, Eva, had taken a great liking to Chrissie and thought she was just right for her boy. She taught Chrissie the art of making pastry which she thought to be a prime wifely attribute. Ted Shrimpton, Chrissie's old fella, wasn't fussy on Jagger. But he was worried that his girl would be perceived as 'living in sin.' For a time Jagger stalled. Then he made his mind up. In the summer of 66, he bought an upscale apartment at 52 Harley House, Marylebone Road, by spacious Regents Park. He promptly installed Chrissie Shrimpton there, telling her she could be his mistress but would never be his wife.

What went for Jagger applied equally to the rest of the band – Charlie Watts alone apart. When reporters questioned Brian Jones about his intentions over Anita Pallenberg he haughtily replied "we don't see marriage as the logical outcome of our relationship." Instead Jones and Pallenberg shacked up in a sumptuous, bohemian apartment at 2 Courtfield Road, South Kensington.

As for Bill Wyman, he'd married his bank clerk wife, Diane, three years before joining the Rolling Stones. By this time his conventional marriage was no more than an empty shell as he plunged into the groupie scene right up to the hilt. By 67 he'd dumped Diane in favour of a nineteen-year-old Swedish model, Astrid Lundstrom. Wyman and Lundstrom would be together for sixteen years but marriage would never enter the equation.

In the final verse of 'Sittin' on a Fence', the singer recoils from the prospect of a lifetime marriage based on a wrong choice in the first place. Perfectly fitting music to lyric, there's a ritardando while Jack Nitzsche's creaking harpsichord personifies an old man reflecting too late on the blunder of his youth.

As far as the Rolling Stones were concerned, the lyric of 'Sittin' on a Fence' was total understatement. Junking the churchy doctrine of 'living in sin' with total abandonment, they unhesitatingly opted for untrammeled sexual pleasure regardless of empty ceremony.

The Rolling Stones' version of 'Sittin' on a Fence' was shelved by Andrew Oldham who'd earmarked the song for his protégés on the Immediate label, the anodyne London pop duo, Twice As Much. They got in the Top Forty with a dumbed down version. Meanwhile, the

Rolling Stones' original, which should of course have been included on 'Aftermath', gathered dust for a full eighteen months before belatedly seeing the light of day on the 'Flowers' compilation.

For all the other instrumental highlights of 'Sittin' on a Fence'– Nitzsche's harpsichord, Bill Wyman's gurgling bass- and, above all, Keith Richards' subtly subdued contrapuntal rhythm guitar- it's Brian Jones' neoclassical lead acoustic which remains in the mind's ear. Virtually suppressed in its own era and never performed on stage, the track has resurfaced triumphantly since being uploaded to YouTube in 2010.

CHAPTER 30

꧁

Waiting- But For Who Knows What ?

THE SECOND SET of sessions required to complete the 'Aftermath' album took place at RCA Hollywood between March 6 –9 1966. It must be said that these sessions produced a lot of mediocre work. Much of it's in country style, formulaic filler designed to load the album with sounds compatible with the American mainstream. 'Flight 505' saw Ian Stewart back in harness with jangly piano. 'High and Dry' wastes Brian Jones' harmonica skills on boozy country, 'What To Do' is banal in the extreme and 'It's Not Easy' is simply atrocious. 'Long Long While', by contrast, was designated as a B-side. Aimed at teenage girls, it featured a pathetic piece of apologetic supplication as its vocal. Stewart's on organ for this number as he'd been for 'It's Not Easy.'

In the circumstances – and particularly the fact that the schedule was much tighter than for the December sessions – it was nothing short of astonishing that the Rolling Stones produced other tracks which rank among the finest iconic pop of the Sixties.

'I Am Waiting' is perhaps too leftfield to be included among these but it's a remarkable piece of work just the same. By this time Brian Jones had mastered dulcimer and he perplexed the 'Ready Steady Go' TV audience when he demonstrated it seated, a wry smile playing round his lips as he plucked the ancient Appalachian instrument with a quill. Soon the beautifully subtle melody dissolves in lovely counterpoint with a bespectacled Charlie Watts' earnest claves, a characteristically expressionless Bill Wyman's understated bass and Keith Richards' laid-back acoustic guitar.

Mick Jagger scowls as he delivers an enigmatic lyric, determined, so it seems, to withhold the slightest clue as to its meaning. He begins with the title phrase then insists that a mysterious someone can't hold out.

162

Just when the listener begins to wonder if this is a song of seduction, the mood alters abruptly against a thunderous chord change and lines about something being censored from our minds.

The phrase about mental censorship hints at Freudian psychology yet a further fulminating change seems to shift the song into a political context. The singer loudly calls out escalation fears with dire warnings about withered stones before the track slows down and finishes.

The entire early Sixties passed in the shadow of potential nuclear conflict, seen as its most alarming in the Cuba Crisis of 1962 which was played out in the early months of the Rolling Stones' existence. What's more, American involvement in the Vietnam War had escalated during 1965, first with saturation bombing of North Vietnam and later with the large scale deployment of US ground troops.

While Vietnam was only marginally discussed in a non-involved UK, it was a very hot topic on American university campuses and the Rolling Stones, who toured the States on a regular basis, would have been well aware of this.

If there's a clue as to the meaning of 'I Am Waiting', it may lie in an interview which Mick Jagger gave to the filmmaker, Peter Whitehead, six months earlier. He said "in the last two or three years, young people – this especially applies to America – have gone through a transition. Instead of just carrying on in the way their parents told them to...... they're anti-war and their sex lives have become freer. And they want to change society, a lot of them. It could be changed, the whole basis of society and values and it could definitely be changed for the better."

In comments such as these Jagger was going well beyond what he felt he could say in the heyday of Andrew Oldham between 63 and 65. At that time the Rolling Stones felt obliged to defend themselves from criticism of their hair styles and silly talk about their alleged lack of personal hygiene. Yet now, in parallel with Bob Dylan's impact on the pop lyric and the Beatles' greater frankness, they could express themselves on a far more serious level. Despite their breach with Giorgio Gomelsky, the Rolling Stones retained many of his societal attitudes, ones which they doubtless heard him express during the key months of their partnership early in 63.

During the same interview, Mick Jagger emphasised the new realism in music. He said "if you listen to popular songs from ten years ago, very few of them actually mean anything or have any relationship to what people were doing. Popular music wasn't a real thing at all. It was very romantic in so far as every song was about a boy/girl relationship. Songs didn't have any relation to what people were actually spending their lives doing. They were just about being unhappy because your girl had left you, or being very happy because you'd just met somebody. That's all they were about – 'the moon in June' and 'the sky is blue'and 'I love you.'"

Clearly the lines in the song about fears piercing the bones of withered stones may be a jibe at an older generation slow to come to terms with new attitudes. That said, any attempt at total interpretation of such an enigmatic lyric could only be guesswork; 'I Am Waiting' is memorable above all for its beautiful and unusual sound. Quickly fading into obscurity, the track resurfaced as a point of reference in the 1999 independent film, 'Rushmore', and the melodic charm of the song was widely commented on.

CHAPTER 31

'Lady Jane': Sounds from a Bygone Century

THE TWENTY-FIVE SECOND contrapuntal intro to 'Lady Jane' is startlingly different to anything which the Rolling Stones had ever done before. As Keith Richards' sublime acoustic guitar meshes with Brian Jones' archaic dulcimer, the listener's moved back centuries in sonic time. Bass and drums are entirely absent and the only other instrument to be heard will be the harpsichord.

The vocal begins to the riffing melody of the dulcimer but, after four lines of the first verse, jumps to a bolder tune for the remaining three lines. The same pattern's repeated in the second and third verses of this extraordinary ballad, separated by a reprise of the intro, this time extended to include Jack Nitzsche's delicate harpsichord. Mick Jagger's vocal is impeccably sung, with immaculate diction and an ability to reach deep down in the register with ease.

In total contrast to the enigmatic 'I am Waiting', the lyric of 'Lady Jane', highly unusual though it is, leaves no room for doubt as to its meaning. The narrator is a courtier from a bygone century. Addressing the aristocratic Jane, his inferior social position compels him to use subservient language. Yet, though he's officially her humble servant, he boldly addresses her as his lover, pledging himself to her on bended knees.

The whole time the narrator has been paying court to Lady Jane, he's also been dallying with another highborn lady- one by the name of Ann. Yet the time has come for her to be kissed off. He tells his former lover that he's plighted his troth with Lady Jane. Then, as the narrator falls silent to let the impact of his treachery sink in, guitar and dulcimer resume at length in perfect counterpoint.

The third female in this scenario is Ann's maid, Marie, who's acted as the narrator's go-between and possibly also as his lover. The narrator tells Marie that he's finished with Ann and, revealing the depth of his cynicism, he tells her the reason. He expects to marry Lady Jane -for the sake of his security! With music perfectly matched to words, the track ends abruptly on a plunging chord.

The musical inspiration for 'Lady Jane' was without doubt the work of Richard Farina which had greatly impressed Jack Nitzsche and Brian Jones. Yet, as Keith Richards recalled, "Brian dug Richard Farina but we were all listening to a lot of Appalachian music at that time." Farina's status in the world of folk was such that he was being talked about as the one to step into the breach created by Bob Dylan's move to electric music. Tragically, the twenty-nine-year-old songwriter lost his life in a motorbike accident on the very day of his singer wife Mimi's twenty-first birthday - as it happened only a fortnight after the UK release of 'Aftermath.'

Over the decades there would be much irrelevant talk about the coincidence of the two named heroines with figures from Tudor times such as Jane Seymour, Jane Grey and Ann Boleyn. This flew in the face of Mick Jagger's remark —"all the names are historical but it was really unconscious that they should fit together from the same period." Nevertheless, the notion of a humble courtier marrying a woman of high social status is historically plausible; for example, the Welsh court servant, Owen Tudor, married Henry V's widow, in 1430.

Latter day British musos were pissed off with cultured speculation and sought to whip the song into rock territory with insinuations that it was "really about" pussy or dope. After all, they insisted, Marie plus Jane equalled marijuana and, 'lady Jane'was the term used by the gardener, Mellors, in D.H. Lawrence's newly uncensored novel, 'Lady Chatterley's Lover', to refer to his upper-class mistress' vagina. And they emphasized that Mick Jagger was known to have read the book,

Although Mick Jagger was in no sense working class, he was well aware, in the deeply class -conscious England of the mid-Sixties, that he was an unlikely consort for young upper-class women. He certainly knew Lady Jane Ormsby Gore, daughter of Lord Harlech, former British ambassador to the US. She and her husband, Michael Rainey, had opened the boutique, 'Hung On You', which was frequented by the Beatles and the Rolling Stones. Yet the notion of a liaison between Jagger and Ormsby Gore never got beyond the realm of rumour.

Certainly Mick Jagger had been intrigued for years by Marianne Faithfull, another of Andrew Oldham's protégés and he relished Oldham's description of her as "an angel with big tits." Faithfull's background was impeccably aristocratic. Her father, Major Robert Faithfull was an intelligence officer in the British Army while her maternal grandfather was a scion of the Habsburgs, the former ruling dynasty of Austria- Hungary. And her mother's great-uncle was Leopold von Sacher-Masoch, the Austrian nobleman who wrote the erotic novel, 'Venus in Furs.' In 65, however, Jagger had been frustrated in his clumsy attempt to seduce the nineteen-year-old Faithfull who'd brushed him aside as what she called "a bit of a yob."

When 'Lady Jane' was debuted on TV, the girly screams were mostly for Brian Jones not Mick Jagger. Hs facial appearance was still seen as a drawback and, only a couple of years before, he'd been mocked by Covent Garden porters when he had Chrissie Shrimpton on his arm. Indeed the market had been convulsed with mirth when he'd been struck on the head with a cabbage hurled by a porter- along with the insult "you ugly fucker!"

Mick Jagger admired the relaxed upper-class confidence of the Old Etonian antique dealer and fashion guru, Christopher Gibbs, and began to frequent Gibbs' soirées in Cheyne Walk, Chelsea. Eager, as he confided to designer Michael Fish, "to learn to be a gentleman", Jagger reinvented himself as a smooth talking fashion plate who took his time with posh women. Marianne Faithfull was fascinated by his transformation and, in October 66, she became his mistress.

While Jagger would dismiss the lyric of 'Lady Jane' as being little more than stream of consciousness, it's in fact cleverly thought out, three very inventive verses which correspond perfectly with the antique instruments Brian Jones and Jack Nitzsche are using.

Although Brian Jones would never be credited for his role in the creation of 'Lady Jane', the song was just as much his work as it was that of

Keith Richards and Mick Jagger. Although Jones preferred to describe the dulcimer as "an old English instrument", he'd talked in the music press about applying it to compositions. This is precisely what he did on 'Lady Jane' where the dulcimer carries the counter melody in response to the main theme vocalised by Mick Jagger. That said, the sumptuous sonic beauty of the track resides above all in Keith Richards' delicate acoustic guitar.

Andrew Oldham was for a long time dubious that Rolling Stones' fans would appreciate a sound so different from the band's usual output. He released 'Lady Jane' as the B-side of 'Mother's Little Helper.' Yet, despite minimal radio play, it started gathering sales independent of those for the A side. Indeed it reached #24 on the Billboard Hot 100 and doubtless would have risen far higher had it been properly promoted.

'Lady Jane' reappeared on YouTube in April 2010 over a beautiful montage uploaded by Zara Agali. The images were not of the Rolling Stones but of paintings by the 19th-century Peruvian artist, Albert Lynch. Lynch specialised in portraits of strikingly beautiful women from the Belle Epoque era.

Albert Lynch's images from a bygone century proved highly appropriate to meld with the sounds of the Rolling Stones and they help to contradict the facile description of the band- by radical feminists and others—as heartless misogynists.

Over the course of seven years, Zara Agali's upload has attracted three million views.

CHAPTER 32

— ❧ —

Sexual Politics

RARELY HAS SUCH a cool sound been deployed in support of such a crass lyric as on 'Stupid Girl.' It's by far the weakest of three tracks recorded not quite consecutively and all too often wrongly lumped together.

We hear not just the five Rolling Stones regulars but an augmented band, bringing back Ian Stewart on organ and bringing in Jack Nitzsche on electric piano. The result is an irresistible dance track yet, long before the lyric's complete, its silly sentiments are a complete turnoff.

The singer's a lad determined to vent his frustration with a girl's alleged antics. Making sure to emphasise that he's not talking about her fashion trend or her hairstyle, he rails against her vanity plus her bitchy gossip and throws in a sneer about her frigidity – before concluding that she's the sickest thing on the scene.

This pathetic lyric would be a source of embarrassment in future years to Keith Richards, who said "it was a spin-off from our environment... bad hotels and too many dumb chicks" before hastily qualifying himself with the remark "not all dumb by any means but that's how one got." Mick Jagger probably got closer to the truth when he admitted "it was very adolescent – going back to my teenage years." Whether the young women the Rolling Stones knew would have been willing to excuse Jagger on the grounds of immaturity might have been another matter.

The previous year Brian Jones' secondary girlfriend, Dawn Molloy, had told him she was pregnant by him. Andrew Oldham, furious about this threat to Jones' value as a sex symbol about whom teenage fanclub girls could fantasise, put financial pressure on Molloy to sign a dictated letter. It read:

'I received a cheque for £700 from Andrew Loog Oldham Ltd, paid to me by the said company on behalf of Brian Jones, in formal settlement of any claims arising, damages and inconveniences caused by me, by the birth of my son and I understand completely that the matter is now closed and that I will make no statement about Brian Jones or the child to any members of the press or public.'

Dawn Molloy's signature was witnessed by Mick Jagger but the letter wasn't dated. It was executed without Jones' knowledge and the £700 deducted from his later earnings without him even realising it.

Jones himself was a thus a victim of astounding ruthlessness. Beyond that there was clear evidence of misogyny towards Molloy in the phrase "inconveniences caused by me, by the birth of my son." While Oldham had been the prime mover, Jagger had been a central figure in this shameless treatment of a young woman in the acts of conception and childbirth. By contrast, Bill Wyman and Ian Stewart had tenderly comforted Dawn as she sobbed uncontrollably on first learning that Jones had acquiesced in Oldham's warning that he must dump her forthwith.

'Under My Thumb', the second of the tracks in question, is far better than 'Stupid Girl' musically and has a nuanced lyric. Essentially it's updated rhythm and blues with a superbly relaxed beat, soothing to the ear of the listener yet, at the same time, an irresistible invitation to the dancefloor.

Jack Nitzsche doesn't play on this track yet his fingerprints are all over the arrangement, which brings out contrasting yet complementary rhythmic elements-Bill Wyman's fuzz bass is far ahead of its time, Brian Jones' marimbas are the quintessence of cool while Ian Stewart's piano is delicately threaded in between. Mick Jagger's handclaps are blended in Atlantic Records style while the absolute highlight is Wyman's wonderful break which then merges with the marimbas.

As to the vocal itself, Jagger shows what he learned from the better soul singers, his wordless gasps accentuating the rhythm even more. All in all, and not forgetting Charlie Watts' laid-back drumming, this is a peak of teamwork.

The lyric of 'Under My Thumb' provoked little comment at the time of its release on 'Aftermath' but, within a handful of years, it was targeted by the first wave of radical feminists as a prime example of male supremacism. The title phrase was angrily objected to as was a young woman being compared with a squirming dog

By 1976 Mick Jagger felt compelled to defend his lyric by pointing out that it deals with a male who's previously been pushed around. His narrator is a formally supplicating young guy who's proud of having learned to stand up for himself with women. Denying that "there's anything wrong with it" Jagger insisted that it didn't apply to all females, also maintaining that, while the song's sentiments were "really naive... they were still true."

Renegade feminist Camille Paglia implied that, far from objectifying women, the Rolling Stones were speaking from a position of weakness, hinting that men should rather be seen as victims of their own lust for voluptuous girls.

The debate would continue across the decades and would never be on strict gender lines-with some males feeling obliged to apologise for digging the sounds of an allegedly sexist band whilst others admired what they considered to be Mick Jagger's contempt for so-called "shit tests." And while some female listeners recoiled from what they considered an arrogant vocal, others praised the song and had no compunction about admitting being aroused by dominant male attitude.

Beyond the fever stoked up by sexual politics, the song's essentially transgenerational appeal in terms of sheer sound was confirmed after it was uploaded to YouTube in 2009. It has since built up an astonishing 16 million views!

CHAPTER 33

— ✑ —

Out of Time in Swinging London

THE SINGER AND his ex have been in a relationship but she broke it off by going with someone else. When she realised her mistake, she tried to start things up again, assuming he'd be happy to take her back. The singer disillusions her in no uncertain terms, making it clear not just that he's finished with her but also that she's so out of touch with the changing scene that she's out of time.

The singer in 'Out Of Time' has listened to the girl's pleas and now he dismisses her with brutally honest words. He reminds her that she was the one who wanted to run away only to discover that she's had her day.

The background to the singer's rebuff is surely the 'Swinging London' of the mid-Sixties, a haven of cool to which his ex is unfit to belong. She's out of touch, discarded, even obsolete! The narrator of 'Out Of Time' is a very different person from the immature boy of 'Stupid Girl' and 'Under My Thumb.' He's a man who doesn't stoop to callow mockery of girls but resolutely stands his ground against a manipulative young woman who tried and failed to resume a relationship which she'd been the one to break up.

The Rolling Stones build up the track drawing effortlessly on a mix of genres. The intro begins with a rock 'n' roll riff, one Keith Richards wrote for his old buddy, Ian Stewart. Stu was on form, revelling in the warm Californian spring, all smiles with his burly frame encased in a boldly striped chino shirt. His gruff, staccato organ blows a raspberry against the song's target and will be reprised later on to punch home the message - left OUT /out of there without a doubt!

172

There's more than hint of modern jazz in Brian Jones' immaculately cool marimbas, which would deceive some critics into thinking they were hearing vibes or xylophone. And Mick Jagger's vocal is tinged with soul style melisma and shouts of "awright!" and "sing the song!"

Yet more than anything else 'Out Of Time' is updated R&B, rhythm and blues for the Sixties, its socking offbeat stemming from Charlie Watts and Bill Wyman, intensified by Jack Nitzsche's pounding piano, Keith Richards' backing vocal whup and Jagger's finger snaps.

One of the greatest tracks the Rolling Stones ever laid down was not designated for single release. Andrew Oldham had earmarked it for Chris Farlowe and it was recorded on Immediate by the Islington -born singer, with Mick Jagger credited as his producer.

Chris Farlowe was a sincere performer, his style was strictly soul and his delivery was notably relaxed. His version, replete with strings is one-dimensional compared to that of the Rolling Stones. Yet his voice had a warmth about it which took it right to the top of the UK chart albeit only for one week. On TV, Farlowe came across as a working-class bloke, not someone who'd ever be identified with 'Swinging London.' Before turning pro and being spotted by Andrew Oldham fronting a band at the Flamingo, he'd been a carpenter by trade and a part-time pub singer. No feminists would ever fasten on Farlowe's version of 'Out Of Time.' He sounded no more menacing than a young guy who'd had a tiff with his girlfriend and they'd split, 'no 'ard feelings, y'know what I mean.' It could be argued that his joyful rendition of the song had opened it up to a wider audience than the Stones' fanbase.

Yet, while that might be true as far as the UK was concerned -and specifically in late July 66- there's little doubt the Rolling Stones would have more than surpassed that chart performance, particularly in the US, had they been given the chance. Jagger's vocal has a cutting edge which Farlowe's lacks and the overall band performance is on another level entirely while still radiating positivity and danceability.

On 'Aftermath', the Rolling Stones clocked in at five minutes thirty-seven seconds for their version of the song, more than two minutes longer than Farlowe's single. In due course Oldham sanctioned its release, in a truncated form, on 'Flowers.' Whilst it would be churlish to begrudge Chris Farlowe his moment of fame, it's still a shame that the Rolling Stones, playing a modernised R&B song at their absolute peak, should have been deprived of the widest possible audience.

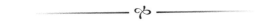

CHAPTER 34

'Paint It Black': Masterpiece of Grief

ON MARCH 8 1966 the Rolling Stones recorded their most extraordinary song, 'Paint It Black.' Despite its musical complexity, its impact is instant and total, immediately seizing the listener in its grip and compelling attention throughout the three minutes forty-seven seconds track. It alternates between a droning, yearning, hypnotic melody stemming from classical Indian sitar and a driving quasi- rock 'n' roll counter. It opens with a delicate guitar figure from Keith Richards, subtly seeming to slide back the curtain before sitar and guitar mesh.

'Paint It Black' is Charlie Watts' finest hour, a tour de force which finds him constantly varying the rhythm from a pounding 4/4 to a cymbals- clipping rock beat. Watts' drumming is the hook on which the entire track is built.

Massively popular in the year of its release, the song was revived on stage by the Stones in 1989 and, since then, has regularly figured in their concert set lists. Funk, folk and philharmonic performers have vied with bands from every subgenre of metal, not to mention an urban contemporary effort, in over fifty cover versions throughout its half-century of existence.

The lyric of 'Paint It Black' is perfectly subtle enough in its own right without being burdened with many completely unhistorical interpretations which are totally out of sync with the world of 1966. And it's not a song about depression rather one about grief, arising from the death of the singer's girlfriend. The cause of her unforeseen demise isn't given and this leaves open the issue of suicide or perishing by accident.

Originally Keith Richards and Mick Jagger aimed for a slow, folk/blues arrangement in the style of the Animals 'House of the Rising Sun' which had been a huge hit two years earlier. This didn't work out and they considered scrapping the number.

At this stage it was rescued by Bill Wyman who was himself dissat-isfied with the bass track he'd laid down. Simply, it wasn't fat enough. Thinking out of the box, he called to mind the band's co-manager, Eric Easton, who had a background as a cinema organist. It would later be put about that he was trying to take the piss. This was something he strenu-ously denied – indeed he had considerable respect for Easton.

Thwarted by the stiff pedals of the studio Hammond, Wyman got down on his hands and knees and played them with his fists. Many years later Keith Richards paid tribute to his bandmate with the words "what made 'Paint It Black' was Bill Wyman on the organ because it didn't sound anything like the finished record till Bill said 'you go like this.'"

Vital as Bill Wyman's inspired intuitive musicianship was in kick-ing the session off after it had stalled, Richards' account skirts round the issue of Brian Jones' role in the song's composition. Jones didn't stand up for his musical rights probably because he didn't want a confrontation with Andrew Oldham. Nevertheless, he was the author of the droning tune just as much as Keith Richards originated the counter- melody.

Charged with copying George Harrison's sitar on the Beatles' 'Norwegian Wood' from the 'Rubber Soul' album released at the end of 65, Jones indignantly retorted "what utter rubbish! You might as well say we copy all the other groups by playing guitar."

Jones had no issue whatever with George Harrison and indeed they were friends. He admired Harrison's sitar on 'Norwegian Wood', saying "it's my favourite track by the Beatles and George's use of the sitar was very effective." What angered Brian Jones was the critic's ignorance of the fact that he'd been studying the sitar himself on and off for years and had sought out the Indian master, Harihar Rao, for advice.

Brian Jones was the first to grasp the link between African-American music and that of the Middle East and South Asia. He said "on 'Paint It Black' I used a flattened third in fret position. The sound you get from a sitar is a basic blues pattern which results in the flattening of the third and seventh as a result of the superimposition of primitive eastern pentatonic scales on the well-known western diatonic."

Jones' influence on 'Paint It Black' may have gone further than the creation of the droning melody. Charlie Watts tended to be vague when asked about the genesis of the pounding rhythm whereas Jones was known to be keenly interested in North African drum sounds. These were subjects of discussion amongst musicians, the likes of Graham Nash from the Hollies, who knew Brian Jones quite well and who visited Morocco in 1966. Two years later, Jones would record the musicians of Joujouka whilst on a trip to the Atlas Mountains.

Whilst musically 'Paint It Black' is effectively Nanker-Phelge, the lyric is entirely the work of Mick Jagger. It's complex, subtle and poignant before it concludes on a note of total rage. Blending perfectly with the music, the first two lines of each verse vent the narrator's distress along with the sitar drone while the third finds him despairingly seeking to come to terms with his loss, albeit fired up by rock 'n' roll staccato.

In the first verse, the narrator pours out his heart, speaking of it as a red door stained black. So even though he can't help noticing girls in summer clothes, he can't respond despite their sensual allure.

The second verse describes his beloved's funeral. Yet, to casual pass-ers-by, this is nothing more than a humdrum sight, albeit one from which they avert their eyes – death like birth is a fact of life.

In the third verse his resolve seems to weaken and, having possibly toyed with the idea of killing himself, he seems indifferent to whether he lives or dies.

The fourth verse finds the sitar on its own as the narrator suspends the contrast between red and black, preferring one between two other colours, the oceanic green which surrounds him now and yesterday's placid blue. Thus, while his girlfriend was alive, her love was strong enough to free him from storm and stress and he sailed on smooth waters. Then (while Charlie Watts kicks in the beat again) come lines which suggest that the whole thing has been a terrible nightmare from which the narrator is about to awaken. If he stares into the sunset, his girl will return to him in happy laughter before the dawn.

The death of the girl is only too real, however, and the fifth verse reprises the first. The bleak atmosphere is intensified by a section of

humming by Jagger and Richards over the insistent drumbeat and a finger picked guitar riff -all topped up with heavy reverb.

But the vocal has yet to end and the singer's previous emotions give
way to raw existential anger at the shocking death of a young woman
whom he'd loved with all his heart. Shouting ferociously in jump blues
style, he calls for the obliteration of the sun itself. The track ends with a
long outro where Keith Richards brings in a bolero rhythm.

It was 'Paint It Black' which led some interviewers to suggest to the
Rolling Stones' frontman that, after all, he must "really be an intellectual."
Jagger's features creased with mirth at the very idea. In contrast to Brian
Jones, potential Oxbridge student, top echelon IQ and esoteric music
theorist, he was nothing of the kind. Yet Jagger, a man determined not to
be stereotyped, had a verbal mastery and a superb grasp of imagery to
which Brian Jones could never aspire.

'Paint It Black' is a flawless masterpiece to which all five members of
the original Rolling Stones made a major contribution. It was released
as a single in the US on May 6 1966 and in the UK a week later. It was a
number one hit in both countries, staying there for ten weeks in the UK
and a week longer on the Billboard Hot 100. What's more, it boosted
the American sales of 'Aftermath', on which it appeared as the lead-off
track. Although the lyric was light years beyond the shallow teen pop
'death ditties' popular in the early Sixties, this was clearly no barrier to its
popularity.

It wouldn't take long before the song was freighted with misinterpretation by people who preferred to read things into the merest trivia or
who belonged to the "now what it's really all about is this" imaginings of
people who couldn't be bothered with lyrical analysis.

The most absurd of these arose when a grammatical error by someone at Decca Records introduced a comma between the title words 'Paint
It' and 'Black.' Immediately the idea of a racial undertone was suggested,
something without the slightest basis in fact. Then there was that old
chestnut of the 'what it's really about' school, namely drugs. It's of course
possible that some of the song's imagery suggested itself to Mick Jagger

while on an LSD trip but as he remarked himself, "'Paint It Black' is painting it black."

A more plausible misinterpretation was the notion of an indirect reference to the war in Vietnam. The young Mick Jagger had absorbed some quasi -anarchist ideas from Giorgio Gomelsky and, in March 68, he was to join the anti-war protesters outside the US Embassy in Grosvenor Square. By this time the issue of the war was being widely discussed in British universities, something which was already the case on American campuses when the song was being written.

Certainly the song resonated with American soldiers serving in Southeast Asia and, in due course, it featured in the closing credits on the soundtrack of Stanley Kubrick's movie, 'Full Metal Jacket.' This was not, however until 1987. In truth the essence of the lyric is a pure feat of imagination by Mick Jagger, who had not experienced a personal bereavement similar to that of the song's narrator.

'Paint It Black' would lose none of its appeal in the 21st-century. Rock buffs and progressive pop fans alike would salute it. Yet the Stones' VEVO upload, described as 'the official video', which appeared on YouTube in 2015 has two negative aspects. It treats Charlie Watts' wonderful drumming as if it was some kind of remorseless frenzy, hurling scattershot ink blots in red and black as the powerful sounds fill the screen with lyrics crudely daubed over them in whitewash. Worse, whoever was responsible had failed to listen with care to the dramatic final verse and crassly misquotes the singer's last words. Despite this deplorable dumbing down, the video at least gave widespread currency to one of the greatest songs of the Sixties and a total of 69 million views has been amassed.

Considering the lyric, rock critic Tony Viscounti would insist that Jagger had lifted the line "I have to turn my head until my darkness goes" verbatim from James Joyce's 'Ulysses'. But he offered no evidence beyond the coincidence of the two lines themselves. Beyond that, the lyric of 'Paint It Black' compares very favourably with various works of modern poetry in its own right and is in no way derivative or flawed. In contrast, WH Auden's overrated 'Funeral Blues' contains the powerful lines "the stars

is about

er-

...ut every one; pack up the moon and dismantle
with bathos by such naff phrases as "prevent
a juicy bone."

...cally and musically, is a masterpiece, ranking
...est songs of the Sixties, a decade rich in pop greatness.

CHAPTER 35

'Aftermath' and 'Revolver'

'AFTERMATH' WAS RELEASED in the UK on April 15 1966 and two months later in the US. It went to number one on the UK chart and number two on the Billboard Hot 100 and it was favourably reviewed by British critics.

Despite a nucleus of superb material, 'Aftermath' would have been far better had it not been burdened with filler, weighed down with country crap and deprived of some of the best tracks recorded at the Sunset Sessions. Clearly, 'Mother's Little Helper', 'Lady Jane', 'Out Of Time', 'Under My Thumb' and 'I Am Waiting' were all outstanding songs. Yet, had 'Paint it Black' also been included – as it was on the US version- plus 'Nineteenth Nervous Breakdown' (both pulled for single release)- and had 'Sittin' on a Fence' and 'Ride On, Baby' not been suppressed, then the full strength of the Rolling Stones' creativity and performance would've been exposed.

This worked to the Rolling Stones' disadvantage four months later when the Beatles' album, 'Revolver' was issued in the UK. Raved over by the English intelligentsia of the day and raised to the status of high art by Ian McDonald's 'Revolution in the Head' three decades later, 'Revolver' swept all before it as critics vied to heap praise on a variety of innovative recording techniques. These included automatic double tracking, Leslie speakers, varispeed, tape loops, reversed tapes and close micing. 'Revolver' was simultaneously saluted for what it drew from contemporary classical composers such as Stockhausen. What's more, the Beatles were lionised for the introduction of psychedelia and for moving away from love songs to explore such themes as mortality and transcendence. By contrast, the Rolling Stones were wrongly perceived as bogged down in the blues and out of their depth when they looked to move into high class pop.

The cumulative impact of the Beatles' three mid-period albums, 'Rubber Soul', 'Revolver' and 'Sergeant Pepper' would be to identify them as 'rock' artists. The arrangements, instrumentation and general atmosphere of these albums combined to suggest to the critics that the Beatles were 'improving' on simpleminded, obsolescent rock 'n' roll. In appealing, whether intentionally or otherwise, to European cultural snobbery and in striking an unintended chord with American racism and classism, the Beatles effectively dissociated themselves from rock 'n' roll and rhythm and blues. In truth, they'd come a long way from the Cavern and the Kaiserkeller. But it was a journey that had estranged them from their most vital musical roots.

'Revolver' was presented as a genuine work of art with fourteen progressive pop tracks, no filler and an arresting piece of graphic design (by German musician, Klaus Voorman) for its sleeve. It did contain genuine high-quality material such as John Lennon's 'Tomorrow Never Knows', 'I'm Only Sleeping' and 'She Said She Said.' Nevertheless the praise lavished on it by British critics went clean over the top and was rooted in English class consciousness.

The Beatles were favoured by the Establishment and Prime Minister, Harold Wilson, had nominated them for the MBE. Manager Brian Epstein was seen as cultured and respectable in contrast to the brash Andrew Oldham who'd deliberately promoted a 'bad boy' image for the Rolling Stones.

Producer George Martin was certainly musically gifted but, despite humble social origins, had carefully cultivated a smooth, bourgeois image. The Beatles themselves were not seen as threatening – McCartney was eminently sensible, Ringo was a cheery Scouser, Harrison anonymous and John Lennon was an endearingly eccentric dreamer and not yet a radical critic of the status quo. As for the Liverpool whence they came, its image was still –in contrast to future decades- upbeat and positive.

The Rolling Stones seemed to most critics like polar opposites of the wholesome Beatles. Mick Jagger was viewed as sneering and lewd, Keith Richards as insolent, Bill Wyman as inscrutably surly and Brian Jones as a sybaritic dandy. Only Charlie Watts seemed 'normal.' Whereas the Beatles hung around with 'nice people from good backgrounds' such as Jane Asher- daughter of a Wimpole Street consultant and a Guildhall music professor-the Rolling Stones' entourage extended to thuggish East End elements such as chauffeur Tom Keylock and builder Frank Thorogood. And the band had originated in the back streets of sleazy Soho side by side with strippers and porn shops.

'Revolver' had of course been produced in London at a long -established studio, Abbey Road, in classy St John's Wood. 'Aftermath', on the other hand, had been made in the USA at showbiz capital, Hollywood. Arranger Jack Nitzsche and engineer Dave Hassinger were Americans, little-known figures in the UK.

'Revolver' reflected cross-fertilisation from contemporary classical music. Paul McCartney was open about the influence of Stockhausen and his extravagantly praised song, 'Eleanor Rigby', was set by George Martin for a string octet. In fact it was a pretentious effort, morose even morbid, gloomy with sombre cellos.

Nevertheless the biggest reason for the downgrading of 'Aftermath' was not the prejudice of the critics but Andrew Oldham depriving it of some of the finest work from the RCA sessions in December 65 and March 66. It would have been perfectly possible for Oldham, had he so chosen, to have green-lighted an album containing the following tracks (in whatever order he saw fit), listed here in alphabetical order: 'I Am Waiting'; 'Lady Jane'; 'Mother's Little Helper'; 'Nineteenth Nervous Breakdown'; 'Out of Time'; 'Paint It Black'; 'Ride On, Baby'; 'Sittin' on a Fence'; 'Stupid Girl'; and 'Under My Thumb.' Add on the eleven minute epic 'Goin' Home' and there's a saleable package of normal album length. The classics-loving, Beatles-worshipping critics would scarcely have been able to disrespect tracks such as 'Paint It Black', 'Lady Jane', 'Sittin' on a Fence' and 'I Am Waiting.' But, at the same time, there would have been items to please the likes of Janice Nichols, famed on 'Juke Box Jury' and Cathy McGowan, presenter of 'Ready Steady Go' who spoke for young women seeking danceabilty over other criteria.

Andrew Oldham's flawed decision-making would soon be highlighted again when work began on 'Aftermath's' follow -up album, to which he gave the nebulous name, 'Between the Buttons.' It was started appropriately at RCA in the first week of August 66 during the Rolling Stones' US tour. Yet, by the end of the month, production had been switched to IBC Studios in London. Within a few days it was adjourned and the bulk of the recording was done in November at the newly opened Olympic Studios in Barnes – with the occasional sortie to Pye Studios.

The transition from California to England removed both Jack Nitzsche and Dave Hassinger from the helm. Nitzsche would fly in to play on some of the tracks but essentially he became a session musician, no longer an arranger. The engineer would now be Glyn Johns, a competent technician but no Dave Hassinger. Andrew Oldham took complete charge of production and Bill Wyman tersely summed up Oldham's approach. He said "Andrew still had dreams of being an English Phil Spector, if only by cranking up the reverb to 11. Production subtlety was not his bag."

Weighed down by Oldham's crudity, the Rolling Stones themselves were also badly at fault. On the one hand, they couldn't help the fact that, as Keith Richards phrased it, "it was the first record we made when we hadn't been on the road and we weren't shit hot from playing gigs every night." On the other, they had only themselves to blame for the fact that, as Richards admitted, "everyone was stoned out of their brains." It was in the final months of 66 that the English music scene became suffused with cannabis and LSD. Musicians began to delude themselves that hallucinogenic drugs would greatly boost their creativity and that psychedelia was the way forward.

An insight into the prevalent mindset came with photographer Gered Mankowitz' reflections on the cover artwork for 'Between the Buttons', which he shot on Primrose Hill in November 66. Common sense might have suggested that a shoot at 5.30 in the morning after the band had been recording all-night was scarcely the optimum time. But Mankowitz was motivated by other considerations. "We were aiming to capture the ethereal, druggy feel of the time, that feeling at the end of the night when dawn was breaking and they'd been up all night making music, stoned", he loftily proclaimed.

Mankowitz deliberately opted for a home- made camera filter con-structed of black card, glass and vaseline, seeking to create the effect "of the Stones dissolving into their surroundings." Soon the photographer was furious with Brian Jones. He would earnestly recall "I was frustrated because it felt like we were on the verge of something really special and Brian was messing it up. He was lurking in his collar and it seemed like he didn't give a shit." Certainly Jones was the only band member who was looking down and grinning while the others stared earnestly at the cam-era but this didn't justify Oldham and Mankowitz seeking to portray him as at best a damn nuisance and at worst a half -crazed destructive force. In actual fact he had a down to earth sense of humour and was quick to see through pretentious nonsense.

Bill Wyman, who kept well away from drugs, recorded in his diary the way in which the Olympic sessions were infiltrated by various outsid-ers, not only lovers or friends of his bandmates but also sheer hangers -on. Among those he listed were Brian Jones' mistress, Anita Pallenberg, his friend Prince Stanislas Klossowsky and Mick Jagger's secret lover, Marianne Faithfull. Yet the group extended to include Tony Sanchez, who scored drugs for Keith Richards, and such icons of 'Swinging London' as photographer Michael Cooper, art gallery owner Robert Fraser and comedians Peter Cook and Dudley Moore. Wyman's comment on the effect of this crowd is telling- "these sessions were notable more for the dopey camaraderie than for the music they produced."

Bill Wyman was not alone in taking a dim view of 'Between the Buttons.' Within only a couple of years Mick Jagger said "it's my least favourite Stones album" and effectively gave the game away about drugs when he added "I can't even remember doing it." Speaking five years later, he was even more emphatic when he said that, with the exception of one song, "it's a terrible album, more or less rubbish." In later years Jagger was more specific about the technical flaws of 'Between the Buttons.' He recalled "we recorded it on four- track machines and we bounced it back to do overdubs so many times we lost the sound of most of it."

Few critics were as clearheaded about 'Between the Buttons' as were its creators. One notable exception was Roy Carr of the 'New Musical

Express', a writer who'd been very enthusiastic about the Rolling Stones' eponymous album and would also praise 'Beggars Banquet' in the future. Carr described 'Between the Buttons' as "a turkey" whose twelve tracks found the Rolling Stones "temporarily drained of all positive inspiration, enthusiasm and direction" and he laid much of the blame at the door of Andrew Oldham. Significantly, Roy Carr was a practising musician himself in contrast to the likes of Dartmouth English major, Robert Christgau, the so-called 'dean of rock critics' who devoted many words to it and absurdly hailed it as "one of the greatest rock albums."

Despite 'Between the Buttons' manifold flaws, it contained one outstanding song, 'Backstreet Girl.' What's more, the IBC sessions produced another, 'Have You Seen Your Mother, Baby, Standing in the Shadow?', designated for single release. As for those at Olympic, they yielded one of the Rolling Stones' greatest tracks, 'Ruby Tuesday', which became part of a double A side.

CHAPTER 36

Standing in the Shadow

At IBC on the last day of August 66, Keith Richards set up his most ambitious project yet. It's a song in the key of G major which ends in D major. The chorus has a crackling rock 'n' roll melody, there's three blues-derived emphatic verses and a bridge which begins as little more than a murmur before becoming fiercely insistent. Richards intended to begin the track with boisterous guitar clangour and to end with feedback. The title would be 'Have You Seen Your Mother, Baby, Standing in the Shadow?'

At this point Keith made a sad mistake. He brought in Mike Leander as co-arranger. A graduate of the Trinity College of Music, Leander was considered in cultured circles as a youthful alternative to George Martin. Indeed the following year he'd play a minor role in the Beatles' 'Sergeant Pepper' album. Pissed off because Martin had a prior commitment for a couple of days, Paul McCartney drafted in Leander to arrange the song, 'She's Leaving Home', which Martin reluctantly consented to use when he was free.

Keith Richards knew Leander from working with him on the Stones' version of 'As Tears Go By.' This was a song Jagger and Richards had written at the instigation of Andrew Oldham for the recording debut of the then seventeen-year-old Marianne Faithfull. Mike Leander had acted as producer on Faithfull's original version of the song and had cloaked her feeble voice with oboes, harps and suchlike. Apparently persuaded that Leander was just the man to add horns to the track, Richards brought him in.

Things didn't work out. Richards said "we tried trombones, saxes and all permutations of brass. Everything but the trumpets dragged." But, while the trumpets certainly don't drag, their presence denies space for the rest of the band on a track which, at a mere two minutes and forty-three seconds, would be alarmingly brief. In contrast to Jack Nitzsche's driving piano which blends in perfectly, the so-called Mike Leander Orchestra stands out like a sore thumb.

Mick Jagger responds to the challenge, which his pal Keith had set, with a brilliant vocal. Yet the lyric itself is uneven. The narrator reflects on a relationship with a girl whose eyes he claims to have opened but the context is ambiguous. The second verse nearly unravels as he seems to say he was only dallying with her- before contradicting this with a plea for her sympathy. He ends with an ultimatum – she must choose between the brave old world or her own imminent decline. It seems an odd alternative for someone who was being urged to get with the 'Swinging London' scene. 'Brave New World', the title of Aldous Huxley's futuristic novel, whose author was known as a pioneer of LSD tripping, might have been the preferred choice had it scanned.

This was complex stuff, wide-open to bafflement or genuine misinterpretation. Yet that was nothing compared to the confusion sown by the title phrase/chorus. The first impression created by the lyric of 'Have You Seen Your Mother, Baby, Standing in the Shadow?' is one of Mick Jagger using his command of punctuation and his grasp of ambiguity to bamboozle listeners into thinking that the girl's pregnancy was being referenced.

Yet there may be more to it than that. The word 'shadow' is not just part of the song title, it appears no fewer than thirteen times in the lyric. The concept of 'shadow' is key to the theories of the Swiss psychiatrist, Carl Gustav Jung. In 1963, Jung had written "the shadow is for the most part that hidden, repressed, guilt laden personality whose ultimate ramifications reach back into the realm of our animal ancestors and so comprise the whole historical aspect of the unconscious." Soon the idea of the shadow started to seep into the popular domain and was linked with negative emotions such as envy, greed, anger and lust.

While Mick Jagger always poured scorn on the suggestion that he was intellectual, he was doubtless well aware of Carl Jung's work. Certainly the title phrase seems to imply that the girl needs to realise that the dark side of herself is reflected in her mother (not to mention her brother and another of her lovers who are brought in later). Right throughout, above all with the girl herself, the references to "having had another" imply sexual cheating.

Whatever the truth or otherwise about Jungian influence, the theme of 'Standing in the Shadow' is surely one of deceit and this is most power-fully expressed in the bridge where the narrator calls out his ex-girlfriend for lying about how she adored him and takes the shadow as a metaphor for duplicity. Indeed the remaining six lines of the bridge are a soliloquy, sung rather than spoken (as they would be in a Shakespearean drama) venting the narrator's deeply pessimistic thoughts. For many years Keith Richards would be in awe of his best pal's command of English, saying "I always thought Mick had a bit of Shakespeare in him."

Never before had Keith Richards himself ranged so far and wide in his musical imagination. He had every right to expect that the Rolling Stones would be given an extended period of time to bring his ideas to fruition. They wouldn't get it. In future years Keith would complain "it needed another couple of weeks." He went on to say "I liked the track, I hated the mix. There was a fantastic mix of the thing which was just right. But because they were in a rush to edit it down for the Ed Sullivan Show, where we were booked to play it as our latest single, the mix was rushed and the essential qualities of it disappeared."

Bill Wyman would echo his bandmate's dissatisfaction. He said "the rhythm section's buried in the mix and we all felt it didn't create as much excitement as it should have done. Although we took longer to record and mix the single than any of our previous records, Keith always felt it needed more."

Nevertheless, 'Have You Seen Your Mother, Baby, Standing in the Shadow?' remains in many ways a brilliant achievement. The last seconds of the track yield majestic, reverb-soaked feedback, a sustained sound which lingers in the mind, encapsulating the ambition of Keith Richards' project albeit sacrificed to cheap commercial considerations.

'Standing in the Shadow' was heavily publicised and film director Peter Whitehead was brought in to shoot a promo film which featured all five of the band in drag. Yet the single, released on September 23, didn't rise in the charts the way Stones' records normally did. It reached #3 on the UK singles chart and #9 on the Billboard Hot 100. Clearly the odd- sounding mix and the wilfully obscure lyric, had left substantial elements of the fan-base behind. The relative failure of the track wasn't lost on Jagger. Two years later he looked back on it, describing it as "the ultimate freakout. We came to a full stop after that. What more could we say?"

If Mick Jagger was in philosophical mood, reflecting on pervasive treachery, when he wrote the lyrics for 'Standing in the Shadow', he was fully involved in the machinations of deceit only a few weeks later. His dissatisfaction with his lover, Chrissie Shrimpton, came to a head and he made a second approach to Marianne Faithfull, this time successful. Faithfull, nineteen at the time, was cheating on her husband, art gallery owner, John Dunbar. For over two months Jagger and Faithfull kept things quiet yet, shortly before Christmas, Jagger suddenly disappeared from Shrimpton's life, cancelling their seasonal holiday.

A conventional and devoted twenty-one year old who had little interest in 'Swinging London', Chrissie Shrimpton was devastated by the abrupt end of a relationship which had lasted nearly four years and which she'd hoped would culminate in marriage and children. She took an overdose of sleeping tablets and woke to find herself checked into a hospital under a false name -whence she was smuggled out in a wheelchair, driven in the back of a lorry to a private clinic in Hampstead. Andrew Oldham had been desperate to keep news of Mick Jagger's girlfriend's attempted suicide out of the media but, when the tabloids broke the story, the distraught Chrissie finally learned the truth about Jagger and Marianne Faithfull.

CHAPTER 37

'Back Street Girl' : the Fate of a Working Class Mistress

"THAT'S THE ONLY decent song on 'Between the Buttons '" said Mick Jagger about 'Back Street Girl.'Although he didn't dwell on the reasons, it's not hard to see what they were. With the sole exception of 'Lady Jane', where the context was historical, this was the furthest the Rolling Stones moved from rock 'n' roll. Electric guitar was out and so were drums but harpsichord, accordion and vibraphone were in. So there was no way for Andrew Oldham to steep it in Spector stuff.

It's probable that Jagger composed much of the tune himself and his comment – "I wrote this in some weird place which I can't remember; it's got the feeling of a French cafe about it" - seems to imply that. Doubtless Keith Richards fleshed out the melody but it's not clear how the waltz-time arrangement was arrived at. Brian Jones is at the heart of the track but, beyond Richards and Jones, there's yet another first-class musical brain at work. Jack Nitzsche's input to the Rolling Stones' work would be glossed over by future rock critics who brushed him aside with phrases such as "a friend of the band and an occasional contributor." Yet Nitzsche had been there when the track was begun, with Dave Hassinger engineering, at RCA in August 66 and he flew into Heathrow in November, when it was completed at Olympic with Glyn Johns. In contrast to Nitzsche, Nick de Caro, another American, was a highly regarded session accordionist but this would be the one and only time he'd work with the Stones.

The incredibly beautiful melody of 'Back Street Girl' carries a starkly cynical lyric which would mislead many into thinking that Jagger was expressing negative views about women and had got groupies in his sights. In fact he was impersonating a married English aristocrat who keeps a working-class mistress on the side. This ought to have been clear from his effete accent in the vocal and certainly from a reference to his wife.

Addressing his 'backstreet girl' directly, the narrator begins by presenting himself as no more than an honest and realistic man. He doesn't want to raise her hopes or bring her down. He wants her to be around albeit never part of his world.

Although his manner's initially polite, with the word 'please' frequently used, it's not long before his cruel snobbery takes over. He puts her down with a jibe about her poor manners then sneers that's she's common and coarse. While their relationship depends on the 'backstreet girl' providing sexual favours, the upper-class man takes this for granted with his incredibly haughty demand that she must curtsey and look nonchalant just for him.

Throughout the track, music and lyric are perfectly matched. The intro presents Keith Richards playing exquisite acoustic guitar in counterpoint with yet another startling instrumental innovation by Brian Jones. With his keen interest in modern jazz, Jones had always had the vibraphone on his radar and he admired Milt Jackson's vibes work with the Modern Jazz Quartet. But now he uses his mallets on the instrument's metal bars in strictly pop style. The result sounds like a man whistling lightheartedly almost as he shrugs his shoulders and it perfectly incarnates aristocratic smugness.

Jones and Richards accompany Jagger in the fake honesty of the opening lines. Then, as the narrator demands that the 'backstreet girl ' must heed his whispered advice, there's a sharp change as the harpsichord and, above all, the accordion emphasise his casually contemptuous attitude.

In contrast to that, the next contrapuntal between Brian and Keith comes across quite differently – as if they were underlining the essential poignancy of the girl's subservient situation. The mid-track instrumental section last over half a minute with Nitzsche and de Caro joining the four regular instrumentalists. Charlie Watts' delicate tambourine offers a gentle rhythm while the subdued accordion seems to suggest a sympathy for the 'backstreet girl' going well beyond the trademark aural evocation of Paris.

After the narrator's final utterance of the title phrase, Brian Jones comes into his own in the outro with a dazzling final flourish on vibraphone.

'Back Street Girl' would never be performed on stage and, for decades, it remained an almost forgotten item in the Stones' canon. Not only does it present a far more nuanced picture of the band's attitude to women than the material which the radical feminists would pounce on in the early Seventies but it also carries a echo of the great political scandal which erupted in England in March 1963 at the very moment when the Rolling Stones themselves were on the brink of their recording career.

John Profumo, the Harrow and Oxford-educated Minister for War in Harold Macmillan's Conservative government had denied newspaper suggestions that he'd been in a sexual relationship with nineteen-year-old Christine Keeler, one which had allegedly compromised national security. Soon Profumo was proved to have lied to the House of Commons and he was forced to resign.

Christine Keeler was a girl from a humble working-class background who'd been brought up in a makeshift dwelling converted from two disused railway carriages. Later she became a topless dancer in a West End club and was introduced to Profumo by Stephen Ward, an osteopath with an upper class clientele. Ward was charged with living off Keeler's earnings as an alleged prostitute plus those of another dancer, seventeen-year-old Mandy Rice Davies, a former Birmingham shop assistant. Davies herself had been involved with Lord Astor. She had no intention of remaining in the back streets and confidently stood up to herself in court when a barrister put it to her that Lord Astor had denied any relationship, drawing an outburst of laughter with her reply – "well, he would, wouldn't he!"

In contrast to Mandy Rice Davies' remarkable resilience in confronting the Establishment, Christine Keeler descended into depression, broken marriages and poverty. While she made clear that Profumo himself had never verbally abused her, she was dismissed by Prime Minister Macmillan as "a tart" and her situation would remain very much that of a 'backstreet girl.'

While there's no indication that Mick Jagger had Christine Keeler specifically in mind when he wrote 'Back Street Girl', there's no doubt that the Profumo affair, about which the Rolling Stones had heard rumours before the story broke in the tabloids, had a major impact on the band. It had exposed the Establishment as corrupt and hypocritical, proclaiming strict standards of morality while at the same time using young working-class women for sex.

'Back Street Girl' would be rescued from obscurity when the stereo mix which appeared on the 'Flowers' compilation was uploaded to YouTube in December 2010. Since then that version has attracted 85,000 views.

In April 2014, Joe Daugherty (Historicus Joe) uploaded a video which has drawn 60,000 views and which deserves many more. It's a montage of mainly black-and-white shots of the Rolling Stones as they were in their pomp of iconic pop. Among the many images which appear are: all five of them walking through a park with Watts and Wyman immaculately attired, Jagger in a shortie overcoat and Richards outdoing Jones in the dandy stakes; Richards and Jones standing side by side drinking bottles of brown ale; Richards looking like a classical musician, eyes closed, in another world playing an acoustic; Jones sometimes in flamboyant threads yet also in casual gear wearing basketball boots à la Kurt Cobain.

Females are there in abundance; working-class English teens side-by-side with Bill Wyman and Brian Jones; awestruck girls admiring Jones looking dapper in a striped suit; early girlfriends such as Chrissie Shrimpton and Linda Lawrence; Anita Pallenberg and Brian Jones in close-up double portrait, looking like identical twins of different genders; Pallenberg with Jones then Pallenberg with Richards; Mick Jagger first with Chrissie Shrimpton, later with Marianne Faithfull; Brian Jones with Nedra Talley of the Ronettes (she dated him briefly and described him as "a very nice guy, well mannered and gentle").

All in all, Daugherty's video is a splendid evocation of the mid-Sixties, and of the original Rolling Stones in their prime of progressive pop before their decision to opt for hard rock. The timeless appeal of a great song such as 'Back Street Girl' across the generations is amply demonstrated by older YouTube viewers' delight in rediscovering it and younger ones' astonished admiration in finding the Rolling Stones in an iconic pop mode totally different from their image as rock dinosaurs.

CHAPTER 38

―― ❧ ――

Keith, Linda and Brian- the Story of 'Ruby Tuesday'

WHEN THE ROLLING Stones first broke through, in March 63, Keith Richards, then nineteen, had no steady girlfriend. Soon Sheila Klein, who was dating Andrew Oldham, introduced him to her best friend, the seventeen-year-old fashion model, Linda Keith. It was an amusing icebreaker that her surname was the same as his first name but soon the couple were bonding over a shared love of the blues.

The man Linda would remember in future years was someone very different from the hard-boiled 'Keef' of rock legend. She described him as "shy, introverted, very appealing and lacking in confidence." Their relationship strengthened after an incident in June 64 when Linda was hospitalised. Returning to London after seeing the Summer solstice at Stonehenge, she'd been thrown through the windscreen when her friend's car crashed. As soon as Richards got to know about it, he was at her bedside. Linda was distraught, dreading that facial injuries might put an end to her modelling career, a fear aggravated by nurses taking all mirrors out of her sight. "I will never forget" said Linda, many years later "how Keith leaned down and kissed my face. It showed me that I wasn't a monster and I wasn't revolting. And that was Keith!"

Happily, Linda's scars healed well and she was able to resume her modelling career. Had she been on the scene in the Fifties, her beauty, her gentle manner and the fact she was well spoken would all have been in her favour. Still, she would've gone nowhere because she would've been written off as too skinny. But the Sixties was the decade of the ultra-slim model- notably Twiggy (Lesley Hornby)- and Linda Keith fitted right in. She modelled for Ossie Clark and was photographed by David Bailey. Her legs were slender but superbly shapely.

By the spring of 66, the Richards-Keith relationship was on the rocks. The cause was drug abuse – by her, not him. Richards had been on speed and grass for years and had started on cocaine. But he refused point-blank to try heroin, which Linda Keith had dived into. After a blazing row, she left for New York, where she later became involved with Jimi Hendrix.

This time Keith Richards' concern for Linda's welfare infuriated her where, two years earlier, she'd been delighted by it. Although she was twenty, she was not yet an adult under the laws of those days. Richards promptly got in touch with her father who succeeded in having her made a ward of court in New York, giving him the right to bring her home from America.

Linda had broken away from her artistic Jewish family circle in West Hampstead. Her father, born Alexander Kossoff, had changed his surname to Keith. He was an actor, like his famous brother David Kossoff. But Linda and her cousin Paul considered themselves free spirits not bound by family ties. Paul Kossoff became a stellar guitarist in a bluesrock band, significantly named Free, which would have a massive hit with 'All Right Now.' Tragically, heroin abuse would be a root cause of his death at the age of only twenty-five.

When Linda Keith was obliged to return to London, she made clear to Keith Richards that she never wanted to speak to him again. He fully accepted this. If Linda suspected jealousy with regard to Jimi Hendrix, this doesn't seem to have been the case. Richards would always speak well of Hendrix, describing him as "a really nice guy." On the other hand, he'd been at the end of his patience with Linda's unpredictable ways even before she became a hard drugs casualty. Still, he would miss her. And his mixed feelings would be the origin of a great Rolling Stones' song. Its title was 'Ruby Tuesday.'

'Ruby Tuesday' would be credited to Jagger and Richards. Yet Mick Jagger never claimed he'd written it and, in later years, he explicitly denied it, saying "'Ruby Tuesday' is a wonderful song with a really nice melody and a lovely lyric. Neither of which I wrote but I always enjoyed singing it."

LINDA KEITH
Also known as 'Ruby Tuesday'

For many years Keith Richards would deny that Linda Keith had inspired the lyric of 'Ruby Tuesday', pretending that it concerned a groupie he once knew. In later years he opened up saying, albeit vaguely, "it was probably written about Linda Keith not being there. I don't know, she'd pissed off somewhere. It was very mournful, very very Ruby Tuesday and it WAS a Tuesday." Although the title phrase is a brilliant oxymoron, combining a glittering gem with the dullest day of the week, it may also be that 'Ruby' was Richards' pet name for Linda.

After the breakup of his relationship with Linda, Keith Richards was reluctant to hang around Redlands, his newly- bought thirteenth century moated cottage at West Wittering in Sussex. He stayed for a while with Brian Jones and Anita Pallenberg in South Kensington. Those who knew him well observed Richards copying Jones' dandy gear and it seemed he was in awe of Jones' status as a fashion icon and of Jones-Pallenberg as a glamourous couple. Moreover, as the drugs subculture began to take off, Mick Jagger's cautiousness over substances didn't seem to chime with the times whereas Jones and Pallenberg flung themselves into chemical adventure. For a brief period the 'Mick and Keef' friendship was under strain.

In obvious need of a melody to accompany his lyric for 'Ruby Tuesday', Richards turned to Jones. According to Bill Wyman, Jones gave valuable help with the musical composition. Yet probably his contribution went much further than that.

Marianne Faithfull knew Brian Jones intimately. Indeed they'd briefly been lovers before she became Mick Jagger's mistress. Her preference for Jagger caused no problems between them and she always remained Jones' confidante. Faithfull would relate how Jones told her he'd based the melody of 'Ruby Tuesday' on the English Renaissance composer Thomas Dowland's 'Air on the Late Lord Sussex.' Jones said he'd originally suggested a variant of Dowland's melody mixed with a snatch of a bluesman Skip James' tune – intending to provide an album song for the band. But nothing had come of it. In due course, however, so Faithfull maintained, it had provided the musical basis for 'Ruby Tuesday.'

The excellent lyric of the song includes three verses where a man reminisces about a girl whom he once loved. In the opening lines he recalls how she lived in the moment, heedless of yesterday. In the second verse he advises others not to question her need for total freedom. In the last verse he quotes the girl directly on catching dreams before they slip away.

The recording of 'Ruby Tuesday' began at RCA in August 66 and was completed at Olympic on November 16. Not everything came off well. Bill Wyman selected the notes for a double bass and Keith Richards bowed the strings but the effect of this is only to produce a jarring sound. As well as that, Mick Jagger struggles with unusually low notes but, on the other hand, his immaculate diction and cultured pronunciation stress Ruby's posh background.

Much of the sonic beauty of the track stems from the piano. Many listeners would attribute this to Keith Richards because he was seen playing the instrument when the song was performed on stage or on TV. Others were convinced that Brian Jones, a pianist since childhood, was the one who played. In actual fact it was Jack Nitzsche who, for all his important contributions to the band in the days of their progressive pop, would never be seen playing live with them.

Yet the stellar performer is unquestionably Brian Jones. In contrast to his lethargy at the time of Mankowitz' photo- shoot, he was well and truly up for this one and, as was noted by everyone around, "he seemed like a totally different person." Jones believed he had exactly the right instrument to add vital tone colour to 'Ruby Tuesday.' It was the recorder.

Never was a more boring name applied to such a magical instrument-at least in the English language! In other European languages the recorder had always been called by its real name – the flute. Though it wasn't a conventional flute held sideways from the player's mouth, it was a so- called 'sweet flute' or 'beak flute' or 'block flute.' This meant it had a whistle mouthpiece, it was played projecting vertically from the lips and it had a particularly sweet tone. Jones had been keenly interested in baroque composers for years and had mastered the recorder. Now, in his hands, when 'Ruby Tuesday' was waxed in the studio, it became truly a magical flute.

Linda Keith was well and truly on Brian Jones' radar at the time of the Olympic recording. It wasn't just that he was smitten with her stems– Brian and Linda would become lovers twelve months later – but he considered her a kindred spirit. Jones himself was impetuous by temperament, quick to take up ideas and to drop them almost as fast while always eager to take risks. This would find an outlet in his major contribution to 'Ruby Tuesday.'

Keith Richards was temperamentally the polar opposite of Linda Keith. Although his lyric shows how well he knew her, it also reveals his exasperation with her impulsiveness –underlined in the chorus by Charlie Watts' almost impatient volleys of drums. The chorus is repeated three times with the singer venting his frustration with her volatility. Yet he's compelled to admit how much he'll miss her.

In the verses themselves it's the recorder which sets the tone. First heard under enigmatic words about bright suns and dark nights, it's become a piping flute as it expresses Ruby's sudden appearances and departures. And, by the time of the last verse, the flute's become an all -embracing swirl as the singer quotes Ruby's words about death, mad-ness and the loss of dreams. Brian Jones was not yet ready to fall silent and his outro solo, although barely ten seconds long, is unforgettably poignant.

'Ruby Tuesday' was originally designated as a B-side. The A side, 'Let's Spend The Night Together' has a la-la melody and a cheerful, jaunty beat. But the title phrase shocked Ed Sullivan rigid and he insisted that the words "the night" must be replaced by the innocuous "some time" before he would allow the number to be performed on his show. When Andrew Oldham realised American radio programmers were equally uneasy about the song's sexual implications, he promoted 'Ruby Tuesday' to the A-side in the U.S. 'Let's Spend The Night Together' had been # 3 on the UK chart but 'Ruby Tuesday' topped the Billboard Hot 100 in its own right. That was in January 1967.

Brian Jones was not credited for 'Ruby Tuesday' and when Stones' accountant, Stan Blackbourne, rebuked him with the words "don't you realise you've as good as written Mick Jagger a blank cheque?", Jones reacted with a resigned shrug of the shoulders.

Linda Keith would finish with Brian Jones after their tempestuous affair in 68. She made contact with Keith Richards many years later and, in his autobiography, he mentioned that she settled in the United States and had brought up a family there - having doubtless got her life back on track after kicking hard drugs.

In the fifty years of the song's existence, there have been more than a score of cover versions. With one exception, they're of scant significance. But the version recorded by twenty-three-year-old New York singer -songwriter, Melanie Safka, on her album, 'Candles in the Rain', released in April 1970, is a complete reinterpretation. Taking the verses at a gentle pace, lingering on some words while emphasising others, she brings out all the beauty of the lyric. Then, as she delivers the chorus, her raw voice shivers with emotion as she bids Ruby farewell.

So powerful is Melanie's reinterpretation that some would contend it left the original in the shade. This is not so. As a woman, she could treat Ruby as a lamented lost best friend. By contrast, Mick Jagger was obviously singing from a male perspective, that of the former lover of a girl who was at the same time fascinating and exasperating.

The Rolling Stones' first televised performance of 'Ruby Tuesday' was uploaded to YouTube by Ruudtes, from the Netherlands, in July 2013 together with his detailed commentary. The footage is eye -opening. Mick Jagger sings the vocal with total confidence. His movements are relatively restrained and he concludes with a dignified bow. Brian Jones is immersed in his recorder while Bill Wyman and Charlie Watts solemnly play their instruments.

The odd one out is Keith Richards. After briefly giving a silly grin as he mimes shielding his eyes against the lyric's bright sun, he then crouches uncomfortably over the piano sitting side-by-side with Jones. There was of course an element of sheer fakery there in that Jack Nitzsche was the pianist on the track and not him.

Nevertheless, the casual televiewer might see Richards almost as an intruder, a gawky lad who'd been called on stage to mime along with the band. Few would recognise him as the author of such a subtle and perceptive lyric. Herein lies the enigma of Keith Richards, a truly gifted songwriter yet a man crippled by shyness, deeply ill at ease in the limelight and indeed with fame itself.

Future rock writers would hail Richards as the hard-boiled 'Human Riff ' but, before he quit progressive pop for hard rock, the women in his life would all emphasise his shyness and sensitivity; above all, his mum, Doris, and his first lover, Linda Keith. Then there was Marianne Faithfull, who fondly recalled her one night stand with him. The man they knew was the one who wrote the lyrics to 'Ruby Tuesday ', one of the greatest songs ever composed.

'Ruby Tuesday' was the climax of a wonderful two year outburst of creativity without parallel in English music, going back beyond the 'Aftermath' sessions to those which produced 'The Last Time' at RCA in January 65.

With 1967 opening on such a positive note, it was widely assumed that the Rolling Stones would continue from strength to strength. In actual fact, they were to unravel at startling speed.

Part 6: The Breakup of the Original Rolling Stones

CHAPTER 39

꼭

Drug Bust at Redlands, Treachery in Morocco

As 1967 OPENED, Brian Jones was in upbeat and positive mood. He'd been commissioned to write the music score for the German film, 'Mord und Todschlag' ('A Question of Murder'), starring his lover, Anita Pallenberg, and directed by the highly regarded German director, Volker Schloendorff. He'd supervised such outstanding musicians as Nicky Hopkins, Jimmy Page and Kenney Jones during recordings at IBC Studios and work was almost complete. Shortly the Rolling Stones were due to start another psychedelic album – which would eventually be entitled 'Their Satanic Majesties Request' – and Brian expected to figure largely in its creation, once again demonstrating his versatility on a wide array of instruments.

For all his confidence, Jones remained acutely aware of societal injustice. He was fully prepared to speak out about it and did so during the course of a long interview with 'New Musical Express' journalist, Keith Altham which was published on January 30 1967. He said "our real followers think like us and are questioning some of the basic immoralities which are tolerated in present-day society – the war in Vietnam, the persecution of homosexuals, the illegality of abortion and of drug taking."

He continued "our friends are questioning the wisdom of an almost blind acceptance of religion. Conversely, I don't underestimate the power and influence of those who, unlike me, do believe in God. We believe there can be no evolution without revolution."

This was a remarkably open and lucid expression of opinion which went far beyond what was expected of a pop musician. On the one hand, it anticipated changes in the law which would be enacted later in the year.

On the other hand, it tempted fate in its implicit challenge to the law on illicit drugs

Little did Brian Jones suspect that he had a mortal enemy, a newly promoted policeman, who was dedicated to his downfall. Detective Sergeant Norman Pilcher, seething with ambition, had just been transferred from the Scotland Yard Flying Squad to the Drugs Squad. Pilcher had cultivated contacts with tabloid newspapers such as 'News of the World', 'The People' and the 'Daily Mirror' whose readers' letters reflected a growing resentment against the hedonistic lifestyles of rich young pop stars. Rumours abounded of widespread drug-taking on the music scene and this gave Pilcher the opportunity he craved – to win kudos for himself by arresting successful recording artists. The legislation was already in place. This was the Dangerous Drugs Act of 1965 which imposed draconian penalties for anyone convicted of permitting a house to be used for smoking cannabis.

Norman Pilcher, a prematurely balding, grim-faced, furtive-looking thirty-year-old, longed to get the Beatles but he reluctantly held fire on that one as they were fully accepted by the powers that be, particularly after Prime Minister, Harold Wilson, had recommended them for the MBE two years earlier. So he set his sights on the Stones, disliked by the older generation and detested by the Establishment. While Mick Jagger and Keith Richards were certainly prime targets, Brian Jones was even more prominent in Pilcher's sights. It wasn't just Jones' long hair and perceived androgyny, it was his expressed interest in Eastern cultures and religions. After all, as Pilcher saw it, he was the cissy little bastard who'd smirked as he played that bloody Indian sitar on Top of the Pops.

Two days after recording began on 'Satanic Majesties', Pilcher was tipped off by an informant employed by the Stones that Keith Richards would be hosting a weekend party at his country home, Redlands, in rural Sussex. Mick Jagger and Marianne Faithfull would, he was assured, be there, not to mention various Stones' hangers on, including Tony Sanchez, who scored drugs for Richards, Canadian acid guru David Schneiderman, and famed 'Swinging London' gallery owner Robert Fraser. And above all-as Pilcher saw it- Brian Jones and Anita Pallenberg.

Earlier in the day, February 11, George Harrison and Patti Boyd had also been present at the party but, conveniently for Norman Pilcher, they cleared off, motivated by Harrison's dislike of the Stones' hangers -on. Yet, to the copper's frustration, Jones and Pallenberg had not arrived. Temporarily delayed by the need to complete work on 'A Question of Murder', Jones knew he could be at Redlands within two hours, stepping on the gas of his Rolls-Royce Silver Cloud. He phoned Richards to let him know he was on his way. "Don't bother!" was the retort – "we've been busted!!"

The Drugs Squad had found substances on the premises and, having cautioned Richards, Jagger and Fraser, had taken their findings away for analysis, pending possible charges.

The Redlands drugs bust was a prime factor in the eventual breakup of the Rolling Stones. Jagger and Richards bonded closer than ever as a result of the shared experience. And they blamed Jones for having bragged about drugs at a West End night club, 'Blaises', within earshot of someone who turned out to be a tabloid snitch – and thus a Drugs Squad informant at one and the same time.

The Redlands bust was gold dust as far as the tabloids were concerned and they were soon titillating their readers with stories of sex, drugs and rock 'n' roll. The sex came in via Marianne Faithfull – she wasn't mentioned by name but her identity was obvious. Alleged to have cavorted scantily clad, the only woman at the party, salacious rumours abounded that she'd performed what were described as "kinky sex acts" with Jagger.

With the findings of the police lab not yet established, it was decided to take a 'get away from it all' holiday. This would start on March 12 with the ultimate destination being hippy haven, Morocco. Jagger and Faithfull would fly direct but Jones, Pallenberg and Richards, accompanied by a woman friend of theirs, Debra Dixon, would take a leisurely trip through France and Spain, driven by Stones' chauffeur, Tom Keylock, in Richards' Bentley Continental.

Brian Jones was keenly looking forward to the holiday because it would give him the chance to explore his interest in Eastern percussion by visiting the Atlas Mountains and recording the Joujouka drummers. Anita Pallenberg was experiencing mixed emotions. She was keen to link up with her best friend, Marianne Faithfull. But her attraction to Brian Jones had begun to fade. The issue was surely his ill- health.

Around this time, Jones' asthma worsened. What's more, he started to have blackouts. In future years Pallenberg would say that, when these happened, she would turn him on his side and keep a careful eye on him till he recovered consciousness. Brian himself had no memory of what had happened and scarcely registered the significance of such episodes. Whilst Anita had diligently taken care of him when he was ill, the contrast between a sickly Brian Jones and the robust Keith Richards, recently their guest at Courtfield Road, was doubtless not lost on her.

Within days of the holiday starting, Brian Jones was taken seriously ill. He was hospitalised at Toulouse in France and found to be suffering from pneumonia. His frail frame contrasting with his long hair, he was momentarily taken to be female by the nurses who admitted him. Fortunately. he responded to treatment but was kept in as a precaution. He suggested to the others that they go on without him and that he'd rejoin them as soon as he felt better.

With Jones none the wiser, Dixon flew home to London while Pallenberg and Richards went on, as originally planned, through Spain and thence via Tangier to Morocco. But– at least according to Keylock-the mutual attraction between Keith and Anita rapidly intensified and, whilst he was driving them from Barcelona to Valencia, she gave him head on the back seat behind the heavily tinted windows of the Bentley Continental.

Nevertheless, when Jones let Pallenberg know, by telegram, that he'd recovered and asked her to return to him in Toulouse, she did so. They flew back to London where Jones had medical treatment for an illness which may well have been triggered by asthma.

It wasn't long before Jones and Pallenberg rejoined Jagger, Faithfull and Richards in Morocco. But, within days, Pallenberg left Jones for Richards. While he was tricked into a lone visit to the Atlas Mountains to hear gnauwa music, the others flew back to England leaving him stranded and shattered.

Pallenberg and Richards would allege, as the immediate cause of her breakup with Jones, that he asked her to join him in group sex, namely a foursome involving two Berber prostitutes. When she refused, Jones had allegedly beaten her up so that she'd had to seek Richards' protection.

Whilst this story would become enshrined in rock legend, its accuracy is open to doubt. Certainly Brian Jones revelled in sexual scenarios involving him with at least two women but, according to those who knew them both well, Pallenberg had previously been ready to join in. As to violence, Jones' friends would claim that Pallenberg could give as good as she got.

Brian Jones himself would admit to unprovoked aggression against his later lover, Linda Keith. Yet his earlier girlfriends would deny that he'd ever been violent with them. And so did his final lover, Anna Wohlin. Whatever the truth or otherwise of Pallenberg's accusations, the fact remains that she'd already had sex with Richards while they were in Spain.

Jones was badly shaken by Pallenberg's desertion and even more by Richards' betrayal, to which Jagger had been an accomplice. Richards' own remarks on the subject, taken at face value, show an astounding lack of emotional intelligence on the part of such a sensitive musician. Talking as if Jones was no more than a temporary colleague in Jagger's ad hoc pickup band, he commented: "just because a chick leaves somebody to go with somebody else is no reason to feel guilty. It could have been someone 12,000 miles away but it happened to be the guy who stood on the other side of Mick onstage. And that was that."

Brian Jones himself, a man without a brother, had always regarded Keith Richards and Mick Jagger as his musical brothers–in–arms. Even though hostilities were put on hold for the band's European tour and recording sessions for TSMR, the unity of the Rolling Stones had inevitably been compromised by what happened in Morocco.

Nevertheless, Brian Jones managed to get his personal life on track before too long. He found sexual solace with none other than Linda Keith, Richards' ex – 'Ruby Tuesday' herself. And he befriended Prince Stanislas Klossowsky de Rola. Klossowsky, widely known by his nickname 'Stash', had shared a bill with the Rolling Stones at the Paris Olympia in 66, when he was the drummer in Vince Taylor's rock 'n' roll band. His background was unusual to say the least. The son of a famous French painter, he was descended from the Polish nobility. He was of no musical significance but he shared Jones' interest in art cinema. Beyond that, Klossowski, two metres tall, multilingual, a noted dandy and brimming with confidence, was a magnet for women. He'd been Anita Pallenberg's lover before she became Jones' mistress. What's more, the first time Marianne Faithfull cheated on Mick Jagger, she did so with Klossowsky.

By this time charges had been filed against Keith Richards and Mick Jagger in light of the Redlands raid. Together with Robert Fraser, they appeared at Chichester Crown Court on May 10 1967. Fraser was charged with possession of heroin, Jagger with possession of amphetamines and Richards with permitting his house to be used for smoking cannabis. Outside the courtroom, a tabloid media scrum lay in waiting, beside themselves with anticipation of a sensational outcome.

CHAPTER 40

Mick Jagger's Establishment Pardon

As the world waited with bated breath to see how events would unfold in Chichester Crown Court, Norman Pilcher showed the instincts of a streetfighter as he went for the old one-two. The shifty scuffer switched the focus to South Kensington, ordering his minions to raid Brian Jones' apartment. Jones and Klossowsky had only just returned from the Cannes premiere of 'A Degree of Murder' and they endured the rudest of welcomes as the Drugs Squad busted their way into Courtfield Road.

In next to no time, triumphant detectives had what they were looking for – cannabis. Jones and Klossowsky were bundled into a police van and taken to Marlborough Street Magistrates Court. This time media involvement went beyond the usual tabloid bloodhounds and extended to TV cameramen eager to show footage on the early evening news.

At Chichester both Keith Richards and Mick Jagger pleaded not guilty to the charges they faced. Jagger insisted not only that the amphetamines had been legally prescribed for his girlfriend while they were on holiday in Italy but also that they had the subsequent approval of her GP. Faced with a more serious charge, Richards denied that he'd knowingly allowed dope to be smoked at Redlands. His defence was that Schneiderman– who'd promptly bunked off to Canada– had sneaked stuff in without his knowledge.

Keith Richards showed up in his true colours when it came to cross -examination. Coached by counsel to answer every question with the word 'sir' respectfully included, he let the mask slip. Sneering at the prosecution's assumption that Marianne Faithfull's near-nudity in itself showed that she'd lost her inhibitions because she was high on drugs, he replied "we are not old men – we have no time for petty morals."

On the Temple Heath estate, where the boy Keith had grown-up, the police were not treated with the unquestioning respect shown in the popular BBC TV series, 'Dixon of Dock Green' where popular character actor Jack Warner played the part of a cheery bobby on the beat who ended each episode with a moral homily. Far from it, on the dysfunctional Dartford estate the abusive phrase 'sloppy copper' was often hurled at members of the dreaded 'old Bill.' The notion that the police were tools of the Establishment- and, as likely as not, bent into the bargain- was commonplace.

Richards' working class defiance did him no good. He was sentenced to twelve months imprisonment, significantly twice as long as Robert Fraser received after pleading guilty to the more serious offence of heroin possession. Fraser was, of course, an Old Etonian and an ex-officer in the King's African Rifles.

Jagger was also convicted and sentenced to three months imprisonment. The two Stones were separated and hurried off to jail. But whereas a crestfallen Jagger was in tears when visited by 'Marijuana Faithful' (as the tabloids soon christened her) Richards was quite prepared to tough it out. His status within the band increased as a result. Jagger and Richards were only behind bars for one night, being freed on bail pending an appeal.

Meanwhile, Brian Jones and Stanislas Klossowsky prepared for their appearance at Inner London Sessions which was scheduled for June 2. It was now that a very significant development took place which at once threatened the unity of the Rolling Stones. Brian Jones was advised by his lawyers to plead guilty to the charge of letting his apartment be used for cannabis consumption. Although the maximum penalty was ten years in prison, he was assured that a guilty plea would lead to him being treated leniently. Jones meekly complied despite Klossowsky's best efforts to talk him out of it.

Klossowsky himself freely used recreational drugs but he had no intention whatever of pleading guilty to possessing cannabis; he was convinced the stuff had been planted while he and Jones had been away in France. Jones, for his part, believed it must have been carelessly left behind by one or other of the many girls who'd been at Courtfield Road since Pallenberg had left. "You must plead 'not guilty', Brian", so Klossowsky told him, "because you ARE not guilty." Jones had of course been using grass for years but that didn't necessarily mean that he'd turned a blind eye to others using his house for that, still less of encouraging them to do so.

Brian Jones would not be dissuaded from his plea of guilt. When Mick Jagger and Keith Richards heard this, they were furious. As they saw it, Jones was kowtowing to the Establishment and threatening the prospects of future Stones' tours to America, where a drugs conviction would almost certainly mean no entry. As far as Richards was concerned, he began to despise Jones, his former friend from their days at Edith Grove, but the fact remained that the band was still heavily reliant on Jones' instrumental versatility.

Despite many delays brought about by consultations with lawyers and court appearances, the psychedelic album, 'Satanic Majesties', was gradually being put together. Brian Jones figured prominently on a wide variety of instruments, including organ, flute, soprano saxophone and the newly invented mellotron.

Amidst all the confusion, Andrew Oldham was, after four years at the helm, ousted from the band's management. Mick Jagger, initially deferential to Oldham, had absorbed most of the dark arts of showbiz infighting. Citing his role as a producer at Immediate and vocal coach to Chris Farlowe, he demanded one third share in the label. Stunned by Jagger's chutzpah, Oldham snapped "you can fuck off!"

But Oldham's position would-be fatally undermined when he reacted with terror to police harassment of the Stones. In contrast, Allen Klein, thick- skinned veteran of the Mafia- infiltrated New York entertainment world, was in his element. Jagger and Richards began talks with Klein and, by September, he'd taken full control of the Stones' finances. Mick Jagger became the band's manager on a day-to-day basis and took over production of the psychedelic album. By this time Oldham was on the verge of a nervous breakdown and he volunteered for electro-convulsive therapy before disappearing forever from the history of the Rolling Stones.

Brian Jones himself now faced an anxious wait of almost five months, seeing as the final hearing of his case wasn't scheduled until October 30. Meanwhile, an utterly unpredictable development took place which would have a major effect on the Rolling Stones and, in particular, on Mick Jagger's public image. With the appeal against the Chichester verdict not yet heard, an editorial was published in the Times, on July 1, entitled 'Who breaks a butterfly on a wheel?' Borrowing a phrase from 18th-century poet Alexander Pope, it focused on Mick Jagger and argued that he'd been harshly punished simply because he was a world-famous celebrity.

The author of the editorial, William Rees Mogg, was an Old Carthusian, an ex-President of the Oxford Union and a former Conservative parliamentary candidate. His clear sympathy for Jagger resonated widely and was the first indication of a change in Establishment attitude towards the controversial Stones' frontman. What's more, 1967 was the very year in which liberal attitudes started to permeate the upper echelons of society. Under the Sexual Offences Act of July 67, homosexual acts involving males over the age of twenty-one were decriminalised under English law. And the Abortion Act, a Private Member's Bill permitting termination of pregnancy up to twenty-four weeks, would receive government backing and pass into law in October.

When their appeals were finally heard, Keith Richards' conviction was quashed and, although Mick Jagger's still stood, he was conditionally discharged. It seemed to them both that their defiant stance had been vindicated. The same would later apply to Stanislas Klossowky who, when he pleaded not guilty to possession of cannabis, would find the charges against him promptly dropped.

Brian Jones soon found himself isolated from the rest of the band. Told by Allen Klein to quit Courtfield Road and keep the police guessing as to his whereabouts, he was advised by his lawyers to stay away from Jagger and Richards. Soon, Klossowsky was his only go-between and Mick Jagger was asking "Stash, don't you know where Brian is?" Jones would then ask, almost pathetically "Stash, what are the Stones doing?"- almost as if he was no longer part of the band.

By this time Brian Jones had a new primary girlfriend. She was the model, Suki Potier, who knew Linda Keith well from the time when they both worked with Ossie Clark. Potier was a gentle girl from a posh background who fell in love with Jones and saw it as her mission to look after him. But she proved unable to stop his slide into further drug abuse.

While Jones had resolved to steer clear of cannabis and LSD, he became more and more consumed with anxiety about the possible outcome of his delayed court case. He could not bear the prospect of prison even for the shortest term. His life had always revolved round women and music and, obviously, he would be deprived of both. But what made it even worse was the shame which he knew it would bring on his parents.

Certainly Basil and Eva Jagger had been very upset by the prospect of their son Michael going to jail. But that would be as nothing compared to the reaction of Lewis and Louisa Jones. They were not only the epitome of middle-class respectability but devoutly religious into the bargain. Even though Brian had turned his back on Hatherley Road while still in his teens, he longed to prove himself, to his father in particular, as a successful musician. He was on the brink of being acclaimed as a gifted composer because of his score for 'A Degree of Murder.' Yet now his status was in jeopardy with the media portraying him as no more than a drug - crazed enemy of society. He wrote to his parents, begging them "please don't believe all you read" but their absence of response only deepened his depression.

Plagued with insomnia and drinking more and more heavily, he was prey to persons who plied him with mandrax, the street name for methacqualone, a drug prescribed to combat sleeplessness and promote muscle relaxation. Its use was not yet monitored as it would later be, following the Misuse of Drugs Act (1971).

Jones took the dreaded downers right to the limit and they soon had a terrible effect on him. His features became bloated and there were large. dark rings under his eyes. One side-effect of the drug was lack of muscle coordination and Stash Klossowsky was appalled to see his friend incapable of walking in a straight line and constantly staggering against walls.

Between them Klossowsky and Potier prevailed on Jones to seek the help of a Harley Street psychiatrist. It didn't work. Agitated, deeply depressed and so incoherent he could scarcely begin to explain what had happened to him, he was referred to a private clinic in suburban Roehampton.

It was there that Brian Jones spent most of July being weaned off methacqualone. Gradually his true personality resurfaced and he impressed his doctors as a highly articulate young man with a sharp analytical mind. Ambitious to be recognised as a composer and not merely a pop star, he made clear that he'd never used hard drugs. He made no secret of the fact that he'd been a heavy cannabis user for years but seemed realistically to accept that it solved no problems and only aggravated negative feelings.

By the last day of July Brian Jones had recovered sufficiently to take part in the recording of the Rolling Stones' single, 'We Love You.' The contrived lyric expresses thanks to the band's fans for standing by them in times of trouble and includes a couple of sneering references to the Establishment. The track itself is a dismal, heavy-handed effort, lit up only by Nicky Hopkins' fiery piano.

'We Love You' was accompanied by a promo film directed by Peter Whitehead. It was a pretentious, confused effort tendentiously comparing Establishment harassment of the Rolling Stones under drugs legislation with the prosecution, under Victorian sexual offences laws, of the gay dramatist Oscar Wilde in 1895. Whitehead's promotional film worked to the disadvantage of Brian Jones in that he was featured struggling to keep awake, doubtless as a result of persistent insomnia.

Jones' bandmates tended to think of him as a hypochondriac who could always come up with plausible explanations for his ailments. Yet, except only in one respect, Jones made no attempt to pull the wool over his doctors' eyes. He claimed that he'd learned to cope with stress without resorting to the crutch of cannabis. But he said nothing about his increasing dependence on alcohol.

Much of the work on the psychedelic album had been completed before Jones' breakdown and what remained was eventually completed by early October. On the thirtieth of that month, the case against him was finally heard at the Inner London Sessions. No other member of the band was there to support him. The only one who was sympathetic was Bill Wyman, by now thirty-one, a man of genuine emotional intelligence whose level of maturity far exceeded that of Jagger and Richards.

Wyman was already being taken to task by Astrid Lundstrom for his failure to be proactive on Brian Jones' behalf and it was only many years later that, in his book, 'Stone Alone', he made the telling comment "had one or two of us gone to court we would've learned more about our friend and colleague in half an hour than we'd managed to glean in five years."

In court everything seemed to be going well at first with Brian Jones making a good impression, vowing that he would have nothing further to do with cannabis and playing up to the Establishment by stating that he hoped his case "will be an example to young people who are tempted to try drugs." He reiterated his plea of guilty to the charges; possession of cannabis and permitting his premises to be used for the purpose of smoking it.

Nevertheless, despite his compliant attitude, he was sentenced to nine months in jail, promptly put in a prison van and driven to Wormwood Scrubs. The following day he was freed on bail pending an appeal and, reassured by his lawyers that it would probably be successful, he ceased to live on the run and he and Suki Potier moved into a small new flat at 17 Chesham Street in Belgravia.

On December 8, 'Satanic Majesties' was finally released. Like 'Between the Buttons' previously, it suffered from the continued presence, at recording sessions, of multiple hangers-on. With the exception of 'She's a Rainbow', which featured the elegant piano playing of Nicky Hopkins (but was flawed by a feeble lyric and facile strings) there were scarcely any memorable melodies. This seemed to have little effect on its chart success. It reached number #3 on the UK chart and # 2 on the Billboard 200.

Nevertheless the album would-be fiercely attacked by rock critics, above all Jon Landau in 'Rolling Stone.' The upshot of the criticism was that 'Satanic Majesties' was a pathetic attempt to imitate the Beatles' acclaimed 'Sergeant Pepper's Lonely Hearts Club Band', that it was utterly pretentious and a catastrophic blunder.

For once the rock critics' comments were, for the most part, well justified. 'Sergeant Pepper', released six months before TSMR, was an exceptional album, going far beyond its Beatles' predecessors, 'Rubber Soul' and 'Revolver.' It contains such outstanding songs as 'Lucy in the Sky with Diamonds' and 'Being for the Benefit of Mr Kite' not to mention a masterpiece in 'A Day in the Life.' What's more, a superb double A-side single, 'Strawberry Fields Forever'/'Penny Lane' had been recorded during the Pepper sessions. Although George Martin had continued in neoclassical style on some tracks, he featured other instruments, such as the harmonium and the calliope, to good effect while Paul McCartney effected a brilliant lift from JS Bach's 'Brandenburg Concerto', namely the piccolo trumpet which lights up 'Penny Lane.'

Even McCartney's weaker easy listening songs on 'Sergeant Pepper' have lively melodies and are far ahead of the succession of dismal, lifeless tunes on TSMR. The reasons for the ineptitude of the Stones' psychedelic album were not hard to find and were freely articulated by band members. Many years later Bill Wyman commented- "every day at the studio it was a lottery who would turn up and what – if any – positive contribution they would make. Keith would arrive with anything up to ten people, Brian with another half a dozen and it was the same for Mick. I hated it!"

This was echoed by Mick Jagger who said "there's a lot of rubbish on 'Satanic Majesties.' Just too much time on our hands, too many drugs and no producer to tell us "enough already, thank you very much, now can we just get on with this song." Brian Jones, for his part, described it as "got together chaos."

TSMR had indeed disfigured the Stones' discography. But later generations of musos were well wide of the mark when they implied that the band were incapable of rivalling the Beatles in pop terms. Whilst Jack Nitzsche had been their effective producer at RCA, they had performed brilliantly. But, with Andrew Oldham at the helm and- after his abrupt departure midway through the album- his replacement by Mick Jagger,

there'd been a lack of studio discipline- exacerbated by seri̇
abuse. In contrast, the Beatles, whilst they certainly used recre
drugs during the making of 'Sergeant Pepper' were never stoned o̟
their minds in the studio.

Following the release of TSMR, Brian Jones argued that "the album
is a very personal thing, but the Beatles are just as introspective", adding
"entertainment is boring – communication is everything." Asked about
the advent of progressive pop, he contrasted the optimism of the Sixties
with escapist post-war culture which had lingered on to the end of the
Fifties. He replied "nothing destroys culture, art- and the simple privilege
of having time to think- quicker than a war. And once you get the horror
and terror of a war people have to escape from it. They need the escapist
pop culture that croons about Moon and June and romance. I have never
had to go through those times" he declared, adding – "I thank God I have
not."

Needless to say, Brian Jones' breadth of vision went over the heads of
the tabloids and was ignored by the broadsheets. Within days, they were
avidly reporting the results of his case in the Appeal Court which was
heard on December 12 1967. His prison sentence was set aside but he
was placed on probation for three years on condition that he continued
to receive psychiatric treatment.

Euphoric at the shadow of imprisonment being lifted, he promptly
hooked up with 'Ruby Tuesday' herself. Brusquely dumping the ever -loyal
Suki Potier, he flew off with Linda Keith for a holiday in exotic Ceylon.

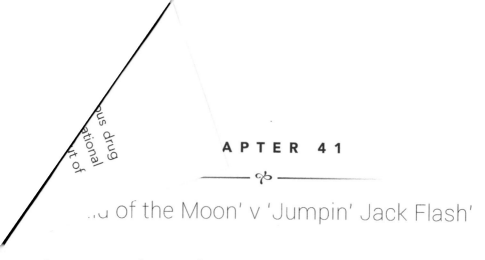

❧

'...d of the Moon' v 'Jumpin' Jack Flash'

STUNG BY THE rock critics' fierce criticism of their psychedelic album, the Rolling Stones realised the need for a new producer who wouldn't tolerate a slaphappy studio atmosphere. They engaged the bustling, Brooklyn-born Jimmy Miller, an expat American drummer who'd achieved success in England as a producer for the excellent BRB group, Spencer Davis.

Keith Richards reckoned he'd had a bellyfull of psychedelia and, in future years, he recalled his attitude in typically forthright language- "I was sick to death of the whole Maharishi guru shit and the caps and bells. A spell in prison will certainly give you room for thought and I was fuckin' pissed off with being busted. So I said 'right, we'll go and strip this thing down.'" He began using open tunings and a capo, especially open D and open E.

The new album would need months to assemble but in the meantime, the Rolling Stones intended to herald it with a landmark single. At this point disagreement broke out as to what it should be. Brian Jones favoured 'Child of the Moon', on which the band had made a tentative start with Glyn Johns in October 67. But Keith Richards argued for 'Jumpin' Jack Flash', a song he'd recently written with Mick Jagger. The compromise was to record both numbers before deciding which should be scheduled as the A side and which the B.

The two songs are almost polar opposites with 'Child of the Moon' essentially ethereal while 'Jumpin' Jack Flash' is dynamic. Between March 29 and April 3, 'Child of the Moon' was completed by Miller at Olympic Studios with Eddie Kramer assisting as engineer. Miller wisely brought in Nicky Hopkins to play both piano and organ. Hopkins had been prominent in pioneer BRB band, the Cyril Davies Rhythm and Blues All Stars. He suffered from Crohn's disease and this had made it difficult for him to work with a band on the road. Yet by this time he was recognised as the finest session musician in England. Always eager to boost percussion, Miller augmented the band with the Ghanaian congas exponent, Rocky Dijon.

'Child of the Moon' is the last great track from the Rolling Stones' era of progressive pop. The sloppy studio indiscipline of TSMR is a thing of the past and Jimmy Miller, a stern taskmaster, opens the track himself with an outburst of startlingly aggressive shrieking, his words angry but incomprehensible.

Determined to stamp out the last embers of flaccid psychedelia, Miller assembled a fierce wall of sound which includes Bill Wyman on fuzz bass, Rocky Dijon on percussion, plus Nicky Hopkins' attacking piano and is driven along by Watts' crackling drumbeat. The barrage soon ceases leaving only Watts' powerful, rattling drums.

The Rolling Stones core trio then take centre stage as the beautiful track unfolds. Mick Jagger has rarely sung better, his impeccable vocal delivering his own poetic lyric to set an almost otherworldly ambience. Keith Richards' ringing open tuned guitar punctuates three verses whose melody, doubtless his own, is country at its best, folk- derived and yearning.

Suddenly there's a sensational chord change launching the first of three choruses whose subtly expanding/contracting melismatic melody has Brian Jones' fingerprints all over it and which, in interview, Jones stated that he'd written. Not to be denied as an instrumentalist, he alternately rasps and shrills on saxophone, the first instrumental love of his youth after he changed from classical music to jazz.

Seeming to address the moon itself, the singer commands the celestial body to open her rainy eyes and smile in the shape of a crescent. In the second verse the singer turns to his lover still asleep beside him. The bedside lamp casts a flickering light across her face as she shivers and stirs. The woman herself is a child of the moon and she will soon be awake and seductively smiling.

MARIANNE FAITHFULL
Was she the inspiration for 'Child of the Moon?'

After a burst of brilliant organ from Nicky Hopkins, the final verse is suffused with pantheism as the singer claims the stars themselves are pining for his lover. Then the poetry of the lyric culminates as the singer orders her to bid the smiling sun to rise silky-faced on a misty day in hues of pearly grey. For all the nebulous tone, the track ends with Keith Richards' ringing guitar and Charlie Watts' crackling drums.

The lyric for 'Child of the Moon' was widely believed to have been inspired by Mick Jagger's passion for Marianne Faithfull, his twenty-one-year-old lover, the woman with whom he'd conceived a child only for Faithfull to suffer a miscarriage. At the time the track was being recorded, she was filming her starring role in the Anglo-French film, 'Girl on a Motorcycle.' The movie featured Faithfull astride a Harley-Davidson clad in tight fitting full-body leathers. Yet beyond her sensual allure she was an actress of considerable intelligence and a lover of European literature who'd introduced Jagger to the works of Charles Baudelaire and Mikhail Bulgakov.

It would be claimed in some quarters that the main melody resembles that of the Beatles 'Rain', an argument favoured by those who obstinately– and wrongly– insisted that the Rolling Stones lacked the intrinsic quality to match the Liverpool quartet's iconic pop.

'Child of the Moon' is significant in being the last song when the moon itself would be considered as a symbol of beauty, mystery and romance. The following year, 1969, would see the Apollo Moon Landings which reduced a celestial body to a lump of rock on which astronauts casually jumped.

Jimmy Miller completed work on 'Jumpin' Jack Flash' at Olympic between April 20 and 27, this time with Glyn Johns as engineer and Ian Stewart on piano. The arresting title phrase was sparked at Redlands after Richards and Jagger had spent a long night trying and failing to get a song going. At dawn Jagger was nodding off only to be alerted by vigorous noises outside. "Who the fuck's that?", Jagger barked and Richards told him it was his gardener, Jack Dyer. Jagger was narked by the way the gardener was leaping about but Richards shrugged it off with the phrase "he's Jumpin' Jack" to which Jagger, on the spur of the moment, added the word 'flash.'

'Jumpin' Jack Flash' begins with crisp guitar and a variant on the riff from 'Satisfaction', which was suggested by Bill Wyman. Then the singer tells how he first saw the light of day in a crossfire hurricane, a possible reference to Dartford, birthplace of both Jagger and Richards and known as the infamous Luftwaffe 'Bomb Alley.' He goes on to describe being brought up by an ugly hag and punished with a strap across his back.

The third verse is the most startling. After hints of Crucifixion imagery-bleeding feet and refusing crumbs of bread-it closes with an unmistakeable reference to Christ's Crown of Thorns. That in itself might, a decade earlier, have provoked a prosecution for blasphemy. But, by the late Sixties, censorship had almost ceased to exist.

In the chorus the singer shucks off all the horrors he's endured as he jubilantly shouts the title phrase over Keith Richards' leering bass. Whilst the title would be grist to the mill of the 'bout drugs innit!' school, the song in fact hails the triumph of a formerly despised man. Jagger himself had been scorned by the Establishment only to be acclaimed by Stones fans and the intelligentsia alike as the ultimate rockstar. Without doubt, 'Jumpin' Jack Flash' is a great rock song- dynamic, exuberant and positive. Its opening bars acted like dynamite to demolish the rotten edifice of TSMR.

The critical hostility to 'Satanic Majesties' had made Mick Jagger consider "getting out of the pop thing", as he later phrased it. Jack Dyer leaping about in the Redlands dawn surely symbolised his own reawakening after a long, fruitless spell of psychedelic pondering. For all his lyrical mastery, he was, throughout the era of iconic pop, struggling for dominance against Brian Jones' multi-instrumental virtuosity. With a return to rock 'n' roll verities that would now be over. There could be no question that he alone was the leader of the Stones.

In Jagger's mind, there was another factor which would conclusively tip the balance in favour of 'Jumpin' Jack Flash'- and that was its danceability; not of course in the sense of the appeal to dancers of the Rolling Stones' rhythm and blues-infused songs. But rather of Mick Jagger himself, the potential cynosure of all eyes as he leaped about onstage. Impressed by the performances of Rudolf Nureyev, the exiled Russian ballet dancer, Jagger increasingly added camp posturing to his earlier gymnastics. For him, dancing was power and his sometime political ambitions were now subsumed using onstage antics as a means of authoritarian control. Shirley Watts had once half-jokingly scolded him for bossing Chrissie Shrimpton about and she'd mock-saluted him with the words "Heil Jagger!" Soon what had been in-group humour would become stadium rock reality.

Latching on to a trend towards promotional films, Jimmy Miller engaged his fellow -expatriate American, the filmmaker, Michael Lindsay- Hogg, to shoot footage to accompany each track. It was a singular error of judgement. Lindsay -Hogg enjoyed an exaggerated reputation, much of which stemmed from him being the son of the great film director, Orson Welles. He was nowhere near the level of Ray Davies, the frontman of BRB band, the Kinks. Davies was a working-class North Londoner but a former cinema student who had a deep love for-and understanding of- the best European art films. His promo films for 'Sunny Afternoon' and 'Dead End Street' were brilliant pieces of work from 1966 which outclassed the pretentious Lindsay-Hogg.

On April 28 Lindsay-Hogg shot the initial promo for 'Jumpin' Jack Flash' with the band miming to a specially recorded version. On May 11 he took the band into the Surrey countryside to shoot 'Child of the Moon' with a ludicrous scenario which travestied the lyric. Brian Jones reacted with barely disguised contempt-much as he had for Gered Mankowitz' equally pretentious shoot on Primrose Hill- and ended up just short of bladdered. Then they returned to the studio while Linday-Hogg filmed them recording another version of 'Jumpin' Jack Flash', this time with their faces garishly painted and Jagger's dancing heavily emphasised.

By this time a decision had to be made and, while Brian Jones opted for 'Child of the Moon', he was outvoted by those who wanted 'Jumpin' Jack Flash.' It was thus the latter song that was performed at the NME Poll- Winners concert at Wembley. It went down a storm and was released as the A side on May 24.

Wowing critics and fans alike, 'Jumpin' Jack Flash' topped the UK singles chart and reached # 3 on the Billboard Hot 100. Reaching only a minority of curious listeners who flipped the disc to hear the other side, 'Child of the Moon' had no promotion whatever and was never performed onstage.

Just as 'Child of the Moon', albeit intrinsically ethereal, begins and ends with raw power, so 'Jumpin' Jack Flash', essentially kinetic, closes with a rapturous outro almost half a minute long.

Keith Richards would be very proud of 'Jumpin' Jack Flash'-and rightly so. Reflecting on its origins in his autobiography, he said "it's almost Arabic, or very old, archaic, classical, the chord setups you could only hear in Gregorian chants or something like that. And it's that weird mixture of your actual rock 'n' roll and at the same time this weird echo of very, very ancient music that you don't even know. It's like a recall of something and I don't even know where it came from."Surely Richards' remarks hold good above all for the outro, one of the absolute peaks of the Rolling Stones on record, with his own sparkling guitar in counterpoint with Bill Wyman's fantastic Hammond outburst.

Virtually suppressed for decade after decade, 'Child of the Moon' was resurrected on YouTube in April 2012. What's more, the uploader, nomadtraveller, posted a video with an impressive montage. It begins with a long shot of a rural landscape by moonlight, continues with the first sunglow of the day, switches to an image of the dark side of the moon bathed in beautiful blue light and returns to the rural landscape, this time shrouded in fog. A young woman is seen in silhouette, her dress billowing in the breeze and the video closes on a close-up of a sleeping female pierrot.

The upload itself received many appreciative posts which were replied to courteously by nomadtraveller herself. The exchanges were in total contrast to the intolerance and hurling of abuse only too frequent in certain sectors of YouTube. The video has now accumulated 194,000 views.

As for the debate within the band as to which track should be the A side, Brian Jones had to accept his error of judgement in underestimating the commercial appeal of 'Jumpin' Jack Flash.' Indeed he went so far as to apologise to the others for having argued against it. It was only as work on 'Beggars Banquet' began in earnest that he realised that 'Jumpin' Jack Flash' was no one- off. A crucial decision had been made in favour of rock and there would be no going back.

CHAPTER 42

The Persecution of Brian Jones

ON MAY 20 1968 the Rolling Stones recorded the last track for 'Beggars Banquet' to which all bandmates would make a significant contribution. 'No Expectations' had been written by Keith Richards, long-time country music buff, in a characteristically yearning style. The rhythm is discreet with Charlie Watts on claves and Bill Wyman pumping occasional punctuation. Mick Jagger's vocal fits the bill and Nicky Hopkins' rippling piano is suitably lachrymose.

The song wasn't really Brian Jones' cup of tea yet he surprised the others with his protracted steel slide guitar contribution, lifting the number from a mere lament to a thing of beauty.

Jones returned from that late-night recording session in an upbeat mood to his new apartment at classy Royal Avenue House off Kings Road in Chelsea where he was living alone. But he was rudely awakened the following morning by the Drugs Squad gaining forced entry. Norman Pilcher was not at their head but he'd deputed Detective Sergeant Robin Constable to take his place. It wasn't long before a cop was triumphantly brandishing a ball of wool with a suspicious substance wrapped inside it.

Despite his protestations that it didn't belong to him, Jones was bundled off to Marlborough Street Magistrates Court and charged with possession of cannabis. According to the evidence of the arresting officer, Jones had replied "oh no, this can't happen again, just when we were getting back on our feet!" before exclaiming "why do you always have to pick on me?"

Jones' comments, which, in future years, would be dismissed by some as self- centred paranoia, showed both his loyalty to the band and his well- grounded fear of persecution. Rolling Stones' press agent, Les Perrin, was himself an ex-cop. Benefiting from tipoffs he got from a contact still in the force, he'd managed no less than seven times to alert Brian Jones to an impending raid and make sure he switched premises to forestall it.

The reasons why Brian Jones, far more than even Mick Jagger, had become public enemy number one as far as the Establishment were concerned were more complex. Unlike Jagger he wasn't politically active. And, although he was a professed atheist, the same applied to all the others in the band. Even beyond his expressions of admiration for Eastern culture, there was another factor which stoked the hostility of the elite.

Jones' long blond hair, flamboyant style of dress- including floppy brim hats, blazers with pink stripes, Afghan fur coats and Moroccan silk scarves- marked him out as a dandy. In late Victorian times, society had viewed dandies with extreme suspicion, taking their mode of attire to signify implicit hostility to the Establishment. After the imprisonment of Oscar Wilde and the early death of Aubrey Beardsley, dandies were far fewer on the London scene in the following decades until the emergence of Brian Jones in the Sixties.

It might well have been easier for Jones had he (like Wilde and probably Beardsley) been gay, newly self-outed in the immediate aftermath of decriminalisation. But his gender blurring, combined with rampant heterosexuality, led to him being widely detested by the older generation.

On March 16, an incident had occurred at Jones' apartment on which the tabloids pounced with undisguised glee. Acting on a tipoff, the Drugs Squad had busted their way in only to find not Jones himself but his girlfriend, Linda Keith, lying naked on a bed, suffering from a drugs overdose and requiring immediate hospitalisation. Linda's suicidal act had allegedly been triggered by discovering Jones cheating on her with another girl. Disappointed as Norman Pilcher was by not getting his man, his failure only made him even more determined to bust Jones once and for all.

Since he first quit Cheltenham for London, Brian Jones had hoped for reconciliation with his parents and, in particular, with his father. From their days at Edith Grove, Keith Richards would recall Jones spending a couple of days in finalising letters to his parents. This time he didn't hesitate to phone his father as soon as he was on bail. He vehemently denied possession of cannabis and insisted that the Drugs Squad had planted it within the ball of wool in the hours between the departure of the previous occupant, an American actress, and his arrival.

Lewis Jones, who'd accepted Brian's guilt over the Courtfield Road arrest, now realised that his son had been stitched up. Although Brian had been hostile to what he saw as repressive, narrow-minded constabulary since his teens, he'd been brought up to believe in their essential honesty. When he heard detectives blatantly lying in court, he was shocked to the core of his being and, when he told his father about this, the reaction was the same.

Even before the Royal Avenue House bust, Brian Jones was in emotional turmoil, trying to revive his relationship with Linda Keith. He began to bombard her with letters and telegrams and harking back to her overdose. In one of these, written on April 4, he wrote "dearest Linda, I'm so sorry that such a tragic thing seems to have severed our relationship. Let me please say darling that I'm deeply aware of your problems. I'm sure you can shake off the devils that haunt you. That you could so often shake off your troubles to help me so lovingly fills me with such deep emotion. I longed to help you Linda, really I did, but a kind of self-preservation instinct erected a barrier every time the longing to help arose in me. This produced the conflicts inside me which resulted in violence, insults and other hurts I caused you."

Jones' letter and follow-up telegrams didn't have the intended effect and, with Linda Keith's failure to respond as he'd hoped, he became desperate and began to plead with her. He wrote "I'm getting two houses together Linda, a good scene, one in town and one in the country. Please be with me, I'm so lonely by myself. I need you so badly and I love you so much. Please let's start again. Please marry me. Please please please."

These letters strongly suggest that, by 1968, Brian Jones was no longer the same man he had been in the early Sixties. He still showed the same untrammelled emotional openness which had drawn women to him since his midteens but his earlier confidence had been drained and he was suddenly supplicating in a way he never would have done with his earlier girlfriends. What's more, he was proposing marriage, something which he'd scorned for years!

Faced once again with serious drugs charges, he at least made up his mind to plead not guilty this time but the public hearing of his case would be postponed until September 26. During the intervening four months, he came close to another breakdown. Terrified at the prospect of imprisonment, he suffered from insomnia and, in next to no time, he was heavily abusing downers the same as he'd done the year before. Flitting from one hotel room to another, living alone with no woman to look after him and apparently with little in the way of culinary skills, he resorted to buying pork pies and drenching them in HP sauce. His evenings were spent swigging wine and there were unsubstantiated rumours that he summoned call girls to his hotel room more to keep him company in the early hours rather than for sex.

Such a lifestyle was bound to affect his appearance and his friends were shocked to see him looking bloated and with swollen eyelids and deep black rings under his eyes. They prevailed on him to return to Roehampton Clinic where he received treatment just as he had done in 67. It was there that Linda Lawrence visited him together with their four -year-old son, Julian. She would later recall that Brian was friendly towards her and affectionate with the boy. But she added the telling observation- "the spark, the life, the energy was gone."

While all this was going on, Keith Richards and Mick Jagger were making progress with the 'Beggars Banquet' album. Despite his earlier contributions to 'Street Fighting Man' and 'No Expectations', Jones was no longer in a fit state to participate. But the plain fact was that he'd been out of sympathy with the project from the outset. He had little interest in the bluesrock style on which Richards had eagerly embarked. Whilst on the ill-fated holiday in Morocco in 67, Jones had become fascinated with the music of the Atlas Mountains, locally known as gnauwa. Dedicated musicologist as he'd always been, he rapidly noted a link with Mississippi blues.

Right out of the blue, well before he was busted for drugs once again, he received an offer from Paul Getty Jr for an all-expenses paid trip to Morocco with the opportunity to go up to the mountains and record the music. Paul Getty Jr was the heir to a vast oil fortune, a young man who rebelled against his father's values to opt for a reclusive hippy lifestyle in Morocco. Jones jumped at the chance and flew out, with Glyn Johns as his sound recordist, their brief absence sanctioned by Decca Records. Unfortunately, the two men didn't get on well and the project foundered.

By the last week in July 68, however, it was up and running once again. By this time Brian Jones had reconciled with Suki Potier. His spirits revived and his health restored at Roehampton, he and Potier flew out to Tangier, on secondment from Decca and with engineer George Chkiantz as his sound recordist. Whereas Glyn Johns, longtime buddy of Ian Stewart, shared Stu's blokeish impatience with what they saw as Jones' unctuous politeness, the more cosmopolitan Chkiantz did not. He found Jones friendly and helpful. Chkiantz, who was no more than an average swimmer, was grateful for Jones' warning about dangerous Mediterranean currents but he noted that Jones was an excellent swimmer who crawled untroubled in the swirling seas.

Jones, Potier and Chkiantz travelled to Joujouka and paid to witness a festival celebrating the god Pan which featured thunderous tbel drumming audible for miles around. Chkiantz would later recall Jones being in his absolute element as the music was dutifully recorded. They slept in a cave and, in the pure, clear mountain air, Jones was completely untroubled by insomnia. The tapes were duly brought back to London but neither Richards nor Jagger showed any interest and Allen Klein refused to promote them. It would take until 1971 for the sounds to be released on Rolling Stones Records under the title 'The Pipes of Pan at Joujouka' with Jones' earlier comment quoted on the sleeve-"what psychic weaklings has western civilisation made of us all!" The issuing of the tapes would prove to be a significant landmark in the history of the world music genre.

On August 1 1968, while Brian Jones, Suki Potier and George Chkiantz were staying at the El Minzah Hotel in Tangier, something happened which foreshadowed Jones' death less than twelve months later.

Jones and Chkiantz had been chatting lightheartedly on the hotel balcony before moving back into Jones and Potier's room when suddenly, without the slightest warning, in the middle of a sentence and without even putting out an arm to break his fall, Jones pitched forward like a log and lay unconscious on the floor.

Chkiantz was totally shocked by what he considered a medical emergency but Potier merely turned Jones on his side and wrapped him in a blanket while casually muttering "fuck him-it happens all the time!" When Jones came to his senses, he had no memory at all of the incident and Potier made clear to Chkiantz that it was the end of the matter.

George Chkiantz was not the first outsider to witness Brian Jones having a sudden blackout. In May 67, two months after Anita Pallenberg left him, Jones met two girls at the Speakeasy Club in the West End. One was eighteen-year-old aspiring folk chanteuse, Sonja Kristina (later lead singer with Curved Air), the other was her friend Romy, who shared Jones' interest in the god Pan. He invited them both back to Courtfield Road where a languourous threesome took place only for Jones' delighted enjoyment to be cut short by abrupt loss of consciousness. Sonja Kristina and Romy carefully tucked him tightly into the bedsheets to prevent him falling out. Presently he came to, albeit in a somewhat confused state. Whether Pallenberg was aware of this episode isn't clear but, after his death, she would comment that "Brian had been in that condition many times before and there'd always been someone to turn him on his side and look after him."

In contrast to the comments of Pallenberg and Potier, Brian Jones' earlier lovers, Pat Andrews and Linda Lawrence, never saw him black out. Nevertheless, his later mistresses were clearly aware how to administer first aid. In fact Jones' symptoms were consistent with an atonic seizure and it may well be that, some time after 1965, he'd developed an epileptic condition. At the very least, he should have been referred to a consultant neurologist for an EEG.

On returning from Morocco, Jones decided to buy a country house where he and Potier would live, away from London and harassment by police and paparazzi. They decided on Cotchford Farm, near Hartfield in Sussex, the former home of the children's author, AA Milne, and they completed the purchase three months later.

As the date for his court appearance at London Inner Sessions approached, Jones relapsed into the same pattern of mandrax abuse as he'd done earlier in the year. He turned up sporadically at the Olympic studio but was plainly suffering the side-effects of poor coordination and thus unable to make any real musical contribution.

On September 26 1968, Brian Jones' second trial on drugs charges was heard at Inner London Sessions. In his evidence Jones vehemently protested that he'd not been in possession of cannabis resin. The court chairman, Reginald Seaton, was surprisingly evenhanded in his summing up. Nevertheless, the jury, doubtless swayed by media hostility to Jones, found him guilty. Seaton then exercised leniency by merely fining him. Interviewed outside court, Jones said "it was such a wonderful relief when I heard I was only going to be fined. I still protest my innocence but everything seems to happen to me." He was driven away from court head bowed and sobbing, comforted by Cynthia Stewart who, in a poignant motherly gesture, flung protective arms around him.

In future years rock critics and others would pour derision over what they saw as Brian Jones wallowing in self-pity. Certainly his reaction to being busted for drugs was timorous and contrasted with Keith Richards' defiance. Yet whereas Mick Jagger had effectively received an Establishment pardon, elite hostility to Jones was absolutely unrelenting. His sheltered upbringing in Cheltenham had left him insulated totally from life's harsher realities. What's more he was an asthmatic and probably an epileptic.

While concern about cocaine and heroin was well founded, Brian Jones did not use these substances. He was being harassed over dabbling in cannabis and the effect of that was only to drive him towards a pitiful dependence on mandrax. His victimisation at the hands of Norman Pilcher– who, in September 1973, would be convicted of conspiring to pervert the course of justice and sentenced to four years imprisonment– was a clear case of Establishment persecution.

CHAPTER 43

— ✑ —

Mick Jagger- Anarchist and Gentleman

By THE SPRING of 68, Mick Jagger was focusing more and more on politics, a subject in which he'd long been keenly interested. Brought up in a comfortable middle-class home in Kent, he didn't absorb his mother's staunch Conservative views. Far from it, he despised Harold Macmillan's Tory government and revelled in its comeuppance over the Profumo Affair. Yet he had no time for the cosy social democracy of Harold Wilson's Labour government which had been currying favour with youth by recommending the Beatles for MBEs.

Well aware of the strength of feeling on American campuses against the war in Vietnam, in which the UK did not participate, he joined the demonstration outside the US Embassy in Grosvenor Square on March 17. It was organised by the Vietnam Solidarity Committee under the leadership of noted Marxist, Tariq Ali.

But Jagger was never remotely a Marxist. In a 1967 interview he'd said "the only glimmer of hope is anarchism" before adding "not the popular misconception of it-men in black cloaks lurking round with hidden bombs-but a freedom of every man being personally responsible for himself." Although he was careful never to acknowledge the source of his views, Jagger had admired the anarcho-capitalist attitude of Giorgio Gomelsky, the Rolling Stones' first manager.

By May 1968, the insurrection of the Paris students was well underway and Jagger followed it avidly, believing that President Charles de Gaulle was about to be violently overthrown. In fact de Gaulle was able to outflank the students and restore order.

This was the backdrop to the Stones' song, 'Street Fighting Man', which was recorded at Olympic in the final week of May. Long before it became a track on 'Beggars Banquet', it was released as a single in the US at the end of August. The timing proved inopportune. In the run-up to the Democratic Convention in Chicago, it was banned by many American radio program directors who simple-mindedly assumed that because Jagger was singing about revolution then he must be endorsing it. It thus reached no higher than # 48 on the Billboard Hot 100. Told that the record was considered subversive, Jagger snapped "of course it's subversive!" Yet he quickly added "you can't start a revolution with a record. I only wish you could."

The superficial impression created by the lyric would be emphasised by the accompanying instrumental – Keith Richards' galvanic acoustic guitar and Charlie Watts' fiercely rhythmic percussion boosted by heavy bass drum played by recruited multi-instrumentalist, Dave Mason.

Yet for all the thunderous force unleashed by Richards, Watts and Mason, there's a deliberate ambiguity in the lyrics which went over the heads of the PDs. The singer begins with words about marching feet and fighting in the street. But he soon counts himself out of direct involvement. He can do no other than sing for a rock 'n' roll band. It's not just a question of being out of place in politically sleepy London because, after shouting "no!!", the singer seems to mock the very notion of anarchist violence.

What's more, the protracted outro is the epitome of relaxed musicality, with Nicky Hopkins' beautiful piano playing, Dave Mason switching to the South Asian shehnai and Brian Jones languorously droning on the tamboura, the long-necked string instrument which for centuries had held sway from the Balkans via the Levant to India. In actual fact the melody of the verses of 'Street Fighting Man', much of which was written by Jagger rather than– as usual –by Richards, is leaden and only offset by the jaunty rock 'n' roll staccato in the chorus.

At this stage in his life, Mick Jagger was pulled in different directions. On the one hand, he still felt himself to be an outsider. The vicious flak he'd taken over his 'non-Aryan' appearance had led him to empathise with African-American music and, politically, he'd been drawn to anarchism as the most radically anti-Establishment ideology. Yet, on the other hand, Jagger was attracted to the luxurious lifestyle of the wealthy Stones' entourage. He loved to drive his Daimler to shop at Harrods and when he and Marianne Faithfull moved into 48 Cheyne Walk, Chelsea, they had a Regency bed installed plus a Louis XV bath.

Later in 68, Jagger dismissed the disorganised second protest demonstration in Grosvenor Square with the sarcastic words "there's not much politesse in anarchy." His attitude contrasted with that of John Lennon who, after he fell in love with Yoko Ono, moved sharply to the left. In 1971 Lennon would compose what is in effect an anarchist hymn, 'Imagine', where he invokes the three bugbears of classic anarchism– nationalism, faith and property. By this time, Mick Jagger, not yet thirty, had relocated to the south of France, enjoying life as a tax exile, the anti-Establishment posture of his earlier years now a thing of the past. And, in 1977, he would be brusquely dismissed by John Lydon, frontman of the Sex Pistols, singer of 'Anarchy in the UK' as a "daft old fart."

CHAPTER 44

— ✿ —

Keith Richards- " I Like to Whip 'Em So Hard"

THE ROLLING STONES' transition to rock began when Brian Jones reluctantly acquiesced in 'Jumpin' Jack Flash' as the single to be released in May 68. After that, his incapacitation and absences accelerated the change.

Keith Richards was the prime mover in the transition. 'Satisfaction' and its follow-up, 'Get Off My Cloud', had seemed to him the way the band should go and the success of 'Jumpin' Jack Flash' reaffirmed that. He explained it this way – "with 'Jumpin' Jack Flash' and 'Street Fighting Man' I'd discovered a new sound I could get out of an acoustic guitar. That grinding, dirty sound came out of these crummy little motels where the only thing you had to record with was this new invention called the cassette recorder. Playing an acoustic you'd overload the Philips cassette player to the point of distortion so that when you played it back it was effectively an electric guitar. He went on-"'Street Fighting Man' is all acoustics. Even the high-end lead is through a cassette player with no limiter just distortion- just two acoustics played right into the mic and hit very hard."

Expanding on his personal guitar technique, Richards said, of 'Street Fighting Man', "on that opening riff, I used enormous force on the strings. I'm not a hard hitter, more of a striker. It's not the force as much as it's a whip action. I'm almost releasing the power before my fingers meet the strings. I'm a big string -breaker because I like to whip 'em so hard."

Another highly important factor in moving to the Stones' rock sound was Keith Richards' adoption of open tunings. He said "until 68 we were on the road so much I had no time to experiment. I knew these old blues

239

guys were obviously using other tunings. I was trying to figure out Fred McDowell shit and Blind Willie McTell stuff. So in 68 I started to get into that and also the Nashville tuning the country boys have. I was working on open D and open E tunings."

These were the factors which established the definitive Stones' sound- visceral, brusque and resonant. They enabled an emboldened Keith to emerge from the shadow of Mick Jagger and take his place side-by-side onstage with the frontman. Many male Stones' fans couldn't identify with Jagger but they could all relate to a hitherto inarticulate guy who spoke through his axe and bonded band and audience in an elemental rite. As a guitarist, Keith Richards contrasted with the likes of Jimi Hendrix, Jimmy Page and Eric Clapton, eschewing intricate solos in favour of punchy licks and power -packed riffs. As a composer, Richards melded rock 'n' roll staccato with the harshness of country blues but he was increasingly influ- enced by country rock as a result of his friendship with Gram Parsons of the Byrds.

Just as Richards changed the sound of the Stones, so Mick Jagger adopted a totally different lyrical stance. Complex wordplay was aban- doned in favour of a heavy emphasis on sex. In America the countercul- ture was rendering the showbiz prurience of Ed Sullivan obsolete and Jagger was quick to take advantage of the effective absence of cen- sorship. What's more, blatantly sexual lyrics fitted in with his onstage dancing. In the early years of the Rolling Stones, Jagger's movements at the mic were relatively restrained. Yet, in the late Sixties, quoted to the effect that dancing was sublimated sex, he switched to what he called the rooster strut -with the aim of incarnating the rampant male sexuality which the older generation found deeply offensive.

On 'Beggars Banquet' there are two blatantly sexual tracks. In 'Parachute Woman', the singer urges the woman to join him for a ride, asks her to blow him and brags that he's in full priapic mode and eager for solid rhythmic action. 'Stray Cat Blues' goes further, with the singer a rock star boasting of his encounter with an underage groupie. Both numbers are trashy but they served the purpose of testing the waters. A couple of years earlier songs like these would have provoked outrage. Now, in the absence of reaction, Mick Jagger knew he was free to concentrate on similar themes but with much cleverer lyrics.

There would be one last lyrically ambitious song on which the Stones would heavily focus during lengthy recording sessions in June 68. This was 'Sympathy for the Devil', which Mick Jagger sang in the persona of Lucifer revelling in his role as instigator of a succession of historical evils from the Crucifixion to the Second World War and culminating in a topical reference to the assassination of Robert Kennedy. His inspiration was said to have been the publication of the long- censored novel by the Russian writer, Mikhail Bulgakov, 'The Master and Margarita.' The book had apparently been a present from Marianne Faithfull.

'Sympathy for the Devil' is a ponderous and dismal effort. It's scarcely a rock song in that the rhythm, settled by Charlie Watts after much experiment, is a samba. And it's weighed down by a dreary melody, chiefly composed by Jagger. There's a high-pitched chorus sung by nine voices including Anita Pallenberg and Marianne Faithfull, consisting of the word 'whoo' uttered over a hundred times on the track. Doubtless intended to be sinister, the effect is merely ludicrous.

Unreleased as a single in either the UK or America, 'Sympathy for the Devil' served its purpose nevertheless. It fascinated the nascent school of rock criticism, delighted that their chosen genre had been linked with an acclaimed piece of world literature. And, in an era when art cinema was still taken with immense seriousness, the Stones got lucky when they were filmed by Maoist French director Jean-Luc Godard, working on the number in the recording studio. Godard's subsequent film, entitled 'One + One', treated Jagger's apolitical lyric as if it was a covert revolutionary text.

Jan Wenner, the youthful editor of newly founded 'Rolling Stone', was granted a sneak preview of 'Beggars Banquet' and his rave review set the tone for its ultimate acclaim not only by young rock critics such as Jon Landau and Dave Marsh but by the wider liberal media. 'Time' savoured what it called "raw vitality and authentic simplicity." Geoffrey Cannon of the Guardian was fascinated with 'Sympathy for the Devil' and what he considered to be its evocation of horror while the Chicago Sun Times'

Carl Bernstein went clean over the top, insisting that "the Stones have released their rawest, rudest, most arrogant, most savage record yet – and it's beautiful!"

Despite the enthusiasm of the intelligentsia, 'Beggars Banquet' didn't succeed in storming the album charts, reaching # 3 in the UK and # 5 on the Billboard 200. For all the heavy emphasis on lyrics, it had no appeal to dancers and, with the sole exception of 'No Expectations', scant melodic charm. But that wasn't the point. The Stones, at one stroke, leaped to the forefront of British rock bands, leaving the Who, Cream, the Jimi Hendrix Experience and Led Zeppelin in the shade. Already Mick Jagger was anticipating the advent of stadium rock where male fans would congregate to hear Keith Richards' vibrant sounds and so-called 'rock chicks' would revel in his own exuberant onstage antics.

CHAPTER 45

—— ✑ ——

Exit Brian Jones

THE DISSOLUTION OF the original Rolling Stones was a long, drawn-out process which lasted seven months. It began on November 17 1968 when the band's founder, Brian Jones, showed open contempt for a song written by frontman Mick Jagger and musical director Keith Richards. The song was 'You Can't Always Get What You Want', a title triggered by Decca Records' rejection of the cover the band wanted for 'Beggars Banquet.'

'You Can't Always Get What You Want', eventually released as a B side, was a number soon dear to the hearts of rock critics, who relished its drug -oriented lyric. But, with a ponderous melody chiefly written by Mick Jagger, it's sluggish and repetitive. Its redeeming feature is the wonderful piano and organ playing of Al Kooper, the superb American session musician, renowned for his work with Bob Dylan.

Although Brian Jones had warmly welcomed the recruitment of Kooper, he couldn't reconcile with the song itself. The plain fact was that Jones was never a rocker. He'd been upset by Jagger and Richards' flirtation with rock, at the time of 'Satisfaction' in 65, and had toyed with the idea of quitting the band then and there. Yet, throughout the period of progressive pop, he'd remained a key figure. Disillusioned by 'Beggars Banquet', he was dismayed at the prospect of an all out rocking album. He showed his studied indifference to the new Jagger-Richards song by languishing outside the studio reading a textbook on botany.

It was scarcely surprising that Jagger and Richards were infuriated by Jones' attitude. It wasn't the first time that breaking with him had crossed their minds but they'd held back for two reasons, one artistic, the other commercial. Jones' multi-instrumental virtuosity wasn't something that could be lightly dispensed with. What's more, there was his still undiminished appeal to girls in the fanbase. Now, however, with Jones in poor physical shape, they began to think different. Bringing in top-class session musicians such as Nicky Hopkins or Al Kooper could flesh out the textures of tracks in the way which Jones had hitherto done. But, sooner or later, they would need to draft in an outstanding second guitarist.

Had Brian Jones himself enjoyed normal health and been in good spirits, it's likely he would've taken the bull by the horns and quit the Rolling Stones. Yet, he was undermined by asthma more and more. His addiction to downers continued even after the threat of jail had been lifted from his shoulders. Jones lived under dark clouds, with only rare moments of sunlight such as when he completed the purchase of Cotchford Farm and when he and Suki Potier took a vacation in Ceylon at the start of 69.

When the Stones reassembled at Olympic on February 9 to begin work on the album later titled 'Let It Bleed', Jones was permitted to play on a couple of tracks. He contributed percussion on 'Midnight Rambler' and auto harp on 'You Got The Silver' before being abruptly sidelined within a couple of days.

Before too long a familiar face reappeared. Jack Nitzsche flew in to supervise the final arrangement of 'You Can't Always Get What You Want.' It was he who invited the London Bach Choir to participate. He was accompanied by yet another front rank American session musician, Ry Cooder, an outstanding exponent of open tuned guitar.

Nitzsche hadn't worked with the Rolling Stones for over two years and was staggered at the change in atmosphere. He said "the next time I saw them they were different people. There were whole different attitudes. It wasn't loose and friendly any more. It had become affected and decadent."

Nitzsche had already picked up hints of change the year before when he wrote the score for the movie 'Performance.' This was an English film written by Stones' hanger- on Donald Cammell and starring Mick Jagger in the role of Turner, an ex-rockstar mixed up with gangsters. Although it would achieve cult status in later decades, it was a pretentious effort. Nitzsche suspected that Jagger was carrying the Turner role over into private life. Arriving at Nitzsche's apartment before they drove together to see rushes of the movie, Jagger was openly cross dressing and wearing lipstick and eyeliner.

Emboldened by his Establishment pardon, Jagger was carrying himself with nonchalant disregard for what anyone thought. Never short of confidence, his demeanour had become arrogant. Said Nitzsche "a whole new attitude comes over Jagger in these moments-this aloof look when he looks down on everybody and he'll dance whenever he gets the chance and say nasty things once in a while."

At Olympic Jack Nitzsche witnessed at first hand Mick Jagger's sarcastic bullying of an enfeebled Brian Jones. Guitar in hand, Jones had asked Jagger "what should I play?" Jagger had shrugged his shoulders and replied "anything you want, Brian." When Jones played something, Jagger cut him short with the words "no, that's no good, Brian." When Jones tried again, Jagger responded "no, that's no good either, Brian." Next, Jones made an attempt on harmonica only for Jagger to give him a baleful stare before throwing his coat over his shoulder and striding pointedly out of the studio.

There were those who thought that Brian Jones had brought this on himself. Certainly Glyn Johns, who'd replaced the sympathetic Eddie Kramer as chief engineer, felt like that. As to producer Jimmy Miller, he isolated Jones in a special booth, later claiming that Keith Richards had urged him to "just tell him to piss off out of here." But Jones didn't take the hint until one day, in an echo of the Eel Pie Island decree, Jagger told him "just go home, Brian!"

Jagger and Richards obviously needed the support of the other two band members to ostracise Jones in this way. Charlie Watts went along with it, later justifying his attitude with the feeble words "Brian wasn't very nice."Brian Jones' only supporter within the band was Bill Wyman, who resented not being credited for his own musical input beyond bass playing. Although not blind to how difficult Jones could sometimes be, he was the only one to take account of the extent to which his bandmate was suffering from asthma. Whilst no one seeing Jones, inhaler in hand and wheezing desperately, could be in any doubt about that, even Wyman hadn't yet begun to suspect the additional burden of epilepsy. There were no recorded instances of Jones blacking out while in the company of other band members but Wyman later learned the truth from Jones' girlfriends. Without doubt, Bill Wyman's emotional intelligence was on a higher level than that of Jagger and Richards. Still, he didn't confront the other two about their attitude to Jones.

Jack Nitzsche made an attempt to do this. He said "I thought Mick and Keith were being really shitty to Brian. I talked to Mick a couple of times about it but he said he'd tried everything he possibly could to make it work out with Brian and it didn't."

As rumours of conflict within the Stones reached the wider scene, Brian Jones, always well liked by other musicians, received support. Pete Townshend of the Who took Jagger and Richards to task over their attitude to Jones but they said they were determined not to let him drag them down. And George Harrison would later pointedly remarked "there was nothing wrong with Brian that a little more love wouldn't have cured."

Meanwhile, the recording of 'Let It Bleed' proceeded throughout March, and again in the summer before being completed near the end of the year. It contains one or two good songs, notably the powerful 'Gimme Shelter', for which Nitzsche recruited fiery gospel singer Merry Clayton, and the relaxed 'You Got The Silver', a rare number sung by Keith Richards. But it's scarred by crude efforts such as the unsubtle 'Midnight Rambler', the stomping and sleazy title track and the dreadful 'Monkey Man.' Nevertheless, it would be welcomed with open arms by the rock critics. Greil Marcus wrote about it at great length in 'Rolling Stone', wallowing in vague talk such as that its "greatest songs reach for reality and end up confronting it, almost mastering what is real or what reality will feel like as the years fade in."

In their reviews of 'Let It Bleed' some rock critics would insist that it marked the Stones returning to their original blues style. Others would use the term 'bluesrock' to denote the amalgam of blues with rock 'n' roll. But this was not how Brian Jones had described the Rolling Stones' musical policy in his letters to the BBC and 'Disc' in 1963. He made it plain that the band's style would be based on rhythm and blues ranging from Bo Diddley through Jimmy Reed to Muddy Waters.

The rock critics' genre definitions were grounded in ethnicity regardless of actual musical style. For them 'R&B' signified black artists recording for black record buyers. They refused to accept British Rhythm and Blues as a coherent subgenre, asserting that BRB bands were no more than blues imitators- until they gravitated to rock 'n' roll.

The rock of 'Let It Bleed', the album, does have a solid basis in blues but this is the country blues of McDowell and McTell. It has little in common with the rhythm and blues sounds which Brian Jones had described as 'Negro pop music' and which seemed to him the essence of memorable melodies and sheer danceability. But by this time Jones had been reduced to playing the IBC demos from 63, tracks such as Jimmy Reed's 'Bright Lights, Big City'– to anyone who would listen- as templates of the Rolling Stones' original R&B style.

The niceties of musicology held little interest for Mick Jagger. In future years he would dismiss them as "theological disputes" and, in the spring of 69, he was focusing on the prospect of a lucrative American tour. With Brian Jones' drug convictions a probable impediment to that, he was all the more eager to find a replacement. Keith Richards talked it over with Ian Stewart and it was Stu who was given the task of sorting out suitable candidates.

But in April 69, against all expectations, Brian Jones began to revive. A key factor in this was his break with Suki Potier, who'd been steeped in drugs. Three months earlier, at the Revolution club in London, he met a twenty-two-year-old Swedish dancer, Anna Wohlin. Compared to Potier, Wohlin was relatively untouched by drugs and she was delighted to move in with Jones at Cotchford Farm.

Elated by the adoration of his Swedish lover, Brian Jones resolved to clean up his life. Forswearing downers, he began to swim regularly in the luxurious pool at the rear of the house and bought a pair of Afghan hounds. He made every effort to integrate with the locals who, initially suspicious of a so-called 'rockstar' in their midst, were surprised to find him quietly spoken and courteous. And he made every effort to ensure that visitors had no illicit substances in their possession.

Jones was certain he could rely on his housekeeper and his gardener and hoped the same would apply to Stones' staffer, Frank Thorogood. Thorogood was a self-employed builder who'd worked for Keith Richards at Redlands and Jones now asked him to carry out renovations at Cotchford Farm. The only problem was that Allen Klein had left Jones strapped for cash and relying on promises. Meanwhile, Jones let Thorogood stay at the property during the week before returning home to London at the weekend.

Drug-free as he now was, Brian Jones could not yet face the world without the crutch of alcohol. Wohlin hoped to limit him to Blue Nun but couldn't prevent him loading up on wine. What's more, he was still sorely troubled by asthma. Indeed Bobby Korner, wife of his old mentor, Alexis, found him "physically diminished and using his inhalers all the time." He'd invited the Korners, whom he hadn't seen in ages, to visit him and discuss possible music ventures. Although Alexis Korner was pleased to find Jones in an upbeat mood and "happier than he'd been for many years", he noted that Jones was reluctant to play guitar or even harmonica, the instruments with which he first made his name.

By this time Brian Jones told his bandmates that he wanted to record separately with a group of his own but said nothing about a permanent divorce. He contacted his friend Micky Waller, a highly regarded drummer on the London rhythm and blues scene and Waller recruited two up-and-coming young musicians, bassist Boz Burrell and guitarist Martin Stone, who was also a singer. In early May these three joined Brian Jones to demo a couple of songs he'd written. Nothing came of this but at least Jones had made a tentative start to resurrecting his musical career.

Depicted as a stick in the mud blues freak by the likes of Andrew Oldham, Brian Jones was nothing of the sort and, in the summer of 69, he was listening avidly to such records as the Beatles' 'The Ballad of John and Yoko' and 'Proud Mary' by Creedence Clearwater Revival.

Since their turn -of -the year holiday in Brazil, Mick Jagger and Keith Richards – now styling themselves the 'Glimmer Twins'– had been working on a song they believed would be the ideal vehicle for the stadium rock shows they had in mind. This was 'Honky Tonk Women.' The lyric was key. Set wholly in America, the singer's a country loser weeping into his beer and risking a dose of the clap as he resorts to hookers after a failed affair.

Wising up fast, the singer heads north for a sophisticated sexual encounter with a New York City divorcee. He recalls the woman covering him with roses before savouring the memory of a fantastic orgasm. This would be, as Jagger saw it, the ideal scenario for him to stalk the stage with his rooster strut. As for Keith Richards, he'd come up with a truly thunderous riff and could scarcely wait to get it on wax.

Fortunately, Ian Stewart's enquiries had borne fruit. Brian Jones' replacement would be a twenty-year-old Hertfordshire guitarist, Mick Taylor. Young as he was, Taylor, the son of a De Havilland aircraft fitter, was a highly regarded member of John Mayall's Blues Breakers. He jumped at the chance of joining what would soon be billed as 'the greatest rock and roll band on earth.' Cherubic and unassuming, Taylor's looks and demeanour were scarcely Stones- like but he was a prodigiously skilful guitarist and a wholly sincere musician.

On May 24 1969, Mick Taylor joined the others to record 'Honky Tonk Women.' It's a great rock track, powered by Charlie Watts' existentially funky rhythm, devoid of gratuitous soloing but lit up by Keith Richards' guitar open tuned in G (a la Ry Cooder), heralded by Richards' pulverising Telecaster riff and punctuated by Mick Taylor's country -influenced rock licks between the verses. The lyric, sex- oriented yet subtle, reflects the collapse of censorship in the late Sixties.

In terms of music history, 'Honky Tonk Women' is highly significant. It was the song, above all others, which inaugurated the era of stadium rock. Whereas the Rolling Stones' iconic pop songs were aimed first and foremost at dissemination by radio, the switch to rock would summon Stones fans in their thousands to a communal event where they responded viscerally to the beat and exultantly joined in with singalong choruses.

Mick Taylor's successful debut had removed the last obstacle to Mick Jagger and Keith Richards sacking Brian Jones from the Stones. Accompanied by Charlie Watts, they drove down to Cotchford Farm on

June 8, anticipating a confrontation. But there was none. Far from it, Jones seemed relieved about the parting of the ways. There is no evidence that he argued with Jagger and Richards about whether they had the right to appropriate the name 'Rolling Stones' which he was the one to come up with shortly after he founded the band. It's something he might well have argued about had he so chosen -much in the way that Keith Relf and Jim McCarty had effectively obliged Jimmy Page to drop the monicker 'New Yardbirds' and call his band Led Zeppelin.

Although Brian Jones confirmed to the media that he hoped to continue his friendship with the Stones, his press release was telling. He stated "I no longer see eye to eye with the others over the discs we are cutting. Their music is not to my taste any more. The music Mick and Keith have been writing has progressed at a tangent to my own musical tastes. I have a desire to play my own brand of music and we have agreed that an amicable termination of our relationship is the only answer."

Buoyed by his break with the Stones, Brian Jones promptly phoned Cheltenham and invited his parents to stay with him at Cotchford Farm. He'd maintained a tenuous relationship with his father throughout his years in London but now he finally made peace with his mother. Lewis and Louisa Jones were delighted to see Brian evidently settled in rural Sussex and maintaining his determination to stay off drugs. What's more, he told them that he and Anna intended to start a family. As the women talked indoors, Brian and his father strolled round the spacious grounds and Lewis happily nodded when Brian modestly remarked "I haven't done so bad, have I, dad?" After a serene weekend, the Jones parents went home immensely reassured. They were not to know that they would never see their son alive again.

CHAPTER 46

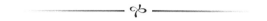

The Unmysterious Death of Brian Jones

On July 7 1969 the East Sussex coroner, Dr Angus Somerville, recorded a verdict of 'death by misadventure' in the case of Lewis Brian Hopkins Jones, a twenty-seven-year-old musician, who had died at his home in Hartfield on July 2.

Somerville was relying on witness statements by Anna Wohlin, Frank Thorogood and a nurse named Janet Lawson who was staying with Thorogood in a flat over the garage at Cotchford Farm. Wohlin, Thorogood and Lawson all described dragging a lifeless Brian Jones from the bottom of the swimming pool. Attempts at artificial respiration proved futile and the police were called to the scene. None of the three could shed any light on the cause of death because, although they'd been swimming in the pool as had Jones himself, they'd returned separately to the house while he stayed in the water.

Somerville relied heavily on the report by Dr Albert Sachs, the pathologist at Queen Victoria Hospital, East Grinstead. Sachs' report was unusually brief and it was flawed by a bad mistake over Brian Jones' height. Sachs stated there was evidence of alcohol ingestion but not sufficient to incapacitate Jones. There was also evidence that he'd taken sleeping tablets but not in sufficient quantity to have any effect other than that for which they'd been prescribed. On the other hand, Jones' liver was badly enlarged. Sachs added that he could find no evidence of an asthmatic attack.

From the witness statements and from Dr Sachs' report, Dr Somerville concluded that Brian Jones had died from drowning - aggravated by drink and drugs. He gratuitously added his personal opinion that Jones had wilfully disregarded persistent warnings about drugs.

It was scarcely surprising that many people remained baffled how Brian Jones, a man known to be an excellent swimmer who swam untroubled in difficult Mediterranean waters, could have succumbed in his own swimming pool on a warm summer's night when the pool itself had been heated to a temperature of 90°F. What's more, witness statements indicated that, although Jones was a bit woozy from having been drinking, he was nowhere near drunk. Certainly he was badly troubled with asthma and hay fever and the pollen count on the night was unusually high. But the pathologist's report had specifically excluded asthma as a factor in his demise. These inconsistencies led to lingering suspicions about possible foul play.

Nevertheless, it wasn't till the mid-Eighties that a series of books began to appear alleging that Brian Jones had been murdered and spreading conspiracy theories. They centred on Frank Thorogood, who'd been the last person to see Jones alive. It was alleged that Thorogood had quarrelled with Jones earlier in the day over wages he was owed for the building work he was doing. Thorogood was of course taller and far more powerful than Jones and he was now accused of holding Jones down under the water. The allegations against Thorogood extended to Stones' chauffeur, Tom Keylock, even though Keylock had not been present at the farm during the specific timeframe.

In his biography of Brian Jones, music writer Paul Trynka extensively refutes the allegations of murder and, whilst dismissing the inquest as flawed, accepts its conclusion of death by misadventure. Whereas the conspiracy buffs rely on incompatible evidence and wild speculation, Trynka's approach is analytical and rigorous.

In actual fact there's no need whatever to postulate foul play on the part of Frank Thorogood, Tom Keylock- or any other mysterious person or persons unknown- to give a logical and sufficient account of the likeliest cause of Brian Jones' death.

Although Jones was never diagnosed as an epileptic, the anecdotal evidence that he may well have suffered from epilepsy is plentiful. Commenting on the circumstances of his death, Anita Pallenberg made a very significant observation. She said "he'd been in that situation many times before but there was always someone there to turn him on his side and this time there wasn't."

Suki Potier didn't specifically comment on what might have happened at Cotchford Farm but she'd earlier said, regarding his blackouts, "it happens all the time." In addition, George Chkiantz witnessed Jones blacking out at Tangier and, previous to that, so did Sonja Kristina and Romy in London.

In the course of time, Bill Wyman became suspicious that his bandmate's death had resulted from an epileptic attack and he succeeded in tracing Jones' daughter, Carol, who confirmed that she'd been diagnosed with temporal lobe epilepsy and had been prescribed medication for it. The symptoms Carol described to Wyman were identical to those suffered by her father at various times.

When Dr Sachs conducted his post-mortem, he was unaware of Brian Jones' history of sudden loss of consciousness and, in terms of Jones' medical record, knew only that he was an asthmatic. Once Sachs had excluded asthma as a cause of death, Dr Somerville felt free to pinpoint drugs.

What really happened, however, may well have been that, a few minutes after he was left alone in the swimming pool, Brian Jones had an epileptic seizure. Even if he'd been sitting on the edge of the pool using his inhaler, he would have immediately lost consciousness with fatal results.

Somerville's censorious comments – "he was warned but he wouldn't listen" – ignore the fact that, during the last months of his life, even though he was still drinking heavily, Brian Jones had turned his back on drugs.

Somerville's conclusions perfectly suited the puritanical moralists of the age, the very people who'd been affronted by the Rolling Stones' hedonism. Equally the conspiracy theories which emerged in the Eighties suited those eager to debunk the so-called 'Swinging Sixties.' While the Coroner didn't have all the facts before him, the conspiracy theorists preferred humbug to evidence.

CHAPTER 47

༺ ༾

Jones, the Stones and the Sixties

ON THE EVENING of Brian Jones' death, the Stones were at Olympic Studios recording tracks for 'Let It Bleed.' With the exception of Bill Wyman, who'd adjourned to a nearby hotel, they were still there in the early hours of the following day when they received the appalling news. It was broken to them by Ian Stewart, who'd been informed in a phone call from Hartfield by Tom Keylock's wife.

The media had already been alerted and soon film and TV camera-men arrived, eager to film the band's reaction. Mick Taylor understandably showed little emotion. He was in an invidious position having replaced Jones, a man he didn't know personally, a mere few weeks before. It was only natural that he felt out of place.

Both Mick Jagger and Charlie Watts were stunned and speechless, slumped and staring into space. It was Keith Richards who broke the silence-with one totally inappropriate word, "finally!" Glaring defiantly at the cameras, Richards swigged a bottle of booze.

The Stones were in the advanced stages of preparation for a free concert to be held in Hyde Park. The intention was to mark their return to public performance for the first time in two years and also to introduce Mick Taylor to the fans.

All this was of course overshadowed by Brian Jones' demise and a collective decision was taken to go ahead with the concert but to treat it as a memorial to him. Thus, on July 5 1969, events went ahead in front of a crowd of several hundred thousand.

Before the gig proceeded, Mick Jagger addressed the assembled throng, displaying more than one aspect of his complex personality.

Ever the showman, he took the stage in a specially designed white dress and summoned the mass release of hundreds of white butterflies. Then he revealed once again his intellectual side, silencing the crowd as he read two stanzas from Percy Shelley's elegy, 'Adonais', written in 1821 to mark the death of fellow Regency poet John Keats. Quoting Shelley on Keats was highly appropriate. The two poets had flourished in the recently ended Regency era, as had Lord Byron. English literature was arguably as fully transformed during that epoch as was English music in the Sixties.

His reading concluded, Jagger tore the dress off to reveal a violet T-shirt and white loon pants. He then dashed across the stage leading the band into a set list including such massive hits as 'Satisfaction' and 'Jumpin' Jack Flash' plus the newly issued 'Honky Tonk Women.' Brian Jones' contribution to the recording of these songs had been relatively minor -and for the last one non-existent-and it was only on the closing number, 'No Expectations', that the Stones played something closely associated with him.

There were those who accused the Stones, and Mick Jagger in particular, of hypocrisy. This was an unjust charge. Bill Wyman would record that Jagger was in tears both on the day the news broke and on the morning before the concert. Wyman himself and Charlie Watts were badly affected and, by common consent, the Stones' rhythm section was a pale shadow of its usual self on the night of the Hyde Park gig. Keith Richards could scarcely be charged with hypocrisy because his one word comment – "finally!" – was as callous as it was absurd.

Brian Jones' funeral took place in Cheltenham on July 10, his cortege wending its way through the streets of his home town before thousands of onlookers including scores of weeping teenage girls. His body was buried in Cheltenham Town Cemetery.

Of the original Rolling Stones, three attended Jones' funeral. Ian and Cynthia Stewart were there, as were Charlie and Shirley Watts and Bill Wyman with Astrid Lundstrom. Mick Jagger had already left for Australia, together with Marianne Faithfull, where he was scheduled to film scenes for a biopic in which he played the role of the outlaw Ned Kelly. As for Keith Richards, who could have attended either with Anita Pallenberg or, more diplomatically, on his own, he decided not to go.

The reactions of the various Stones immediately after Jones' death would be reflected in their attitudes across the subsequent decades. Charlie Watts had previously been critical of Jones at various times but he would later reflect "Brian got a lot nicer in the last few years before he died."

In the days before the Hyde Park concert Mick Jagger had said "I'm deeply saddened. I feel as if something has gone." There's no reason to doubt his sincerity. Whilst Jagger had been guilty of sarcastically bullying Jones early in 69, this didn't spring from any personal animosity. Nevertheless he was ruthlessly determined to oust a bandmate whom he described, accurately at that time, as "not fully functioning."

Two years earlier, when he kicked out a psychologically dishevelled Andrew Oldham, Jagger had made it clear that he himself was the one and only leader of the Stones. Band politics aside, he'd always been fully appreciative of Brian Jones' exceptional musical value– until Jones' breakdown in 67.

Whereas Keith Richards was unequivocally pissed off with progressive pop and with Brian Jones' advocacy of it, Mick Jagger initially had a foot in both camps. He took his time to weigh up the prospects for 'Child of the Moon' and 'Jumpin' Jack Flash' before coming down decisively in favour of the latter.

Keith Richards' callous comment on first hearing of Brian Jones' death would be effectively reiterated over the years, culminating in harsh remarks made in his autobiography, 'Life', published in 2013. They stemmed from a failure to understand the roots of Jones' decline. Richards would never deny Jones' extraordinary musical gifts and would sometimes briefly reminisce about their time together at Edith Grove, describing Jones as "a great guy in those days." But he went on to speak as if Jones had almost willed his own destruction.

Realising the incongruity of him addressing Jones' drug intake, Richards said, in interview, "I know I'm the last person to speak as far as drugs are concerned" before defiantly asserting "but I'm still here!" Richards' decision to quit smack took guts and Jones had never taken a similarly bold step over softer drugs. Yet Richards always enjoyed fundamentally robust health, something which had been denied to Brian Jones since childhood. Richards knew full well that Jones was an asthmatic yet he rarely seemed to take that on board when discussing his former friend.

There was of course a deeper issue than asthma alone as far as Jones' health was concerned. Neither Keith Richards nor Mick Jagger nor Charlie Watts could be blamed for failing to recognise it. They'd never once seen Brian black out while he was with them. Neither had Bill Wyman. But it was to Wyman's immense credit that he later suspected the major cause of his friend and colleague's decline – and probably of his ultimate death. It was not until the publication of Wyman's book, 'Stone Alone' in 1990 that the issue was explored.

The attitude of the surviving Stones was mirrored by that of the rock critics. Their interest in the pre-68 Rolling Stones was secondary and their appreciation of Brian Jones' fundamental role was marginal. It was all too easy for them to dismiss him as an out of time blues freak who brought himself down by reckless drug indulgence.

Discussing the Hyde Park concert shortly after it took place, Guardian journalist Richard Gott wrote that it "was a great and epoch- making event in British social history." Viewed from a historical perspective, Gott's conclusion seems facile. Seen as a cultural phenomenon, the Sixties had begun with the debut of the Rolling Stones at the Station Hotel in Richmond in February 63. Yet by early 67 at the latest both British Rhythm and Blues and progressive pop had been superseded by rock.

The Rolling Stones had been the vanguard of British rhythm and blues, a sub -genre named by Giorgio Gomelsky but never recognised by US rock critics. Their musicology was hamstrung by an insistence on ethnicity. It reflected an American scene where young white musicians steered clear of what was perceived as a strictly African-American form.

In Britain the situation was entirely different. Young Jamaican immigrants didn't relate to R&B, with only rare exceptions such as Roscoe Gordon. Above all they didn't dig white guys playing blues-derived music, as they made clear to Gomelsky when he visited bluebeat clubs with various bands. By contrast, Chicago blues musicians would hail the Rolling Stones as soon as they first arrived at Chess.

Where the Rolling Stones led, a bunch of brilliant British rhythm and blues bands soon followed – the Yardbirds, Manfred Mann, the Animals, the Spencer Davis Group and Them. Unlike the Rolling Stones, they were commercially unsuccessful within that sub-genre. Yet they scored hit after hit once they turned to progressive pop. Lacking songwriters of Jagger and Richards calibre from within their own ranks, the Yardbirds achieved success when they called on Graham Gouldman, as did Spencer Davis when they brought in Jackie Edwards. That didn't happen for Them but, when frontman Van Morrison broke clear and established himself as a singer-songwriter, he was both highly successful and critically acclaimed.

Then there were the Kinks. Frustrated by the band's lack of rhythm and blues success, lead singer Ray Davies emerged as a gifted song-writer, the author of iconic pop songs which were also huge hits. Thus, of the outstanding UK songwriters of the Sixties, even including Pete Townshend – the Who had briefly been an R&B band – almost all of them came from the British Rhythm and Blues movement. The obvious excep-tions were Lennon and McCartney but they too had been strongly influ-enced by R&B.

The BRB movement also yielded stellar guitarists. Whereas Jeff Beck had no problem with playing on progressive pop tracks, Eric Clapton and Jimmy Page turned up their noses. Eager to display their technical accomplishments in protracted solos, they craved rock. Dave Davies of the Kinks had already shown there was a big market for this when he surged into distorted guitar on his brother Ray's song 'You Really Got Me', a number one hit in the autumn of 64.

After that there was a gradual drift to rock notably with the Who. Then, when Jimi Hendrix arrived in the UK in September 66, he was promptly crowned as king of rock guitar. His acclaim by fellow axemen and budding rock critics was soon followed by the formation of his band, the Jimi Hendrix Experience. In the following spring they had a # 3 hit on the UK charts with 'Purple Haze.'

Cream had formed shortly before Hendrix's arrival and soon their former Yardbird guitarist Eric Clapton was capitalising big time on the rise of rock. Ex-Spencer Davis singer/guitarist Stevie Winwood, from April 67 onwards, did likewise with Traffic.

By this time Jimmy Page had transformed the Yardbirds into an all-out rock band and when he and Robert Plant launched Led Zeppelin in October 68 the transition to rock was complete. Whereas the progressive pop of the earlier Yardbirds, the Kinks, the original Rolling Stones– and of course the Beatles– was ideally suited to radio and appealed to both sexes, rock's audience was found above all in concerts and its image was increasingly macho. Above all, it became associated with the heavy use of drugs.

Culturally speaking, there was no such thing as a homogenous 'Sixties.' There was an early Sixties when the Rolling Stones spearheaded a breakout from the drab and dismal world of post-war Britain and, on the other hand, a late Sixties when rock began its generation-long dominance of the music scene. Significantly, the advent of rock was acclaimed beyond the specialist magazines such as 'Rolling Stone.' It was widely hailed by the intelligentsia, notably when the movie 'Blowup' was released in the UK in March 67. Directed by cerebral Italian art cinema filmmaker Michelangelo Antonio, this pretentious, convoluted tale of 'Swinging London' featured a scene where Jeff Beck and Jimmy Page launch into hard rock in front of a grim- faced club audience, smashing guitars as they do so.

The violent scene depicted in 'Blowup' was a world away from what took place at the Ealing Jazz Club on April 7 62 when Brian Jones' slow slide guitar captivated an audience which included Mick Jagger and Keith Richards. It was a matter of weeks before they joined Jones and Ian Stewart in the original Rolling Stones. Whilst a common love of blues brought them together – just as it had linked Jagger and Richards when they met by chance six months earlier – the band was not really up and running until it switched to rhythm and blues at the turn of the year following the recruitment of Bill Wyman and Charlie Watts.

It was the debut of the Rolling Stones at the Station Hotel in Richmond which was the truly epochal event of the decade not the Hyde Park concert. Playing to a handful of curious onlookers not hundreds of thousands of worshipful fans, the five instrumentalists comprised an exceptionally talented group, their collective skill honed by countless hours of dedicated rehearsal. And they played vibrant rhythm and blues with total conviction. Every single one of them – boogie-woogie pianist Ian Stewart, rock 'n' roll refugee Bill Wyman, ex-jazz drummer Charlie Watts, Keith Richards ace guitarist à la Chuck Berry and above all their then leader and arranger, slide guitar specialist and brilliant blues harpist Brian Jones – was an outstanding musician. In front of them stood Mick Jagger, not yet the powerful singer he soon became yet brimful of confidence, a complex character who would later develop into a great lyricist.

Set up in Soho in the spring of 62, at the Bricklayers Arms, the Rolling Stones were thinned to a five piece within twelve months by Andrew Oldham's Eel Pie Island decree. They were dissolved, by mutual consent, six years later, at Cotchford Farm on June 8 1969. This is not, of course, what official history records. But official history needs to be revised in the light of primary sources.

The chief primary source for the history of the Rolling Stones is Bill Wyman's diary. In 2015 Wyman was disgusted by the unveiling of a Dartford Borough Council plaque at Dartford Station attributing the formation of the band to Mick Jagger and Keith Richards, whose childhood friendship was renewed there in October 61. When Wyman challenged them, the Council backed down and altered the wording of the plaque.

Wyman was insistent, throughout his campaign, that Brian Jones was the founder of the Rolling Stones and that he'd recruited the others one by one. Pissed off by Wyman's campaign, Keith Richards protested that "Bill wasn't even there." This remark was factually correct. Although he was present at Eel Pie Island, Bill Wyman hadn't been at the Bricklayers Arms (nor, for that matter, was he at Cotchford Farm in June 69). Richards went on to attribute the formation of the band to Ian Stewart, the guy who'd auditioned him at the Bricklayers. In fact, of course, Stewart himself was the first man responding to Brian Jones' ad in 'Jazz News.'

Keith Richards' confusion over the history of the band was dismissed by Jimmy Phelge with the terse comment– "Keith doesn't remember.

It's the fuckin' drugs talking." An alternative explanation is simply that Richards failed to understand the nature of historical record. Bill Wyman didn't need to have been at 7 Broadwick Street. When he joined the band six months later, he would learn all he needed to know from the everyday conversation of the other members, not least Stu, about events which had taken place a mere six months earlier. Unlike Keith Richards, he was not relying on his memory, something which, after fifty years, could play tricks on anyone, regardless of whether they have or haven't done drugs. Bill Wyman had meticulously preserved his diary and he consulted it thoroughly before the publication of 'Stone Alone' in 1990.

Turning to the dissolution of the original Rolling Stones, formalised at Cotchford Farm in June 69, official history doesn't recognise it at all. Two factors have contributed to this. The foremost is that the name of the band remained unchanged. There are unconfirmed reports that, whilst the discussions between Mick Jagger, Keith Richards and Brian Jones were otherwise amicable, there was a clash over Jagger and Richards' right to retain the name 'Rolling Stones' or whether– as with the Yardbirds' split before Led Zeppelin formed– a new and entirely different name should be taken. Whether Brian Jones tamely acquiesced in relinquishing the name of the band he founded or actively protested against it has always remained unclear. Jagger and Richards have never commented on the matter, nor has the sole other witness, Charlie Watts, a man who prefers to keep clear of controversy.

Whilst the facts remain outside the public domain, the effect of the name chosen by Brian Jones continuing after he quit the band left the secret history of the original Rolling Stones consigned to obscurity. This has served the purposes of first and second-generation rock critics, the same men who brushed aside the British Rhythm and Blues Movement as a mere apprenticeship and who hastened to relabel the progressive pop of the Sixties as 'rock.'

The second factor which has blurred the record is the short timeframe between Brian Jones quitting the band and his death – a mere twenty-four days. Attention rapidly shifted from an event which interested only the Stones' devoted fanbase to one which went viral across the globe.

For a decade and more the coroner's verdict – essentially that Jones had died as a result of drug addiction – was not contested. Yet, beginning in the mid- Eighties, conspiracy theories began to flourish. Wilder and wilder the rumours grew despite a paucity of evidence to back them up. The effect of all this was to distract attention from Brian Jones as an extraordinarily gifted and innovative musician. He would be reduced to an object of morbid fascination for true crime buffs. Even after the publication of 'Stone Alone' the popular imagination would be fed with a caricature depiction of Brian Jones focusing solely on hedonistic lifestyle, scarcely mentioning his persecution by the Establishment or his multi-instrumental virtuosity.

The nadir of this nonsense came in the lurid, cliché-ridden 2005 movie, 'Stoned' -replete with silly subtitle 'The Wild and Wycked World of Brian Jones'- which focused attention yet again on the circumstances of Jones' death. His imagination inflamed by sex drugs and rock 'n' roll stereotypes and having swallowed the conspiracy theories hook line and sinker, director Stephen Woolley hastened to dismiss Brian Jones' music. The key words of the movie blurb were "sordid", "debauched" and "deathbed confession." This was a thinly veiled invitation to a shag and dope fest topped off with Jones' alleged murder by Frank Thorogood. The film would conclude with a ludicrous scene in which the ghost of the dead musician makes an arrogant speech to Tom Keylock.

Throughout the movie Woolley demonstrates not the slightest hint of empathy with Brian Jones, depicting him as a snob whose contemptuous attitude to Thorogood inflamed the East End builder. In real life Jones had shown few signs of snobbery. Whatever the attitudes of his parents in Cheltenham, Jones mixed easily with people from all backgrounds in his career as a musician before he founded the Rolling Stones. And within the band, he bonded closely with Bill Wyman whose impoverished Sydenham family contrasted totally with Jones' comfortable childhood home.

Although the majority of film critics saw through Woolley's nonsense and while he was doubtless disappointed by the movie's box office takings, the effect of 'Stoned' was inevitably to tarnish Jones' legacy.

Nevertheless, nothing that trashy movies could do would ever equal the obfuscation brought about by the band's name remaining the same regardless of Brian Jones' secession in June 1969. In actual fact the original Rolling Stones was a completely different band from the Stones. In terms of music it began by reinterpreting rhythm and blues and continued in progressive pop. Only in the last year of its existence did it become a rock band.

The difference went far beyond the fact that Brian Jones founded one band and broke away from the other. It lay in the interaction of the three core members, Jones himself, Mick Jagger and Keith Richards. Originally united in a shared love of rhythm and blues, their common purpose didn't survive the managerial transition from Giorgio Gomelsky to Andrew Oldham. Right from the start Oldham promoted Jagger as the leader. Jagger himself, always a political animal, was buoyed by this. He was determined to seize control of the band, initially musically – from Jones – and later managerially – from Oldham.

Ambition apart, Mick Jagger didn't see Brian Jones as a threat. He himself was a modestly talented musician, competent on harmonica but nothing more. Conversely, Jones' singing never amounted to more than occasional backing vocals. Equally, Jones was no lyricist. He could express himself very well in writing cogently argued letters to jazz journals or the BBC. But he could never begin to match Mick Jagger's flair for words and imaginative use of language. These were limitations which Jones had accepted from the beginning of the band and, even before that, he was hoping to rely on Paul Jones as his singer. Paul Jones was of course a student of English Literature at Oxford and it may well be that Brian believed Paul would have serious potential as a lyricist.

Having failed to persuade Paul, Brian was relieved that Mick was eager to step into the breach. His early reservations about Jagger's singing had disappeared by November 64 when, at Chess, Mick delivered two great bluesy vocals – one on 'Little Red Rooster', the other on an unreleased version of Bill Broonzy's 'Key to the Highway.' What's more, he came to accept that, as the frontman, Jagger would be the prime focus of media attention.

The massive commercial success of 'Satisfaction' spelt the end of the Rolling Stones as a strictly rhythm and blues band. Yet having toyed with the idea of quitting, Jones opted to stay on. Whilst in personal terms Andrew Oldham remained his bête noire, he soon saw that Oldham wasn't bent on rock. As always the Stones' manager had the Beatles in his sights. When the Liverpudlian quartet ceased to be a touring boy band and retired to Abbey Road, Oldham spied an opportunity for the promotion of progressive pop. Jones was cool with this. Friendly with the Beatles, he admired their musicianship and was confident in his own ability to emulate their sounds- just as he recognised Mick Jagger's growth as a lyricist.

It was a different story as far as Brian Jones and Keith Richards were concerned. The foundations of the Rolling Stones' mastery had been built at Edith Grove where, with Jagger often absent at lectures, the pair of them spent day after day perfecting what Richards would later call "the gentle art of guitar weaving." In those days Keith was full of admiration for Brian both musically and socially. Blown away by Brian's brilliance at the Ealing Jazz Club, he was equally wowed by Jones as a chick magnet. Eager to get laid, he could follow in his bandmate's footsteps and get his fair share of what he would later call "feral females."

After Edith Grove was evacuated and Brian Jones moved to Windsor to live with Linda Lawrence and her parents, Keith Richards relocated to Hampstead where he lived with Mick Jagger and Andrew Oldham. When Oldham outflanked Nanker Phelge and sought to promote Jagger and Richards as a songwriting team, Keith saw his chance and he took it.

From early 64 onwards Keith Richards saw both loot and limelight beckoning. He was avid for one and fearful of the other. Speedily shrugging off the Richards family's socialist heritage, he embraced showbiz capitalism with all the enthusiasm of a Dupree- which he also was. Yet as his mum, Doris Dupree Richards, would confirm, Keith was at heart "a shy and sensitive boy." As he admitted, in his 1964 interview with 'Beat Instrumental', he yearned for a screen between himself and the audience. And in his old pal Mick Jagger he found the human equivalent of that.

Whereas Jagger was a tower of strength as far as Keith was concerned, he struggled to emerge from the shadow of Brian Jones. Yet his trump card was his ability to write songs. In the family home that ability had been fostered from an early age by exposure to Doris Richards' wide-ranging musical tastes going from Ella Fitzgerald to Duke Ellington and beyond to Mozart. Doris herself had absorbed jazz at an early age thanks to her dad, Gus Dupree. And Gus himself was a strong influence on Keith.

In contrast to Richards, Brian Jones had been fed on a strict diet of classical music. He lacked the instinctive pop fluency which Keith Richards evidently possessed. Certainly he had the potential to become a consistent songwriter and, had he survived, he might well have done so. When the Rolling Stones were at their absolute peak in the mid-Sixties, Jones began to contribute as a composer. Several iconic songs should strictly have been credited 'Jagger, Jones and Richards' but this was something Andrew Oldham would never have allowed. By the time Jagger elbowed Oldham out, Jones was in no fit condition to stand up for his rights.

There was of course one great song on which the credit should have read 'Keith Richards and Brian Jones.' That song was 'Ruby Tuesday.' Mick Jagger would always be open that he hadn't contributed to its composition. Yet the trademark credit 'Jagger and Richards' still stood.

Buddies at Edith Grove and companions at Courtfield Road, the friendship of Brian Jones and Keith Richards was permanently sundered when Richards took Pallenberg from Jones.

Many decades later, when Richards was being interviewed about "the early days", he paid what seemed like a grudging tribute to Brian Jones' musicianship but added "bit by bit a different Brian came out – a total ME ME ME!!." Yet if the women in the Stones circle are to be believed, the question should rather be -'did a different Keith come out?'

Linda Keith and Keith Richards became lovers while they were both in their late teens. Recalling him in later years, Linda testified to his sensitivity, tenderness and concern for her welfare. He understood her well -as he revealed in his fine lyric for 'Ruby Tuesday.' Yet he himself went on to pretend that the song had really been about a nameless groupie not about Linda before eventually admitting the truth only to coarsely say – "I dunno, she'd pissed off somewhere."

Marianne Faithfull knew Keith Richards well, liked him and, in future years, said how much she'd enjoyed a one night stand with him. She was also Brian Jones' confidante- and briefly his lover- before she fell for Mick Jagger. As Faithfull saw it, Richards had for years looked up to Jones as a fashion icon he yearned to emulate. Suddenly junking his leather jackets, he began to attire himself as a dandy à la Jones. The next thing was that Anita Pallenberg was out of Jones' bed and into Richardses, a feat of sexual one-upmanship from which he never looked back.

The late Sixties saw Keith Richards swerving musical direction. Gone was the subtle lyricist of 'Ruby Tuesday', departed was the complex composer and arranger of 'Have You Seen Your Mother, Baby, Standing in the Shadow?' In his place was the guy rock critics would admiringly hail 'The Human Riff.' He seemed determined to present himself as a tough guy and a survivor, revelling in an increasingly macho image. Yet, before the decade was out, he'd become a slave to heroin.

Over a period lasting many decades, Keith Richards preferred to avoid reference to Brian Jones but, when he did so, it was in increasingly harsh language. Ten years after his bandmate's death, Richards characterised him as a slacker. Speaking of 'Aftermath', he said "I did all the parts on half the album which Brian normally would have done. Sure, I was mad. It wasn't like now when you spend four to six months making an album. Those albums had to be done in ten days, plus another single. That was a fact of life. With Brian becoming a dead weight on top of the work, it threw a lot of the pressure on me." Here surely is the heart of Richards' enduring resentment of Jones – a bandmate whose instrumental colouring might be heavily praised by others but for him was only a source of stress and insecurity.

Turning from Brian Jones the musician to Jones the person, Richards used the phrase "a complete asshole." Certainly Jones had been guilty of various despicable acts. His alleged physical abuse of Anita Pallenberg is open to doubt but he admitted, in his letters to Linda Keith, that he'd been violent towards her. And, as far as friendship is concerned, he hadn't hesitated to betray Giorgio Gomelsky's trust -and indeed he paid a big price for his treachery when he threw in his lot with Andrew Oldham only to find the Hampstead hustler ready to do him down all along the way.

Yet in total contrast to Keith Richards, others would pay tribute to Brian Jones as a likeable friend, as did Paul Jones and George Harrison. And his penultimate lover Suki Potier recalled his previous kindness to her following the death of her previous boyfriend, Tara Browne, in a car crash – "he made me feel like a woman again."

In the final analysis, the breakup of the original Rolling Stones hinged on the personal breach between Keith Richards and Brian Jones and in their differing reactions to Establishment harassment and the drug bust trials. In terms of music, Richards was unlikely to emerge from Jones' shadow until the decisive shift to rock with the vote for 'Jumpin' Jack Flash' over 'Child of the Moon.' Jones had mastered over a score of different instruments and was beginning to find his feet as a pop composer. But guitar was the one that counted with rock critics and, as a bottleneck specialist, he couldn't match Richards' riff-rocking dominance.

Mick Jagger's comments in the immediate aftermath of Brian Jones' death–"I feel as if something has gone" hinted at a possible nostalgia for the pomp of the Rolling Stones' progressive pop, an era when, as a master lyricist, he was just as much in his element as was Jones in his multi-instrumental virtuosity. Yet Jagger had always craved financial reward more than anything else. From his childhood the prospect of amassing a fortune had fascinated him. His mother Eva hit the nail on the head when she recalled–"money doesn't usually interest little boys but it did Mike. He didn't want to be a pilot or an engine driver– he wanted a lot of money!"

By May 68, when the crucial decision for 'Jumpin' Jack Flash' was taken, it was crystal clear to Mick Jagger that the financial future lay with rock. That had been demonstrated by Cream plus the Jimi Hendrix Experience and Jimmy Page with the Yardbirds. Stadium rock would be Jagger's personal avenue to riches, even more so in the US than in England. He made up his mind to ride Route 66 and he never looked back.

Rock was of course by no means incompatible with artistry – as demonstrated in the rhapsodic outro to 'Jumpin' Jack Flash.' Yet artistry was the epitome of the Rolling Stones' peak of progressive pop. Whether it was his hypnotic obbligato on 'The Last Time', his delicate marimbas on 'Out of Time' or his poignant recorder on 'Ruby Tuesday', Brian Jones left an indelible impression. So did Keith Richards' subtle acoustic on 'Lady Jane', Bill Wyman's witty bass on 'Nineteenth Nervous Breakdown', Charlie Watts' cataclysmic drums on 'Paint It Black' and the intricately woven counterpoint of Jones and Richards in 'Sittin' on a Fence' plus other examples too numerous to mention.

In terms of songwriting Mick Jagger and Keith Richards were a truly formidable team, arguably at their joint zenith in 'Have You Seen Your Mother, Baby, Standing in the Shadow?'-before it was brutally truncated by Andrew Oldham. As a lyricist, Mick Jagger kept clear of the complex but sometimes long-winded thought patterns of Bob Dylan. Equally he shied away from John Lennon-style evocations of childhood. Yet he was second to none as an observer of the contemporary scene.

Both in the Sixties and in subsequent decades it was customary for Beatles buffs and Stones supporters to trumpet their own favourites while shouting down 'the other side' like rival football fans. The Beatles' apogee was undoubtedly the 'Sergeant Pepper's Lonely Hearts Club Band' sessions. There would be no Rolling Stones' equivalents to such magnificent tracks as 'A Day in the Life', 'Strawberry Fields' and 'Penny Lane.' Equally the Stones never descended to easy listening banality such as 'When I'm Sixty-Four.'

Where fans stuck up for the Stones, the intelligentsia didn't. Oblivious to Brian Jones' musicological correspondence with 'Jazz News' and the BBC, regardless of Mick Jagger's subtle lyrics, the critics refused to accept the two most articulate Rolling Stones as worthy of serious discussion. Bob Dylan, by contrast, had been accepted as an intellectual from the word go, emerging as he did from the Folk Revival in Greenwich Village. As for John Lennon, as soon as he became the partner of Yoko Ono, prime mover in the Fluxus avant-garde group in New York City, he was belatedly accepted as an honorary intellectual. Conversely, Brian

Jones would rarely, in their eyes, be anything other than a pretentious little Cheltenham snob who couldn't cope with fame. As for Mick Jagger, a critic could chortle over his rooster strut but couldn't be caught taking his lyrics seriously.

It took the tragic death of Brian Jones and Mick Jagger's Hyde Park reading from Percy Shelley's 'Adonais' to bring about a momentary departure from the usual party line, an all- too- fleeting recognition that the Rolling Stones had played a major part in the counter-cultural revolution.

Postscript: The Rocking Stones

After opting decisively for rock at the time of 'Beggars Banquet', the Stones were dominant in that genre for six years, despite competition from such great bands as Little Feat, Bruce Springsteen and the E Street Band plus the Allman Brothers. Thereafter they were significantly weakened by the departure of Mick Taylor in 1974 and, to a lesser extent, by that of Nicky Hopkins, who played a big part albeit chiefly in the recording studio.

Yet even before this there were signs of imminent decline. Their albums 'Sticky Fingers' and 'Exile on Main Street' were uneven even though they yielded great rock songs such as 'Brown Sugar' and 'Tumbling Dice.' The first man to clock their decline was Jack Nitzsche, who told them face-to-face, while they were on an American tour in 1972, "you've gone stale, you're just repeating your past sound." Nitzsche added a friendly warning that they were in danger of ending up like Chuck Berry, faded but not forgotten.

Jack Nitzsche was both right and wrong in his warning. From a commercial point of view, the Stones would never fade, continuing to pack out stadiums for decade after decade, parlaying their unmatched technical proficiency into riches beyond the dreams of avarice. But their preposterous longevity was bought at the cost of a near -total absence of creativity – 'Start Me Up' in 81 would be their last great rock song.

There were three main reasons for the Stones' artistic decline. The first was that Mick Jagger ceased to be a societal outsider as he undoubtedly had been in the first years of the Rolling Stones. In his early twenties Jagger had been shunned by the Establishment due to his facial appearance and the same applied later due to his flamboyant dancing. But a combination of factors – the crossover popularity of soul music, the sexual revolution and, above all, the acceptance of African-American models as icons of beauty – brought about a huge change in popular attitudes.

From 67 onwards, black women such as Donyale Luna, Naomi Sims and Pat Cleveland began to flourish on catwalks and figure on the pages of Vogue magazine, photographed by the likes of David Bailey. The climax of this trend came with the acclaim of African-American actress Marsha Hunt for her performance in the rock musical 'Hair' and, by 69, Hunt was in a relationship with Mick Jagger.

By 1971 Jagger had consulted the Royal School of Art in search of a marketable rock brand image. He was so taken with the design suggested by undergraduate John Pasche that he used it as the cover for the album 'Sticky Fingers.' The design– soon to be known as the 'Tongue and Lips' logo– was, as Pasche confirmed, based on its designer's reaction to Jagger's most obvious facial characteristics. Highly effective in marketing the album, it might well have been left there. Yet, in parallel with the musical complacency which Jack Nitzsche was soon to identify, the Stones continued with the 'Tongue and Lips' logo indefinitely. Any significance it may originally have had for Mick Jagger in terms of turning the tables on those who'd originally despised him was rapidly dissipated until it became merely the sign of the Stones' celeb vulgarity.

The second factor in the Stones' artistic decline was their relocation to the south of France as tax exiles in 71. Whereas Mick Jagger had previously had his finger on the pulse of 'Swinging London', reacting fast to the constant flux of societal change and reflecting it in masterly lyrics, he was now no more than at best a detached observer. His focus was more and more on America and he was only dimly aware of London's pub rock movement. Wrongfooted by the advent of punk in 77, he was wide open to being dismissed, as he was by John Lydon, as "a daft old fart." The Stones' technical proficiency and dependability in terms of giving their fans memorable concerts meant that they'd soon have the last laugh on the here- today -and -gone tomorrow punk bands. Yet they'd abandoned all pretence of innovation.

On a par with the above was the descent of Keith Richards into heroin addiction. It was never entirely clear when he first lapsed into smack but, from his statements when he kicked the habit in 78, it appears to have been in 69. Whilst his capacity as a great guitarist remained unimpaired, his creativity as a composer was certainly diminished.

In 1982 a BBC documentary marked the twentieth anniversary of the formation of the Rolling Stones. In a rare departure from the adulation with which the Stones were usually showered, the documentary contained a modicum of critical comment. The most telling observation came from none other than Giorgio Gomelsky, who, as their effective manager, had played a major role in their initial breakthrough.

Disillusioned by what he saw as the sell-out of the British rhythm and blues bands to American stadium rock, Giorgio Gomelsky had relocated to France in 1970. Had he been motivated by money, he could doubtless have become a multi-millionaire. But his real feelings would be reflected many years later, when he was living in the US, by a remark he made to music historian, John Strasbaugh: "music is a journey not something mapped out by a lawyer. Human expression is when you make real what you feel. It's about the discovery of reality behind appearances."

Interviewed for the documentary at his home in New York, Gomelsky contrasted the Stones' commercial apogee with their pristine idealism. He said "I think they've sold out. They've lost the spirit of those days. They have tremendous power but they could do something more con- structive with it instead of perpetuating their image and their egos."

Amongst those who were fascinated with the image of Mick Jagger was future Prime Minister, Anthony Charles Lynton Blair. Blair had been an ardent fan of the rocking Stones since his late teens and, between leaving public school and going up to Oxford, he'd set his sights on a career in rock. He soon realised that his band, the Ugly Rumours, had little future but he hoped to make it in the lucrative world of rock management. His idol was Mick Jagger.

Just as the teenage Jagger had dreamt of a political career only to abandon it as he acquired showbiz fame, so the youthful Blair fantasised about being a rockstar, only reluctantly giving up his ambition at the age of thirty when he was first elected to Parliament.

In 1997 Tony Blair, leader of the New Labour Party, became Prime Minister. Although it was his Cabinet colleague, Peter Mandelson, who said "we're intensely relaxed about people becoming filthy rich", Blair enthusiastically endorsed such sentiments. Around this time Mick Jagger had an estimated personal wealth of $360 million. But Tony Blair was upset that his boyhood hero had not been awarded an honour befitting his financial success. This was a deficiency Blair was delighted to remedy when he recommended Jagger for a knighthood in 2003.

It was not only Tony Blair who was fascinated with Mick Jagger. Amongst others was the Californian singer Adam Levine, frontman of the electro-pop group, Maroon 5. In 2011, Maroon 5 had a number one hit on the Billboard Hot 100 with 'Moves Like Jagger.'

Popular taste had been sullied from thirty years of MTV and vaunted videographer Jonas Akerlund knew his brief. Beginning with a black and white clip of a youthful and diffident Mick Jagger confessing he barely expected his career to last two years, Akerlund brought in Adam Levine in full colour, torso emblazoned with tattoos, frantically attempting to mimic the intercut antics of Jagger in his rocking pomp. This was set to a pounding beat of 128 to the minute.

Uttering a dumbass line about not giving a shit, the thirty-two-year-old Levine impersonates a teenage lad desperately trying to impress a girl by bragging that he has moves like Jagger. What's more, now they're naked, he'll show her moves of a different sort if she takes him by the tongue. Thirty-year-old Christina Aguilera plays the part of a teenage girl warning the boy that he'd better learn to rub her right if he wants to own her for the night. Finally the archive interview with the young Mick Jagger ends with him remarking, apparently in all seriousness, that the band might last for another year.

At most, 'Moves Like Jagger' is a piece of lightweight dancefloor fodder. But it would soon be bigged up and not only by interested parties. Adam Levine blabbed "we were lucky to get Mick's endorsement, that's so cool for a new generation of people who don't know how incredible he was." But it was liberal website, the Huffington Post, which unctuously commented "no can one ever touch the original. The best they can do is try to imitate Jagger's greatness." Interviewed on 'Late Night with Letterman', Jagger acknowledged that the tribute was "very flattering" but regretted that he couldn't draw a share of the royalties.

'Moves Like Jagger' summed up where the Stones had reached nearly fifty years after their formation. The band's other surviving original members, Keith Richards and Charlie Watts, were being treated as little more than an adjunct to Mick Jagger whilst he himself was receiving crass adulation not for his singing talents still less for his gifts as a songwriter but only as an icon of modern dance.

Sources

BOOKS

Bockris, Victor	Keith Richards: the biography
Elliott, Martin	The Rolling Stones: Complete Recording Sessions
Norman, Philip	The Stones
Paytress, Mark	The Rolling Stones : Off the Record
Phelge, James	Nankering with the Stones
Richards, Keith	Life
Strasbaugh, John	Rock 'till You Drop: The Decline from Rebellion to Nostalgia
Trynka, Paul	Sympathy for the Devil: The Birth of the Rolling Stones and the Death of Brian Jones
Wyman, Bill	Stone Alone
Wyman, Bill	Rolling with the Stones

WEBSITES
www.allmusic.com/Richie Unterberger
www.ianstewartsixthstone.com Be Herten
www.iorr.org
www.keno.org/gasland
www. timeisonourside.com Ian McPherson
www.nzentgraf.de Nico Zentgraf The Complete Works of the Rolling Stones

VIDEO
Punkcast(Joly McFie Video Interviews with Giorgio Gomelsky)

MAGAZINES
Crawdaddy
Melody Maker
New Musical Express

About the Author

Graham Gordon is a cultural historian. Before turning to music, he specialized in sports history. His books include 'Master of the Ring'(Milo Books 2007), the critically acclaimed biography of Jem Mace, the Father of Boxing and First Worldwide Sports Star.

49063768R00163

Made in the USA
Columbia, SC
15 January 2019